IN OSAKA

Photographs by Yamasaki Ko-Ji

Art Director, Design, Layout,
Emir Shabashvili

Editing
Emir Shabashvili
Daniel Shabashvili

Translation
Emir Shabashvili
Daniel Shabashvili
Yamasaki Ko-Ji

Images by
Yamasaki Koi-Ji

Text by
Yamasaki Ko-Ji
Emir Shabashvili

First published in USA in 2015
by DarkSlide Press

11483 SW 109 Rd #2F
Miami, FLorida 33176
www.darkslidepress.com

Printed and bound in USA
by CreateSpace,
an Amazon.com company

ISBN 9781942180005

Library of Congress
CIP Number 2015939477

The Author is profoundly grateful to all the people he photographed, and especially to the dwellers of Nishinari's slum in Osaka.

Interview with Yamasaki Ko-Ji

Emir Shabashvili

ES: You name, Yamasaki Ko-Ji, is it just a name or it has some meaning or history? As I understand it, Yamasaki is a family name. Then, Ko-Ji should be your first name, right?

YK: Ha-ha, yeah. Correct format might be "Ko-Ji Yamasaki". It is not my legal name; rather, it is a simple phonetic reading of Japanese letters. Anything for a name will be ok. I think it's not important for the sake of our conversation.

ES: Tell me about your first encounter with photography.

YK: I received my first lessons in the craft from my father. He was interested in photography as a hobby. I came to carry around a pocket camera all the time, ever since I graduated from a high school. That camera was Minolta-16 I think. I had been taking snapshots of my friends on a daily basis.

ES: Wow! It is not that easy to work with 16mm film. Have you been developing and printing these photographs yourself?

YK: It was color film. I printed pictures at a shop and enjoyed watching them with my friends. I built my own darkroom in 2004. I was obsessed with the charm of monochrome...

ES: How interesting! 2004 was the year when I, too, set up a darkroom at home and returned to shooting black and white film after a brief escape to digital. So you are developing and printing your pictures. When you need to digitize your images, do you scan prints or you scan negatives?

YK: I scan prints. I don't scan negative film. My scanning method is simple normal mode. When I upload picture to the web, I only resize, no other processing present.

ES: So is that high contrast look of your pictures with blown-out highlights and grainy shadows attributed to the way you print your pictures, the way your develop your negatives, or both?

YK: Both. During negative development, raising the contrast is not the purpose. Getting sharp grain is important. If the grain isn't sharp, the definition of the picture will be lost. I create high contrast by using hard photographic paper (Fujifilm №.4 paper, FM4).

ES: Aside from photography, have you even taken any interest in visual arts? If so, what styles or artists interest you?

YK: I'm not interested in other visual arts. Photography only... Are you interested in any?

ES: Yes! When I was young, I tried to draw and to paint. I quickly noticed that drawing interested me much more than painting. It was nothing serious, but then I self studied the whole history of painting. There was a nice art museum in my town (Kazan, Russia) and I used to go there. I am not sure how it all influenced my photography, but if I see a visual reference to a classical painting in a photograph I definitely react to it.

ES: Did poetry ever influence you? I am asking because in my case the influence was a big one and because I noticed poetic titles you gave to some of your images.

YK: When I started showing my photography on the web, I wrote poetic titles for my photographs. I thought it added something, some additional meaning to the sad feelings I was trying to convey with the image. However, later I decided that it's like making a drama. Necessary things should be told by the photograph itself. I think that a strong image does not need that supplement of words. I'm using photography exactly because there is an emotion that couldn't be explained in words. That said...I still interested in poetic photos.

ES: This brings us to the important question about your relationship to "Provoke" magazine photographers and to early Daido Moriyama's photographs. My impression is that the visual style of your photographs is very close to these images. The mood, on the other hand, is very different: your photographs are poetic, as you just said. Through all that urban craziness of your images I can always feel a sense of strange, subtle harmony. Because of this, your images tend to be more self-contained. This is quite unlike many of Daido Moriyama's images - his photographs really open in series, in his books. So, what is you history with "Provoke" photographers? Did you follow the visual tradition they created? What names are important to you?

YK: Yes, "Provoke" magazine was the greatest influence on my work, as you might imagine. When I was surting the net, I found Takuma Nakahira's pictures. At the time, I was trying to develop my own photo style...there were two images I found. I saw broken composition, rough grain and terrible exposure. But, they matched the state of my mind. "That's it!" I thought. This is the way to express my troubled mind. Since then, I have been reading about Takuma Nakahira. This is about my encounter with "Provoke".

ES: These are beautiful images! What year it was when you got interested in the style?

YK: Fall of 2003?

ES: I know you live and work in Osaka. Osaka is a huge megapolis. It is also very diverse: there is Osaka Bay, the river, numerous canals, bridges, huge downtown, even mountains...what area is yours?

YK: I work in Osaka, I live in Kobe city. But I love Osaka! Especially slum of Nishinari area is good. I drink in the bars there. Do you know the Tsutenkaku tower? Look it up, it's very famous in Japan.

ES: Apart from Takuma Nakahira and "Provoke" photographers, does any master photographer influence you in your work? Anyone outside of Japan?

YK: I like Antoine D'Agata and Josef Koudelka's "Praha".

ES: In your work, what are you looking for? Are you after a single picture, moving from one lucky image to another? Are you rather trying to create a sense of a story or a diary, where several pictures are important?

YK: I do not have much interest in a single photo. My photography is a diary pieced together out of many photographs I have taken, day to day. I feel people I photographed, their life, in this diary, myself included. I think...maybe I am interested more in the visual story my diary tells than the photographs as images, taken separately and independently from the story.

ES: Yamasaki-san, I'd like to thank you for your answers. Of course, I am a very curious person; I always have one more question to ask, but... it has to stop somewhere and twelve questions is a perfect number. Now I know much more about you. After this conversation, I see your work in new light. I even decided to return to a darkroom to print my pictures instead of scanning and printing from computer! I wish you good luck in your life and in your work.

YK: Many thanks, Emir! Return to your darkroom? It's great!

1

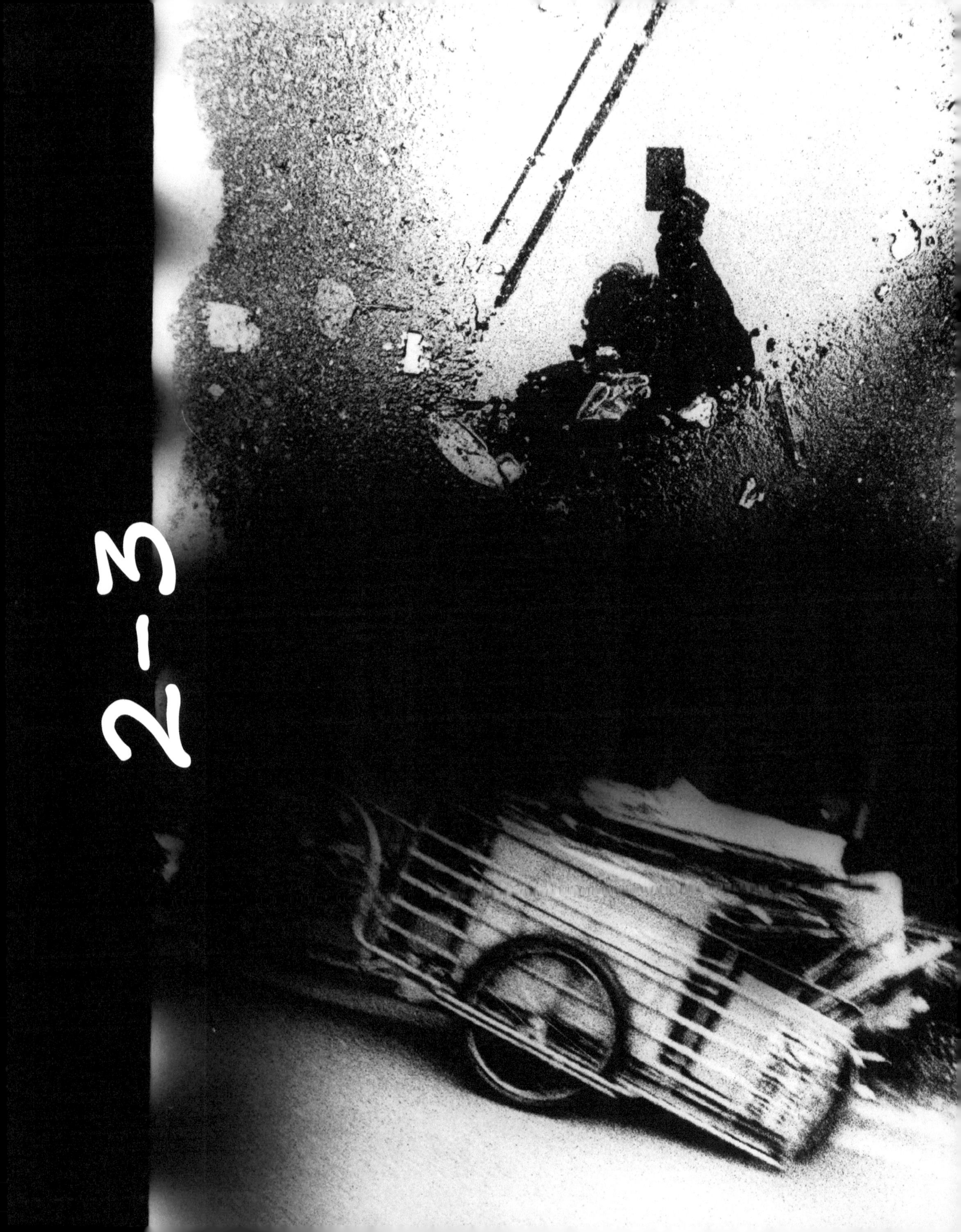

2-3

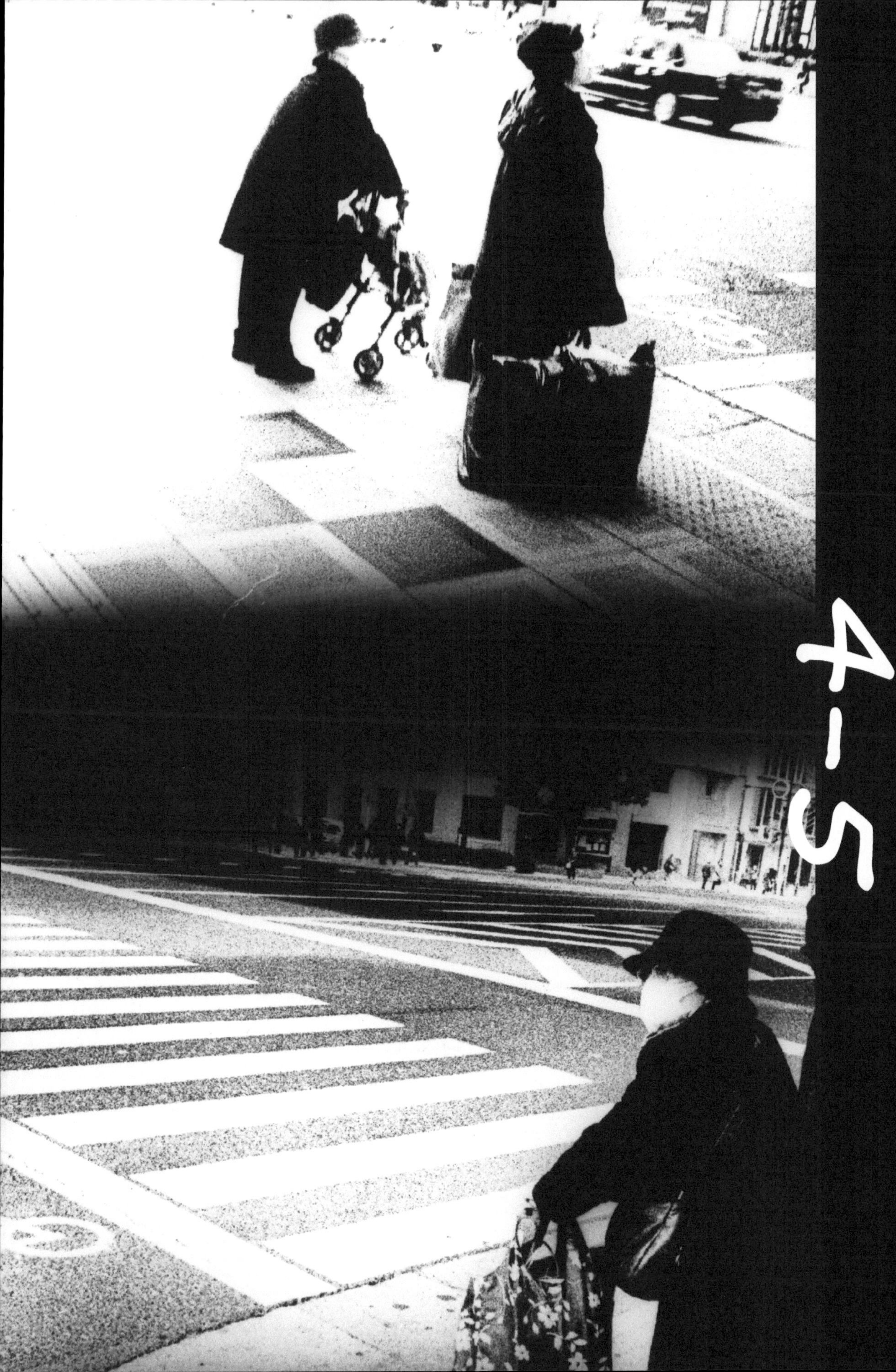
4-5

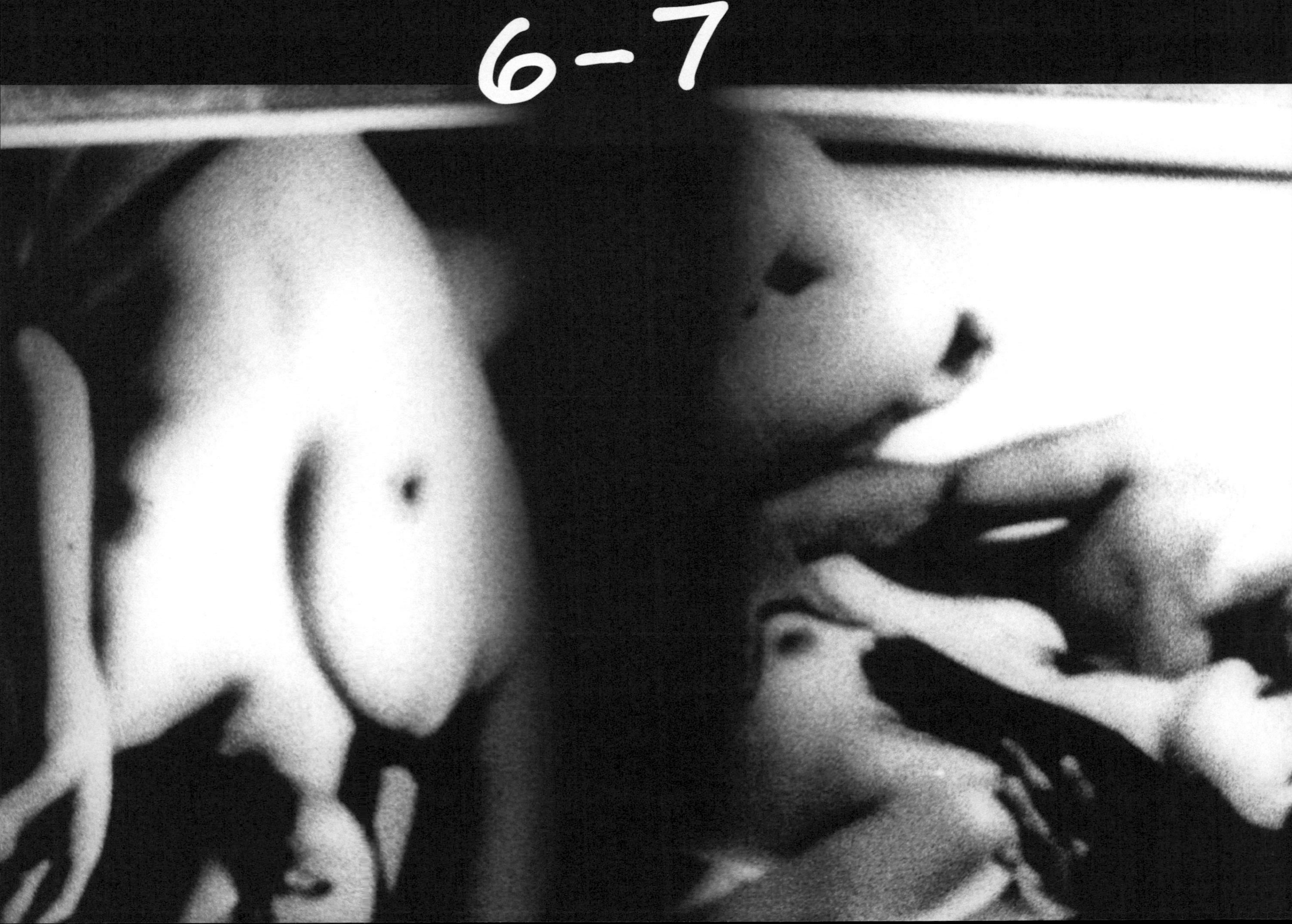
6-7

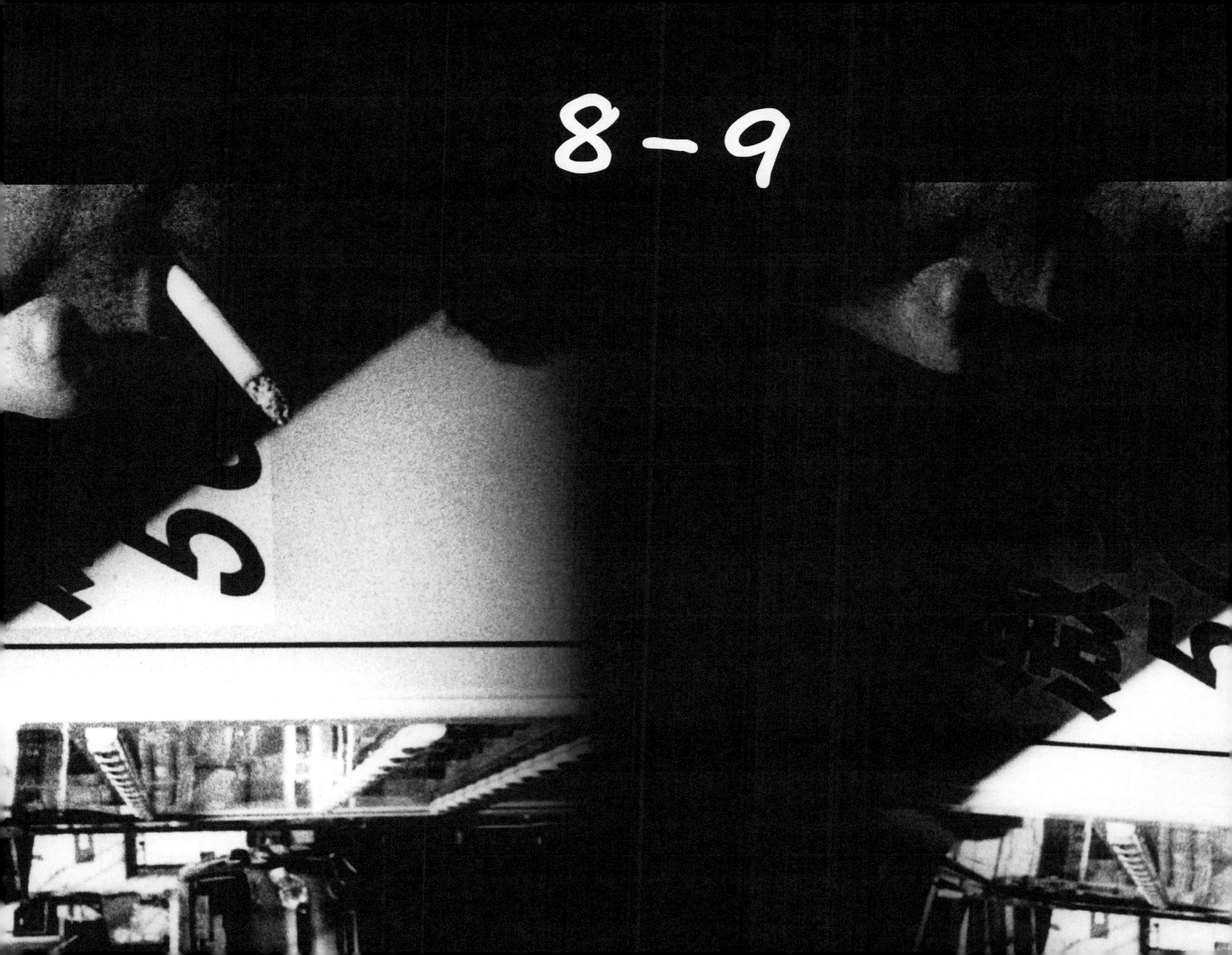
8-9

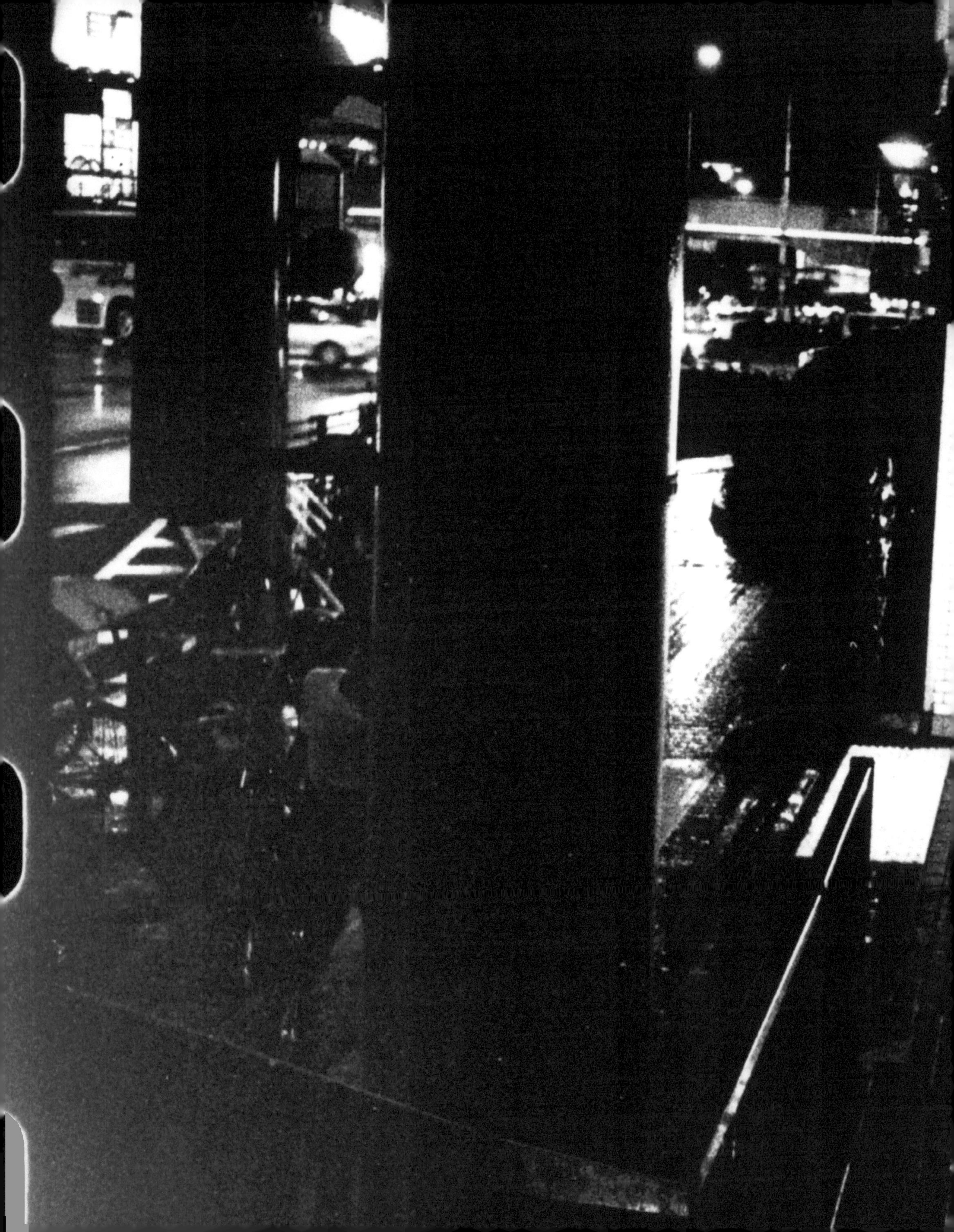

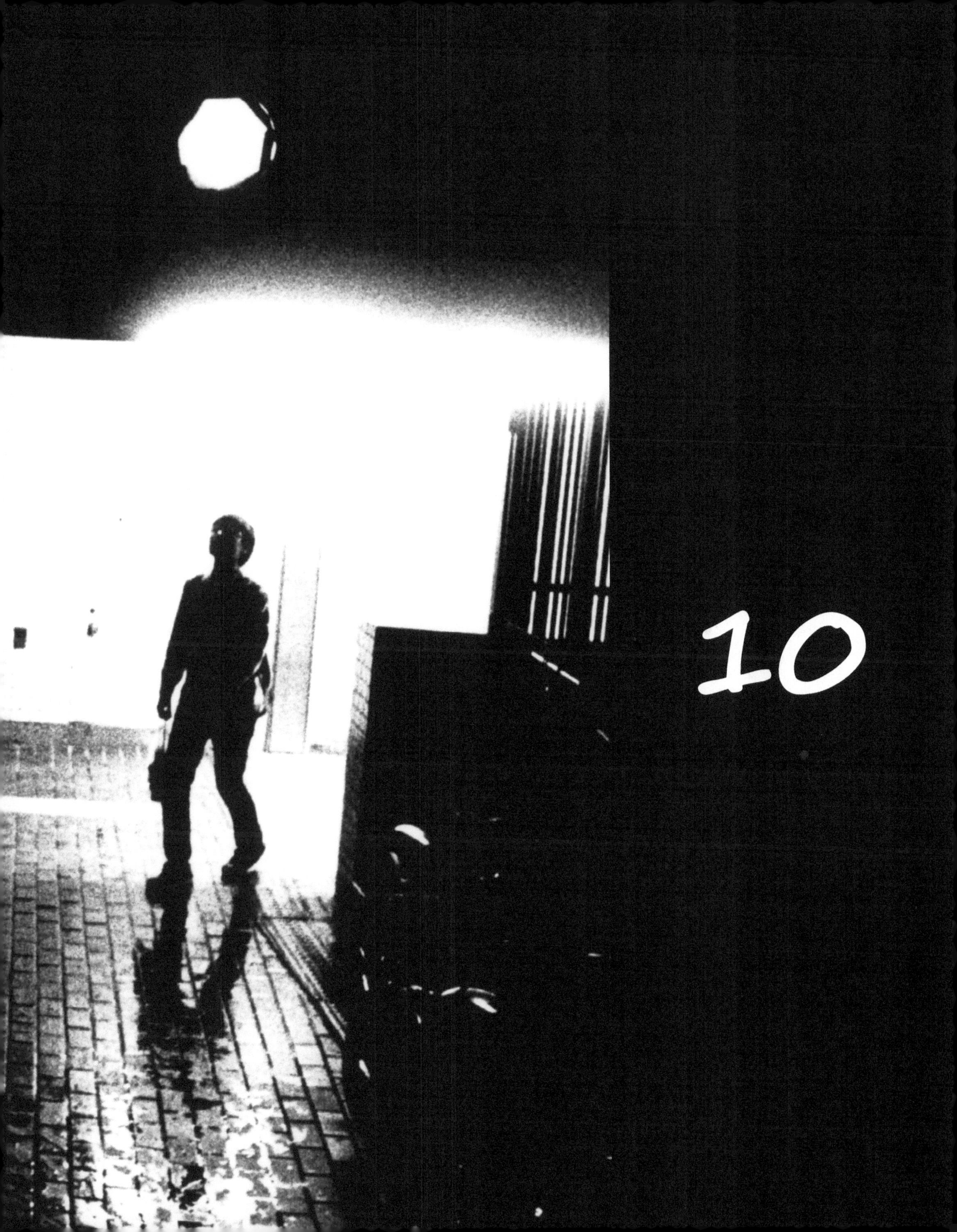

10

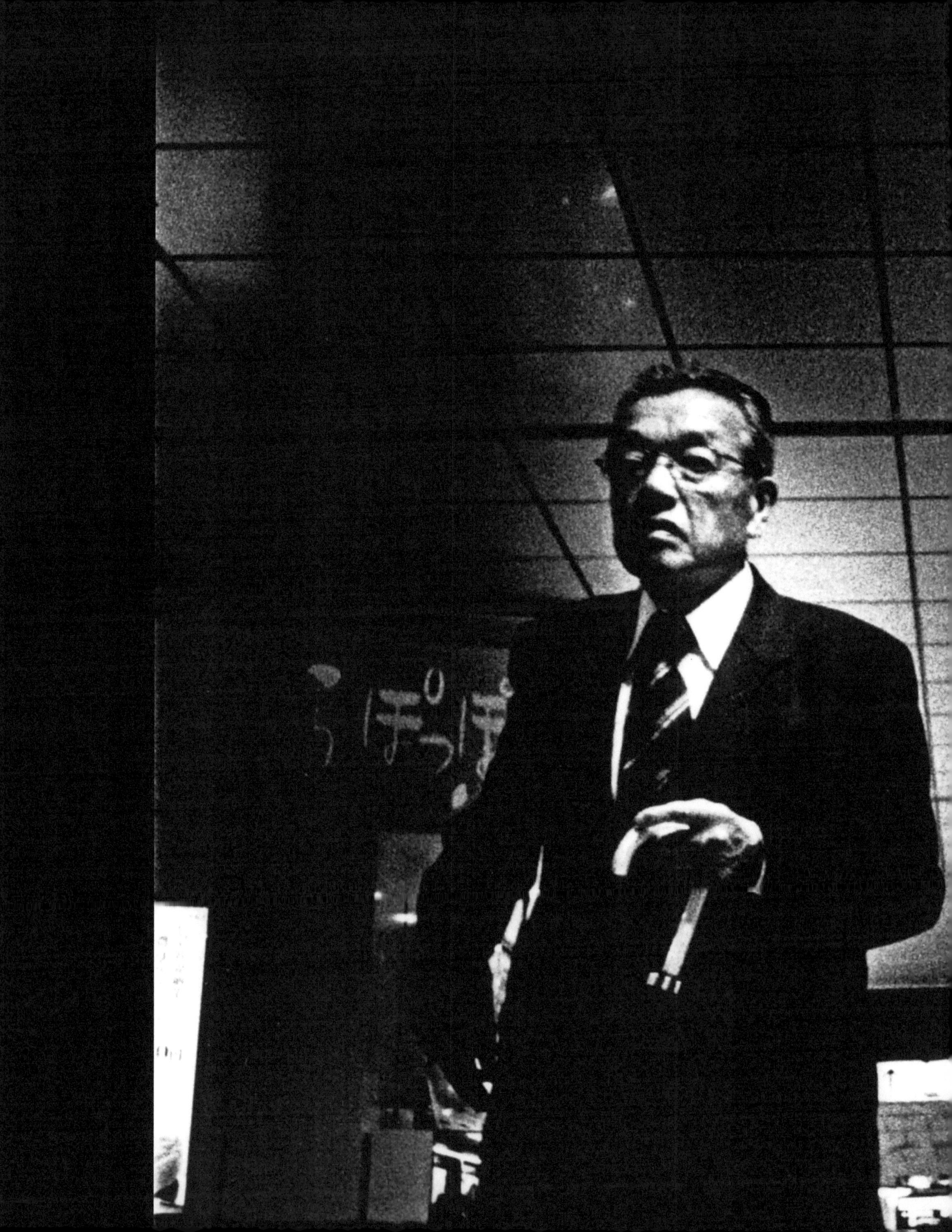
うぽっぽ

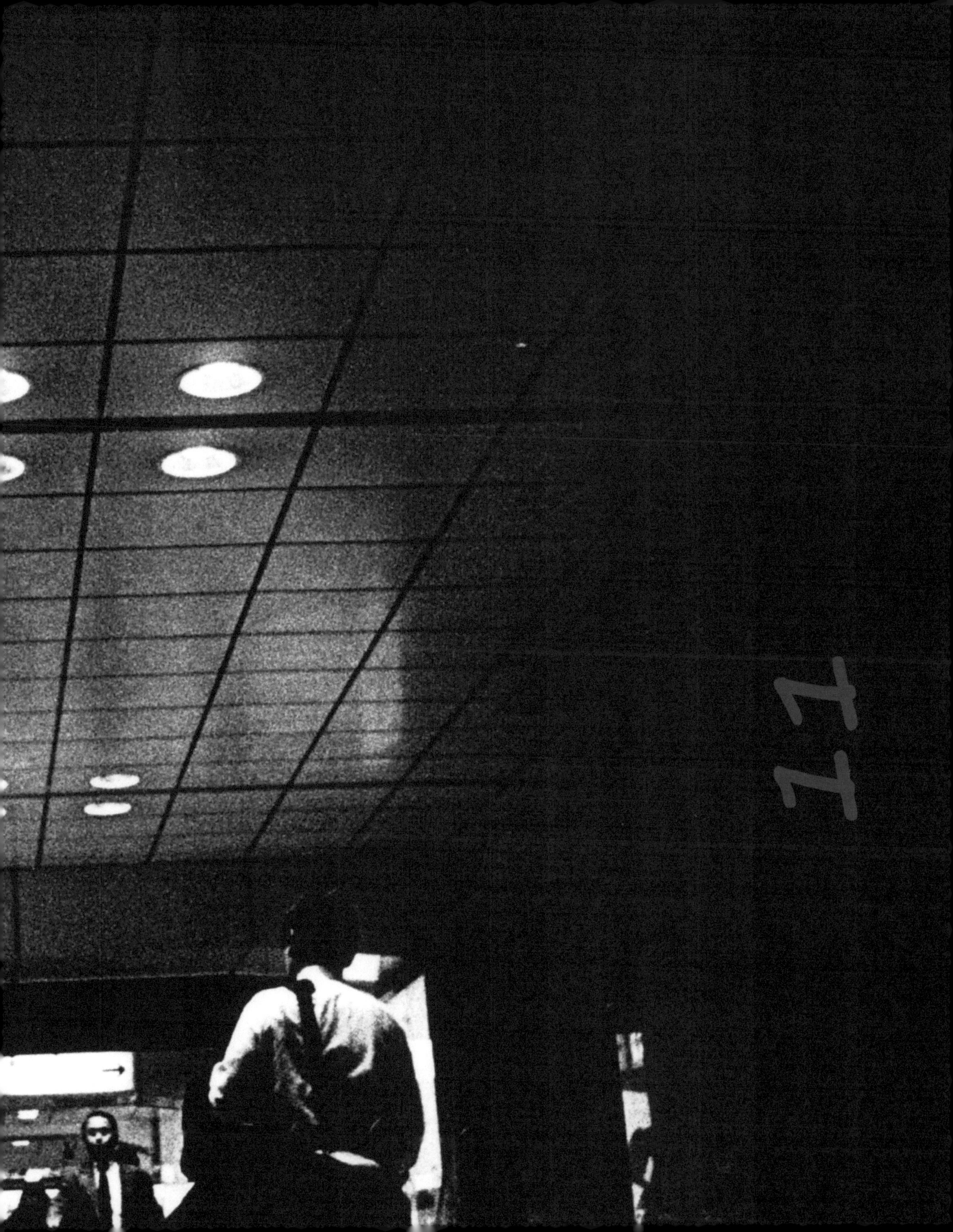

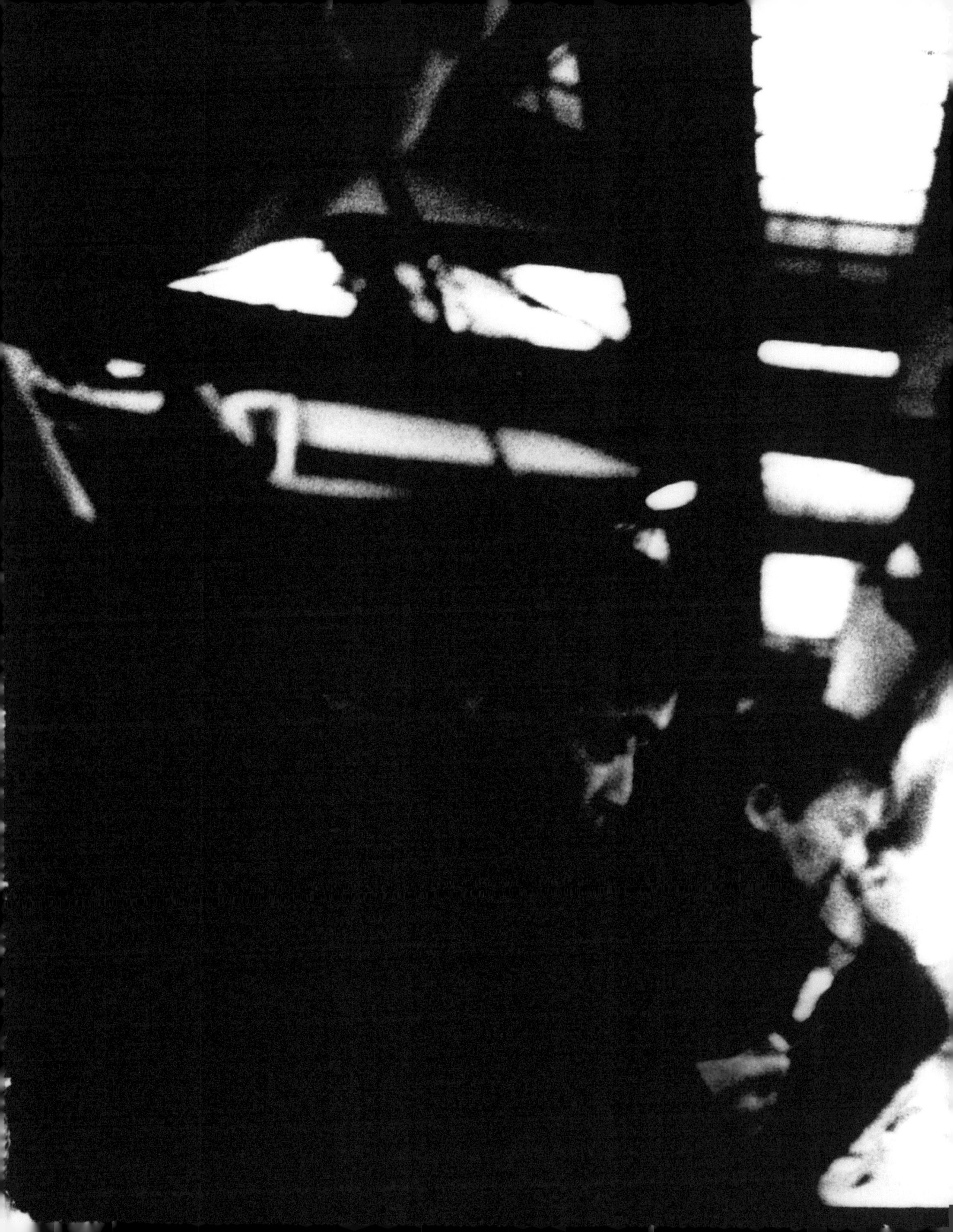

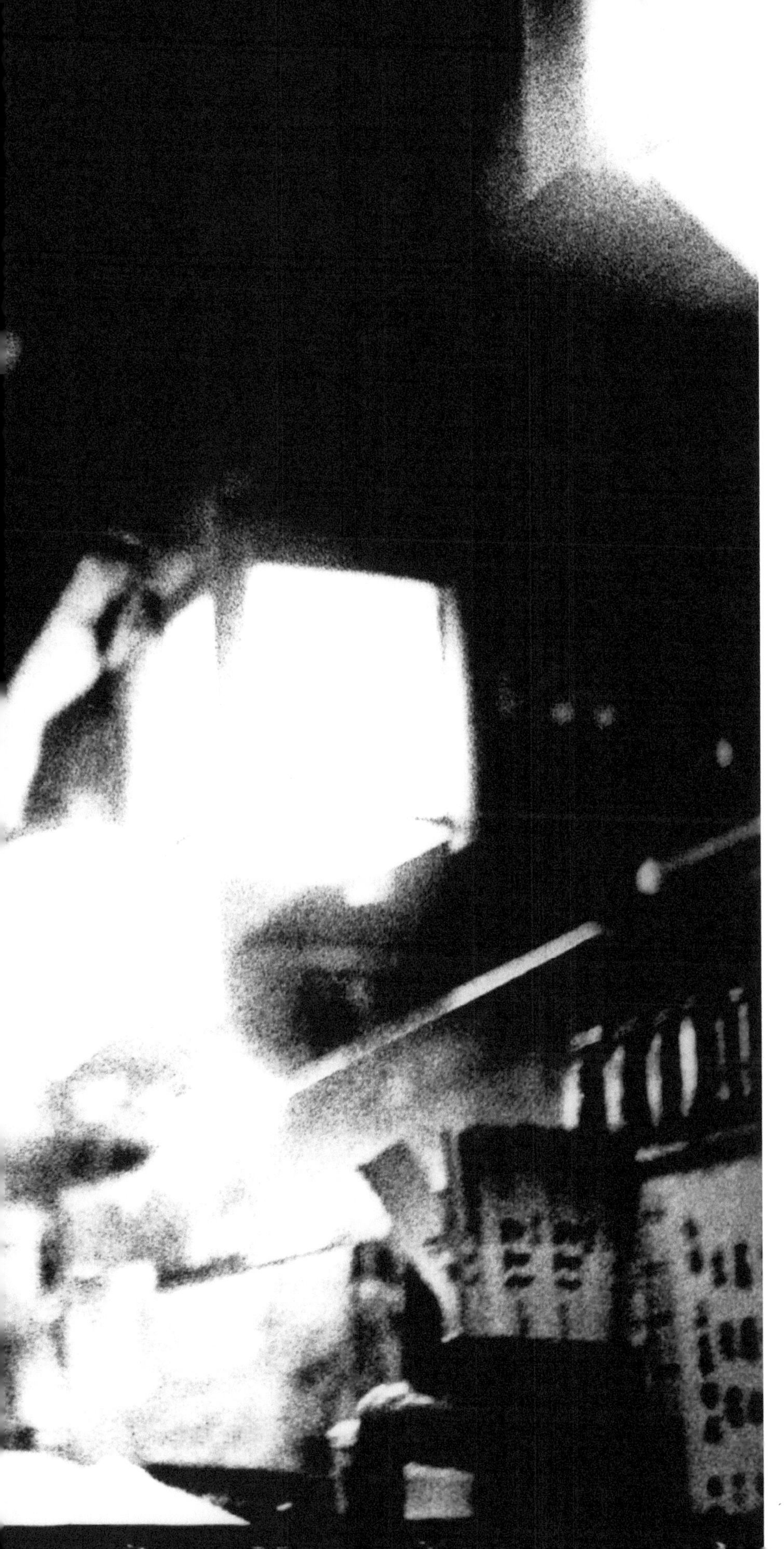

12

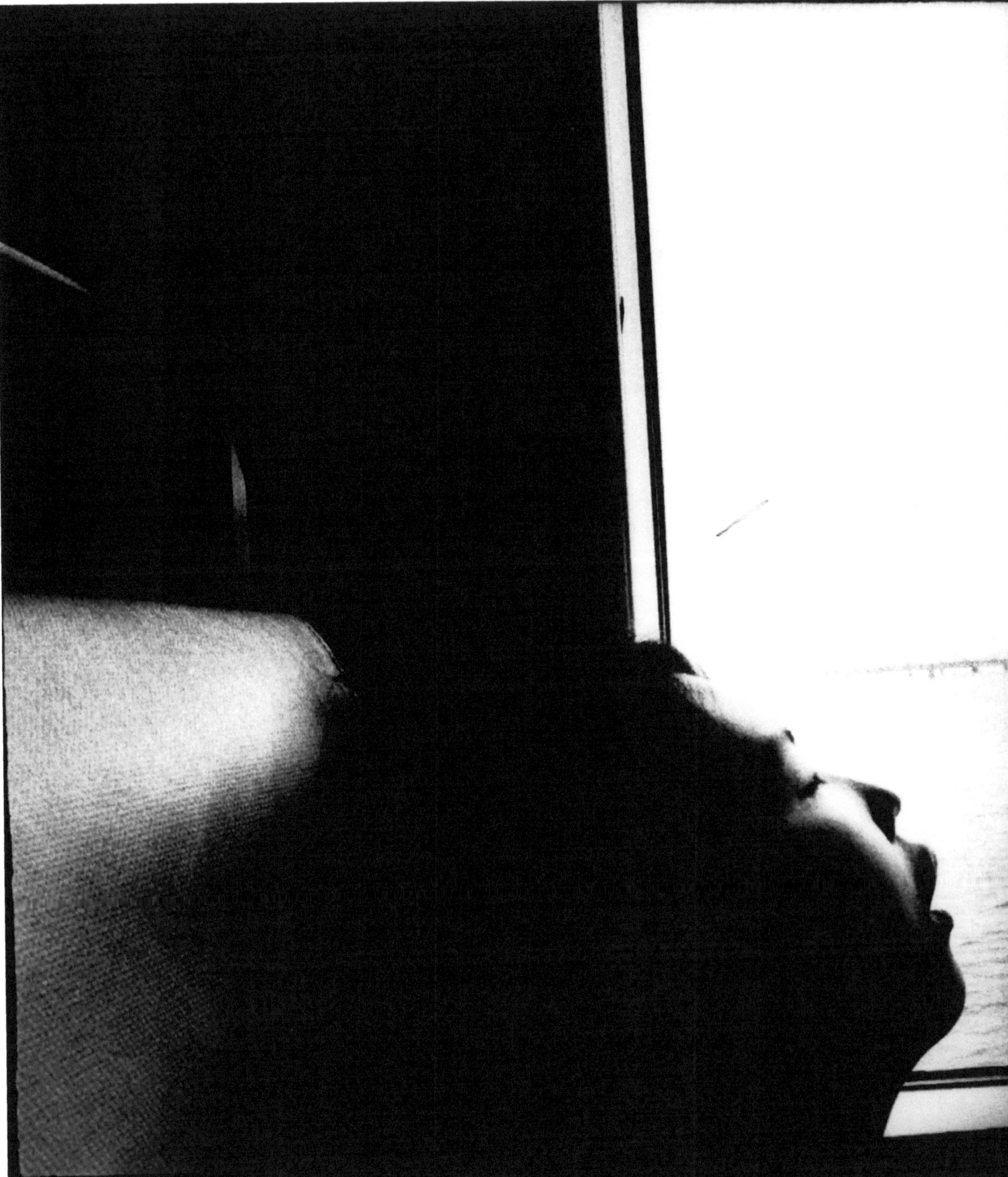

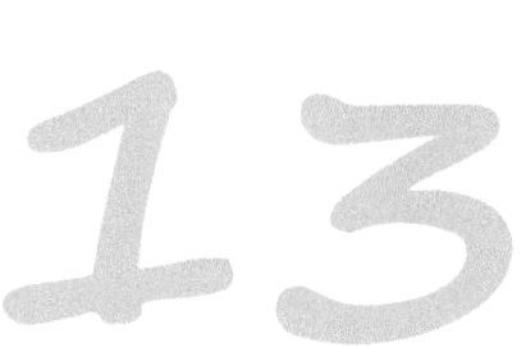

13

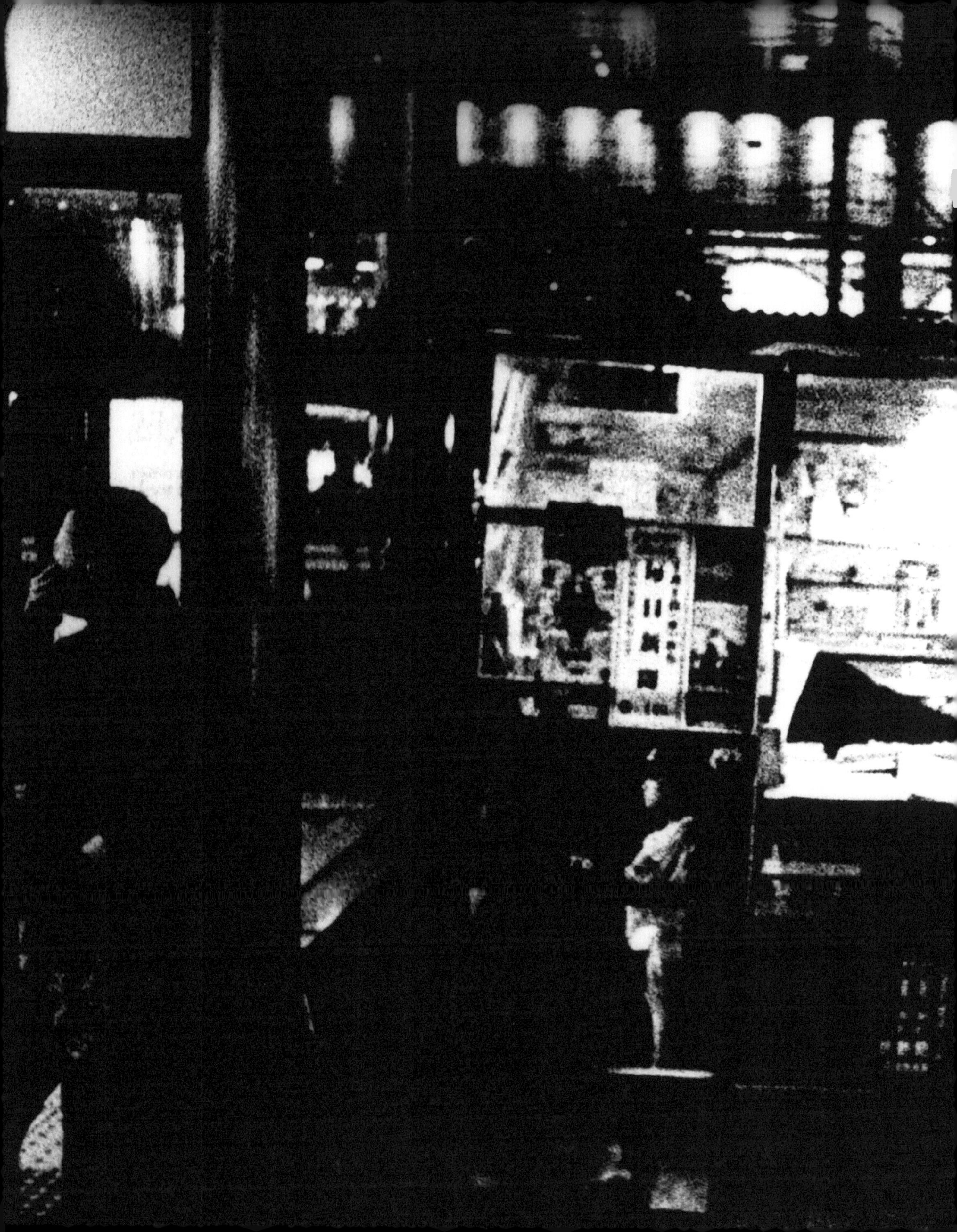

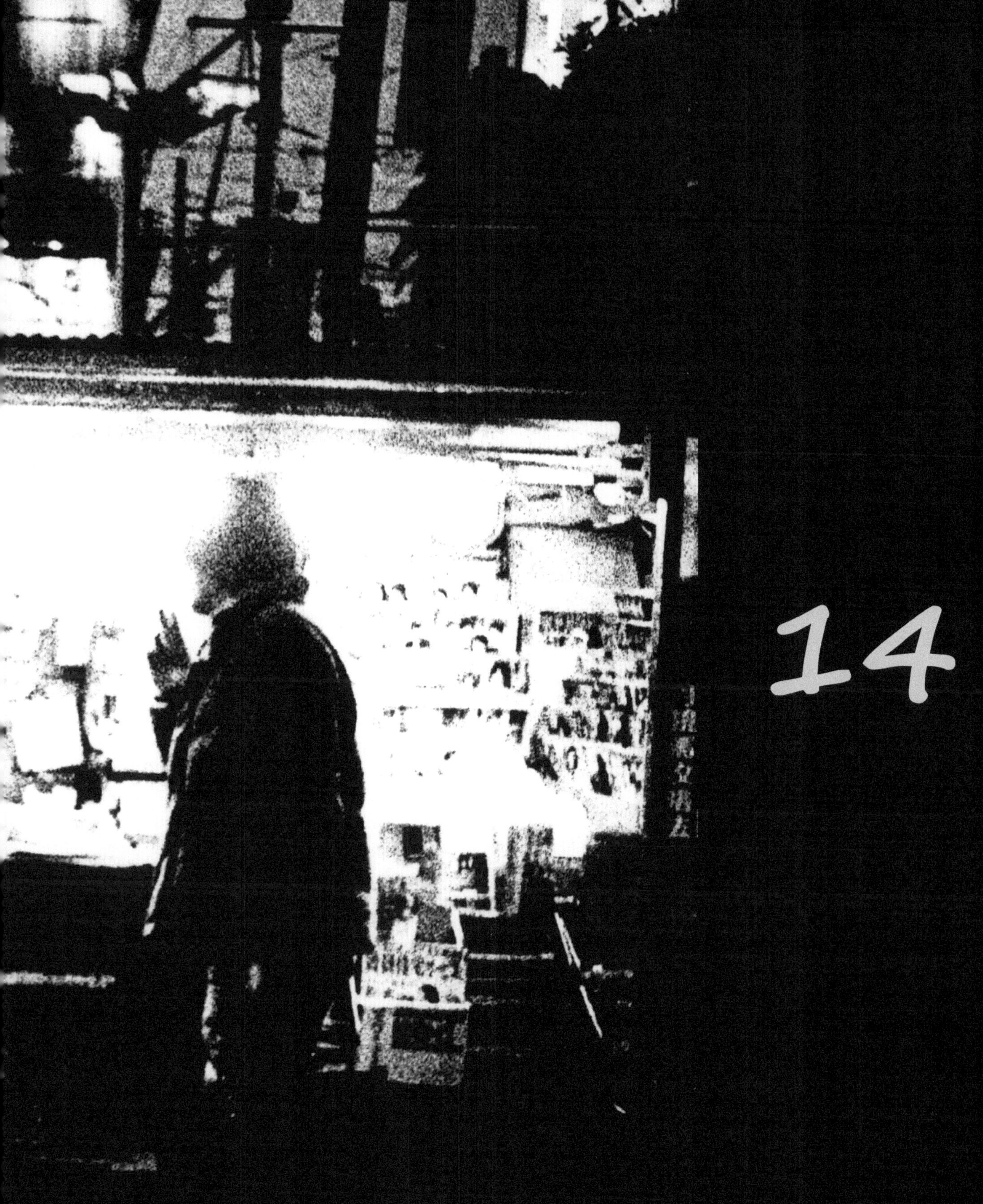

14

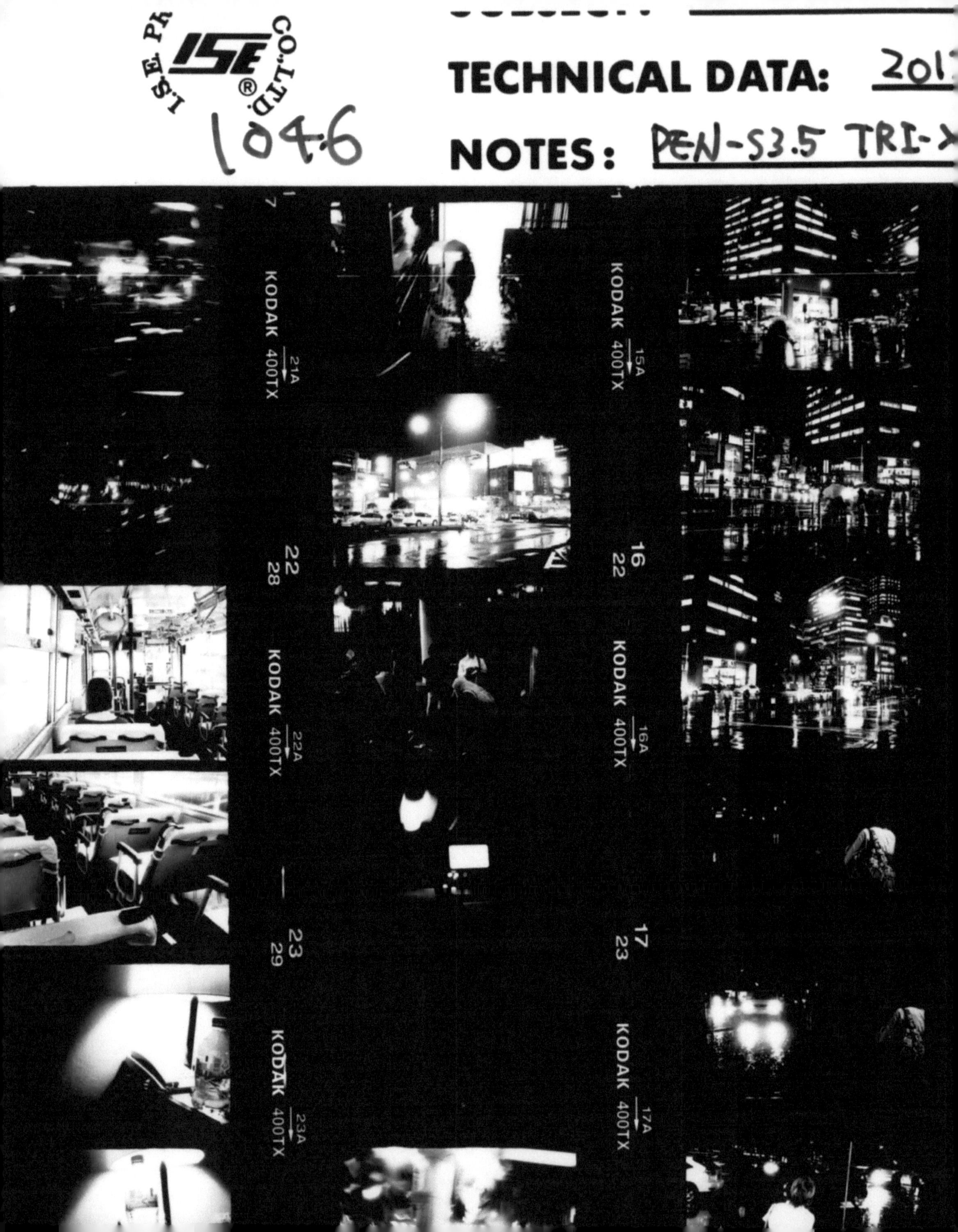

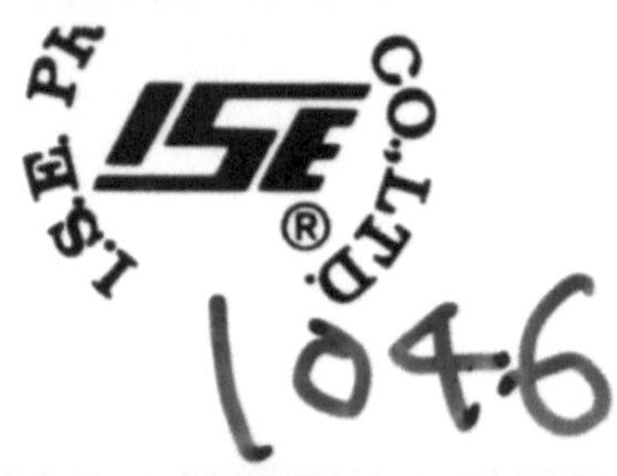

ISE PR
ISE
CO.LTD.
®
1046
TECHNICAL DATA: 201
NOTES: PEN-S3.5 TRI-X
KODAK 400TX
21A
22
28
KODAK 400TX
22A
23
29
KODAK 400TX
23A
15A
16
22
KODAK 400TX
16A
17
23
KODAK 400TX
17A

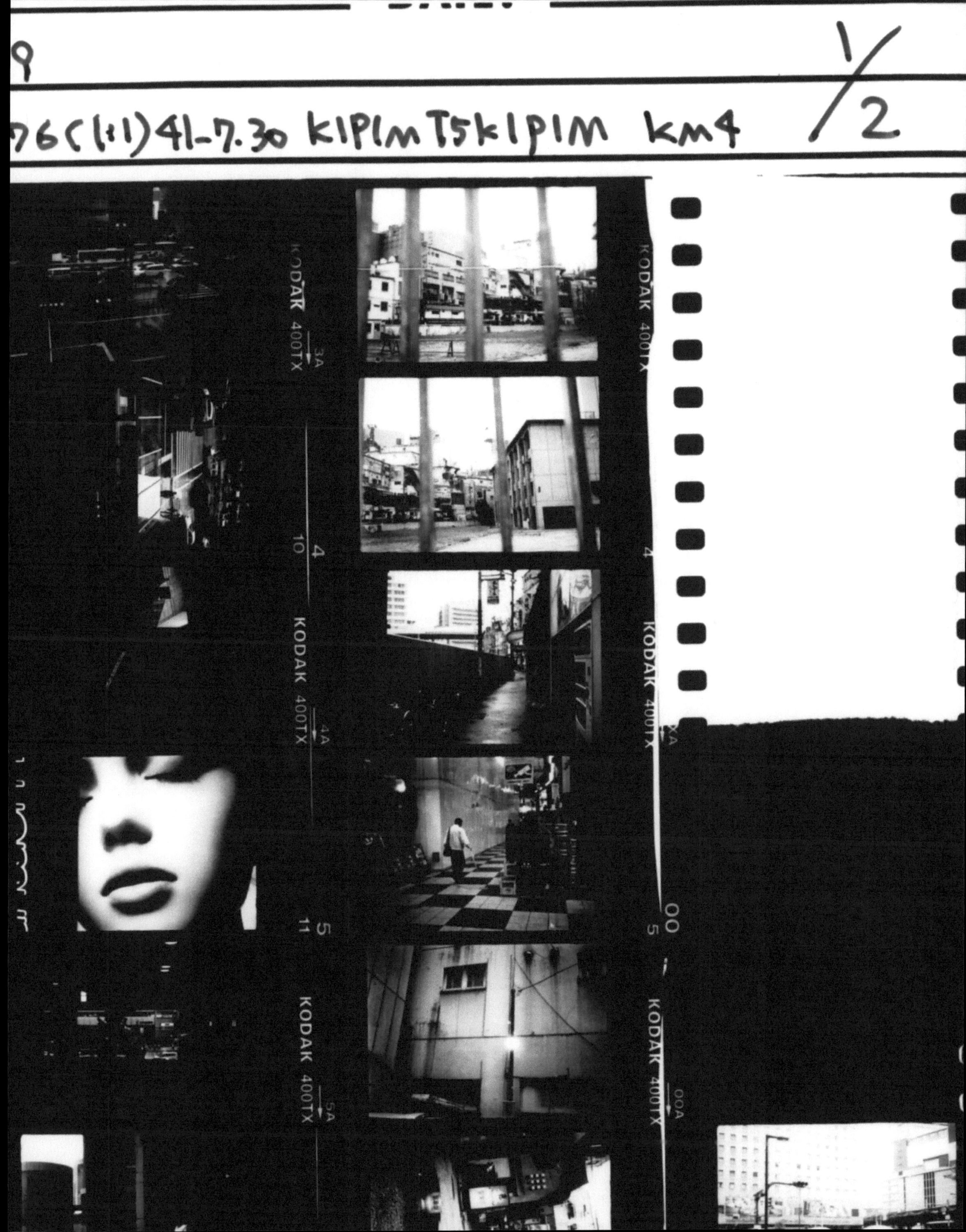

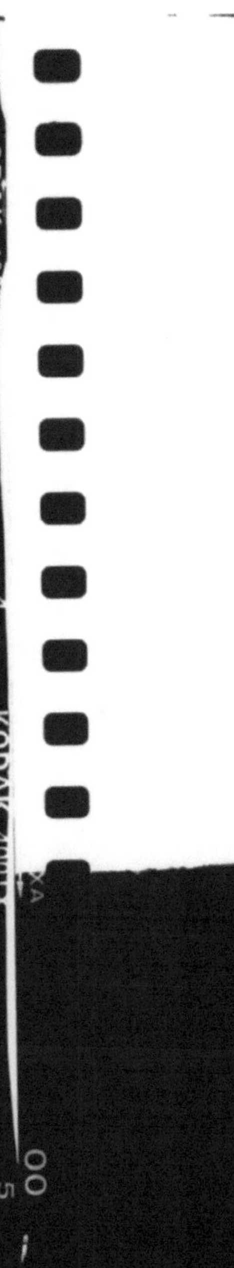
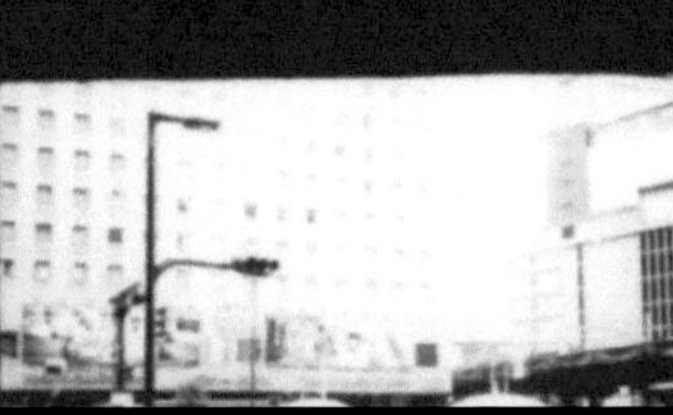

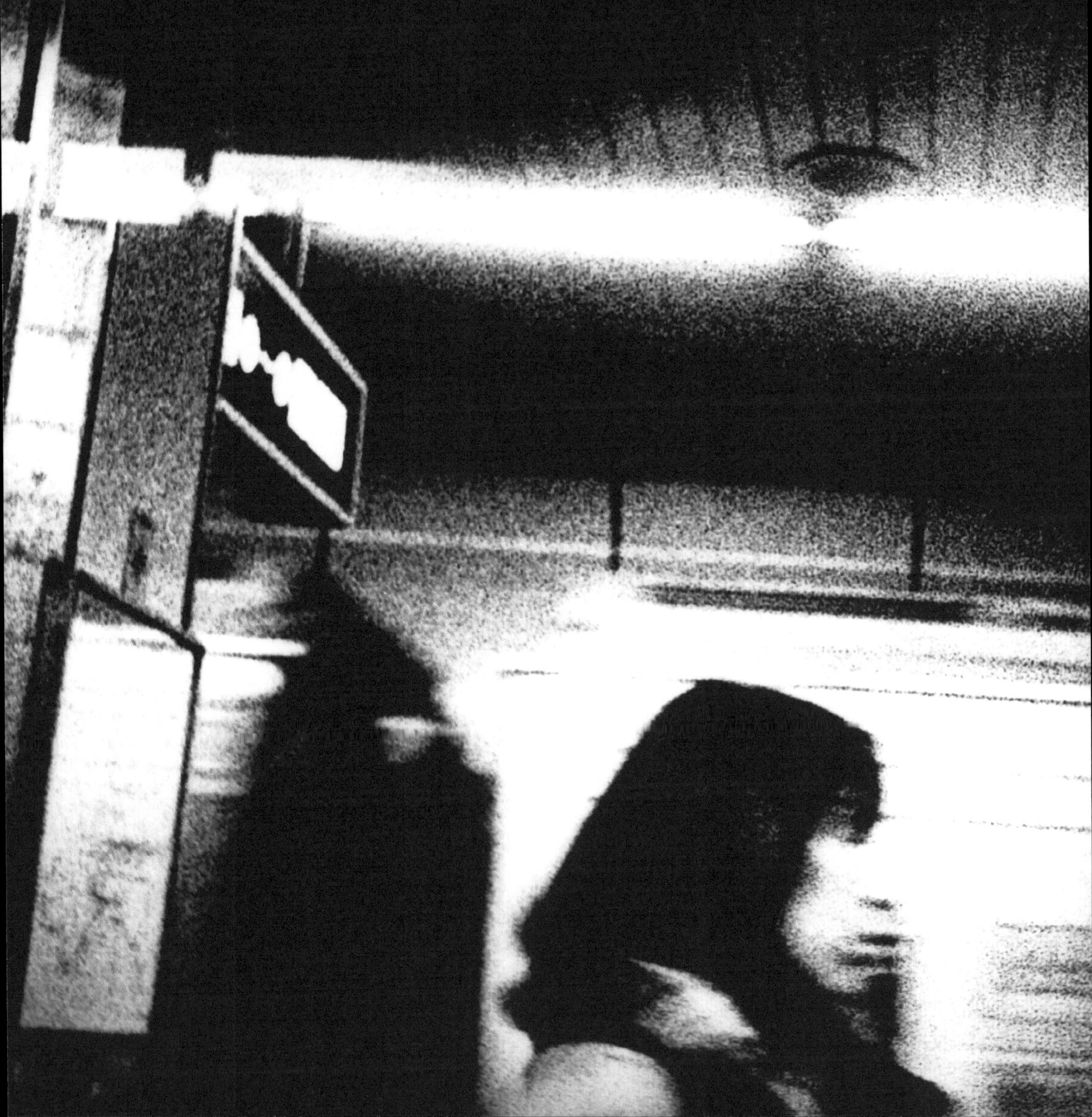

15

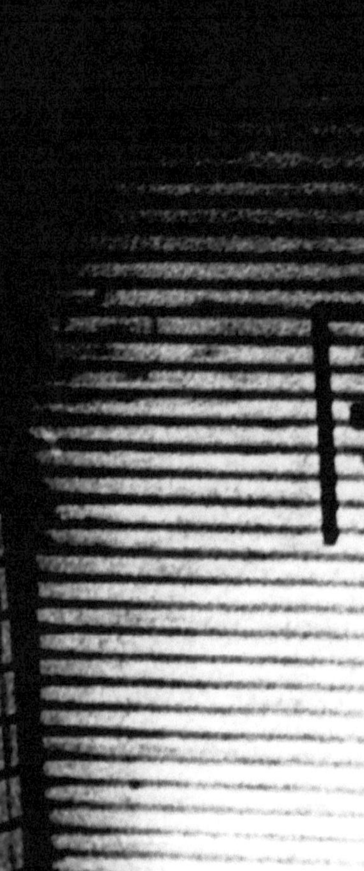

16

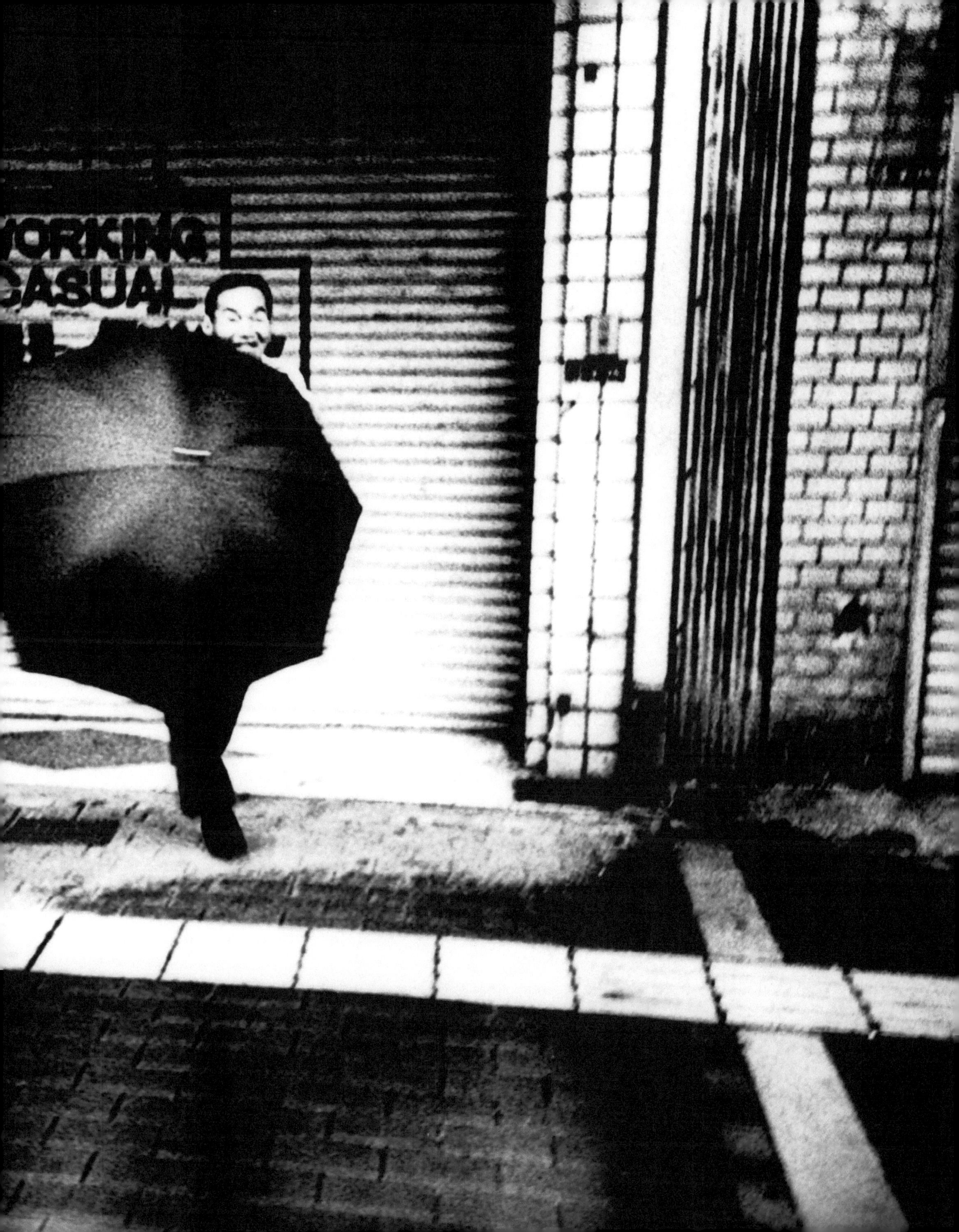

ORKING
ASUAL

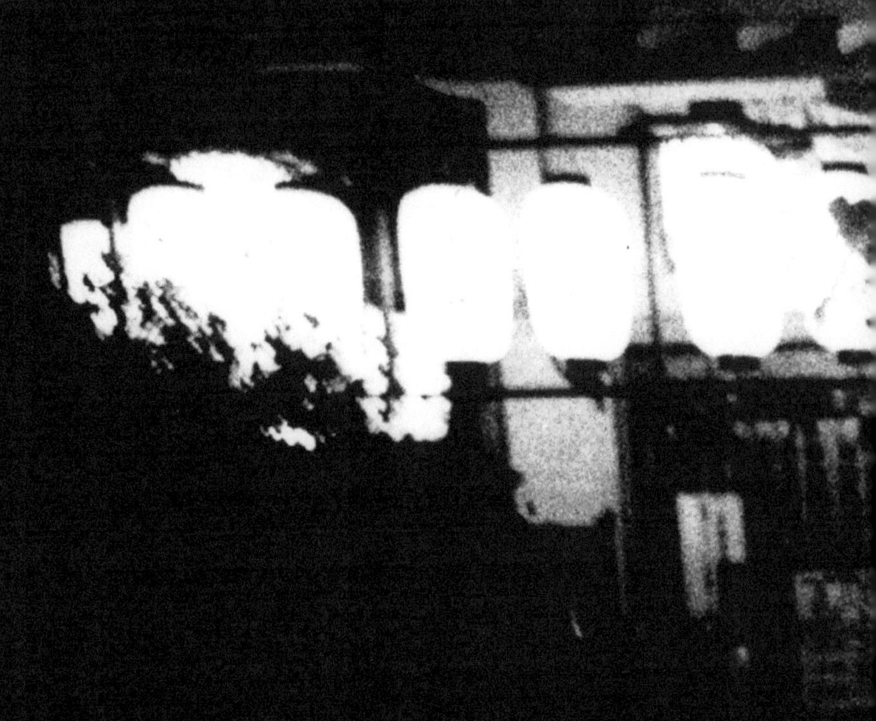

17

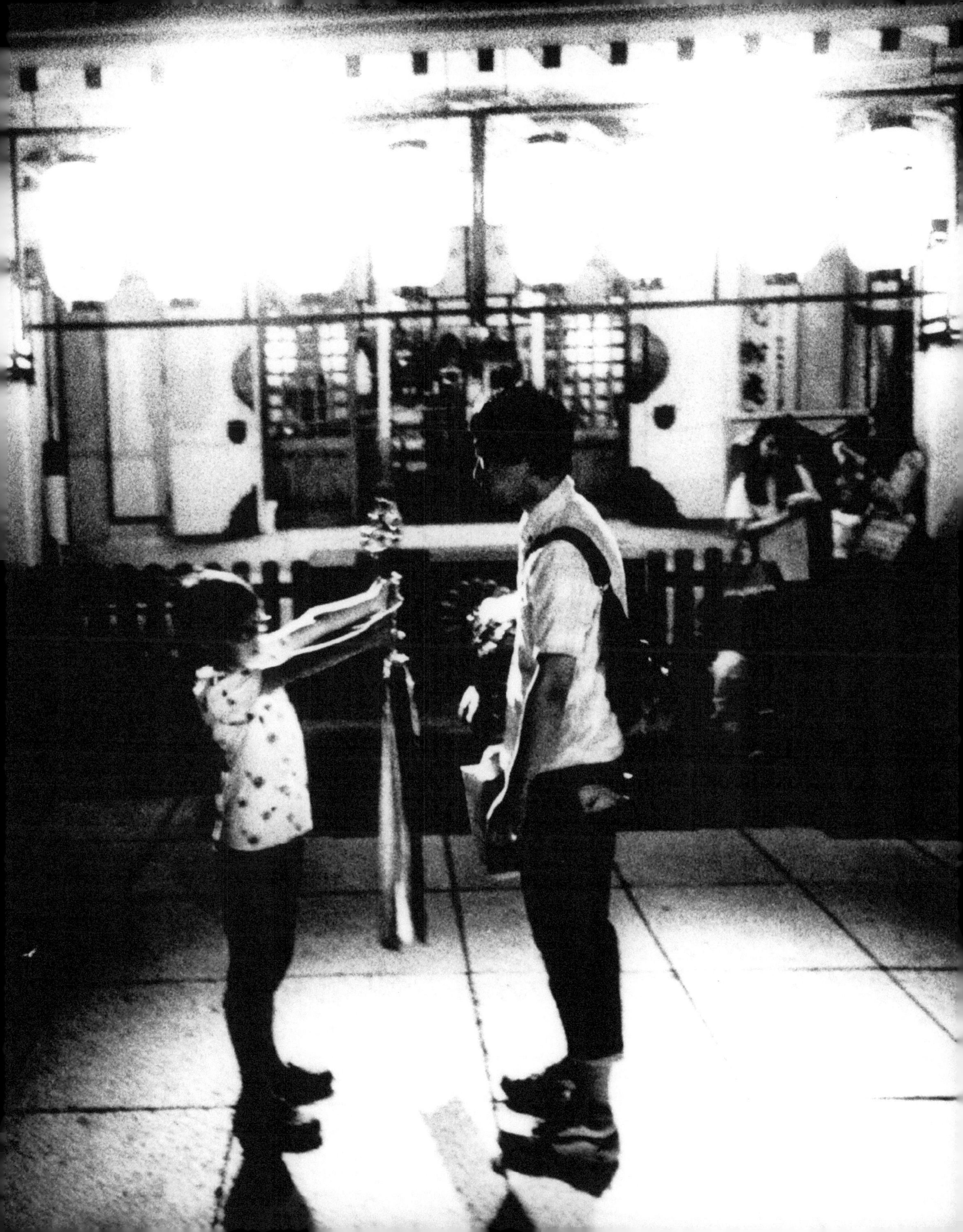

18

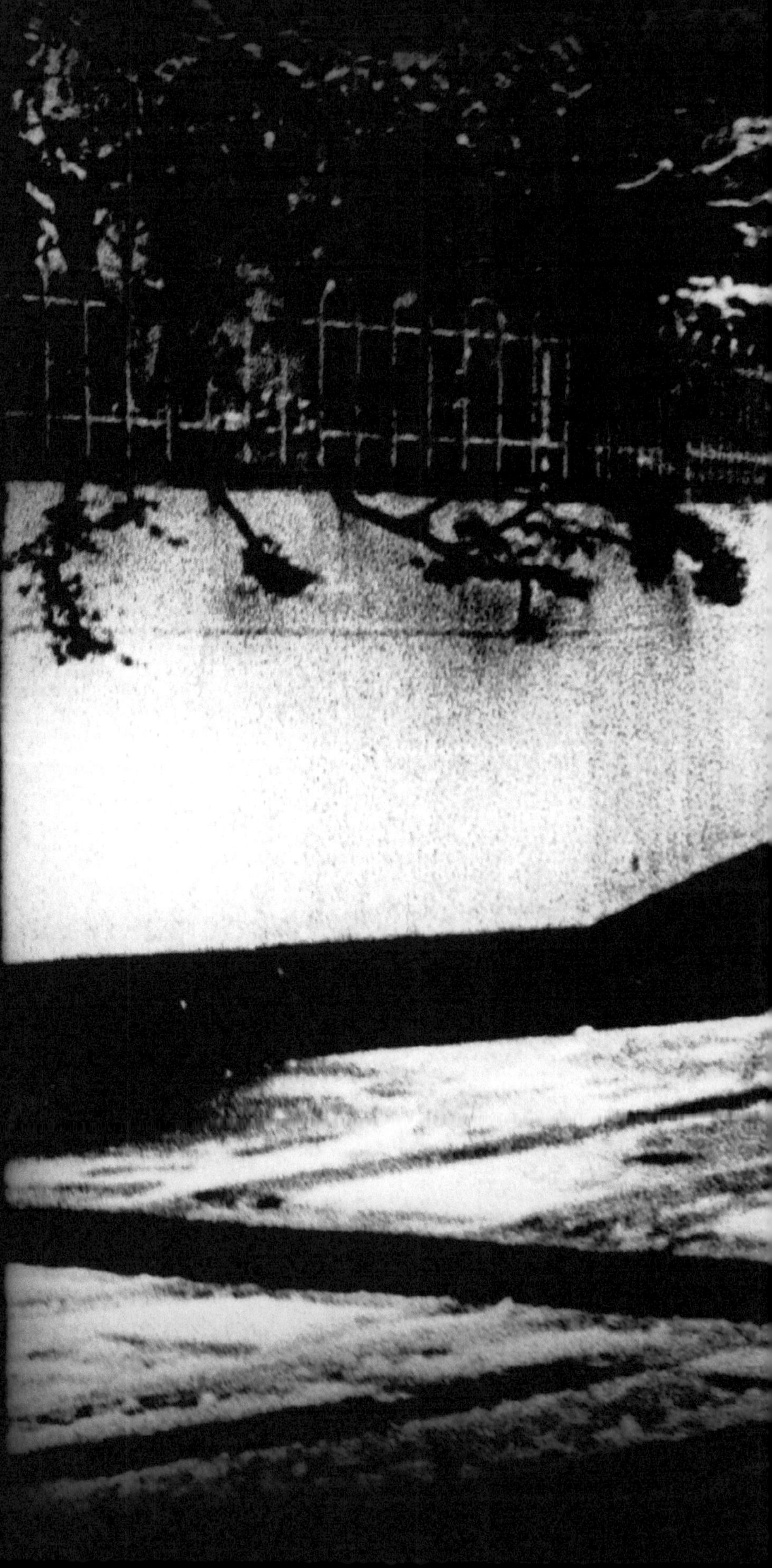

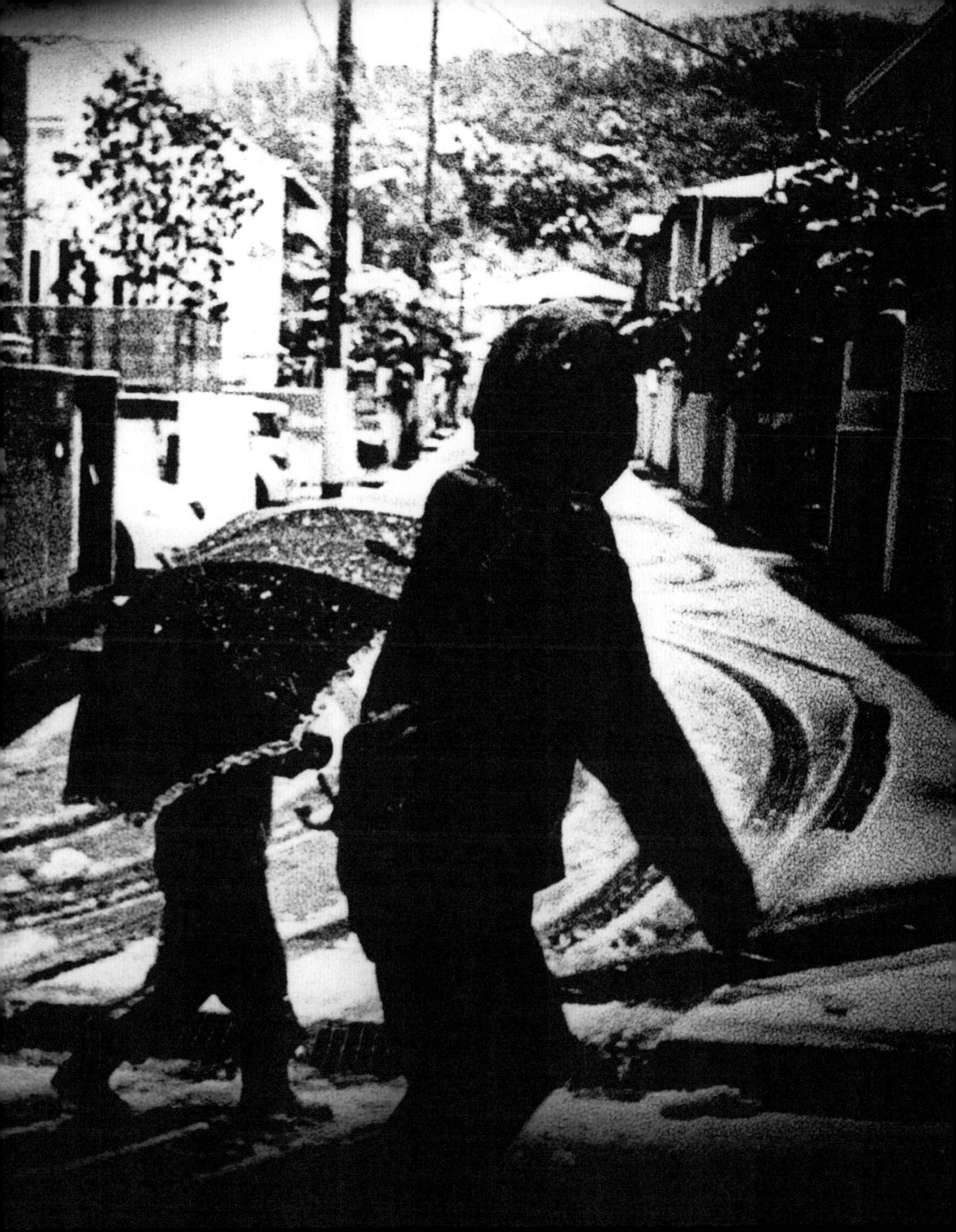

19

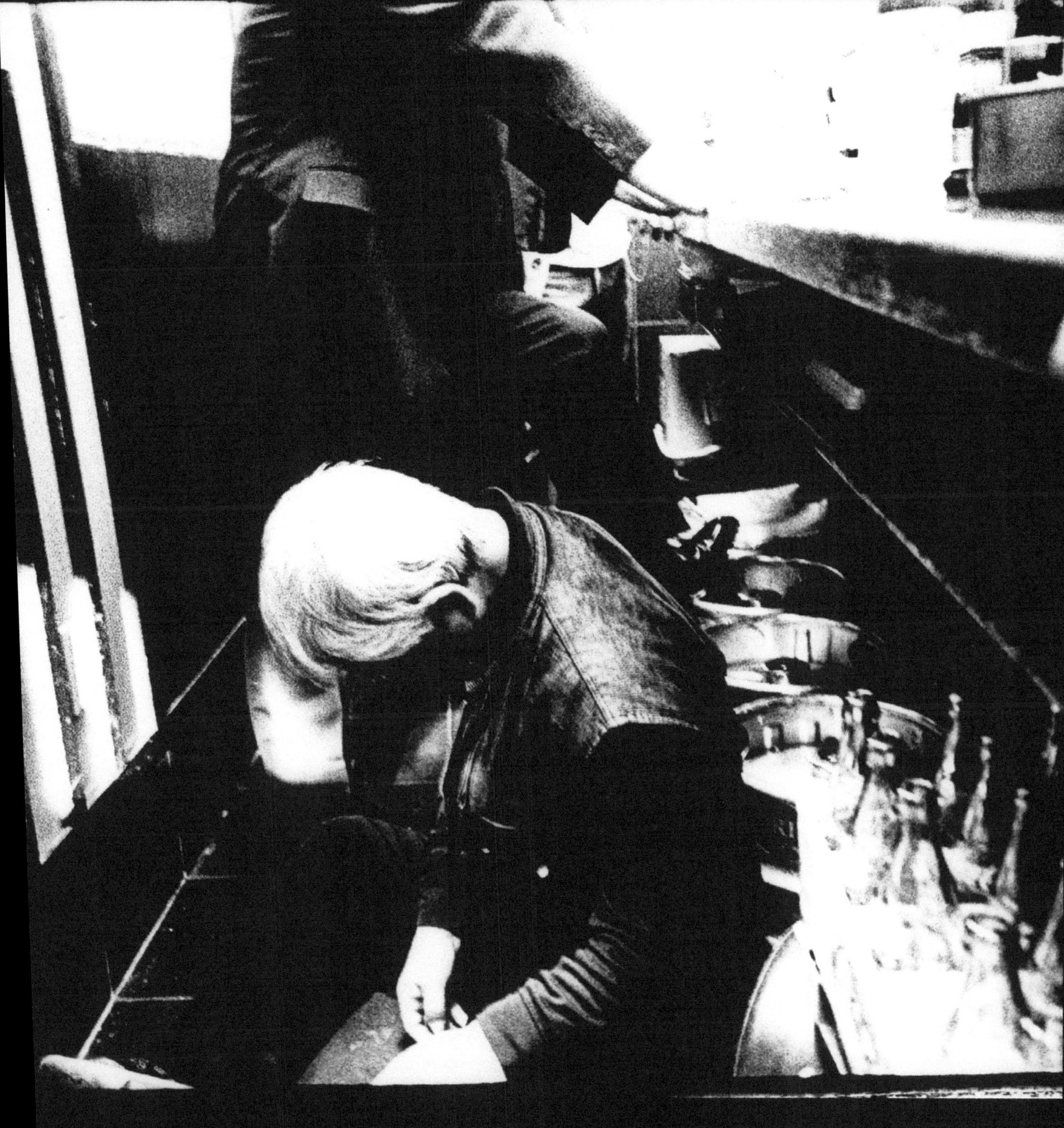

20

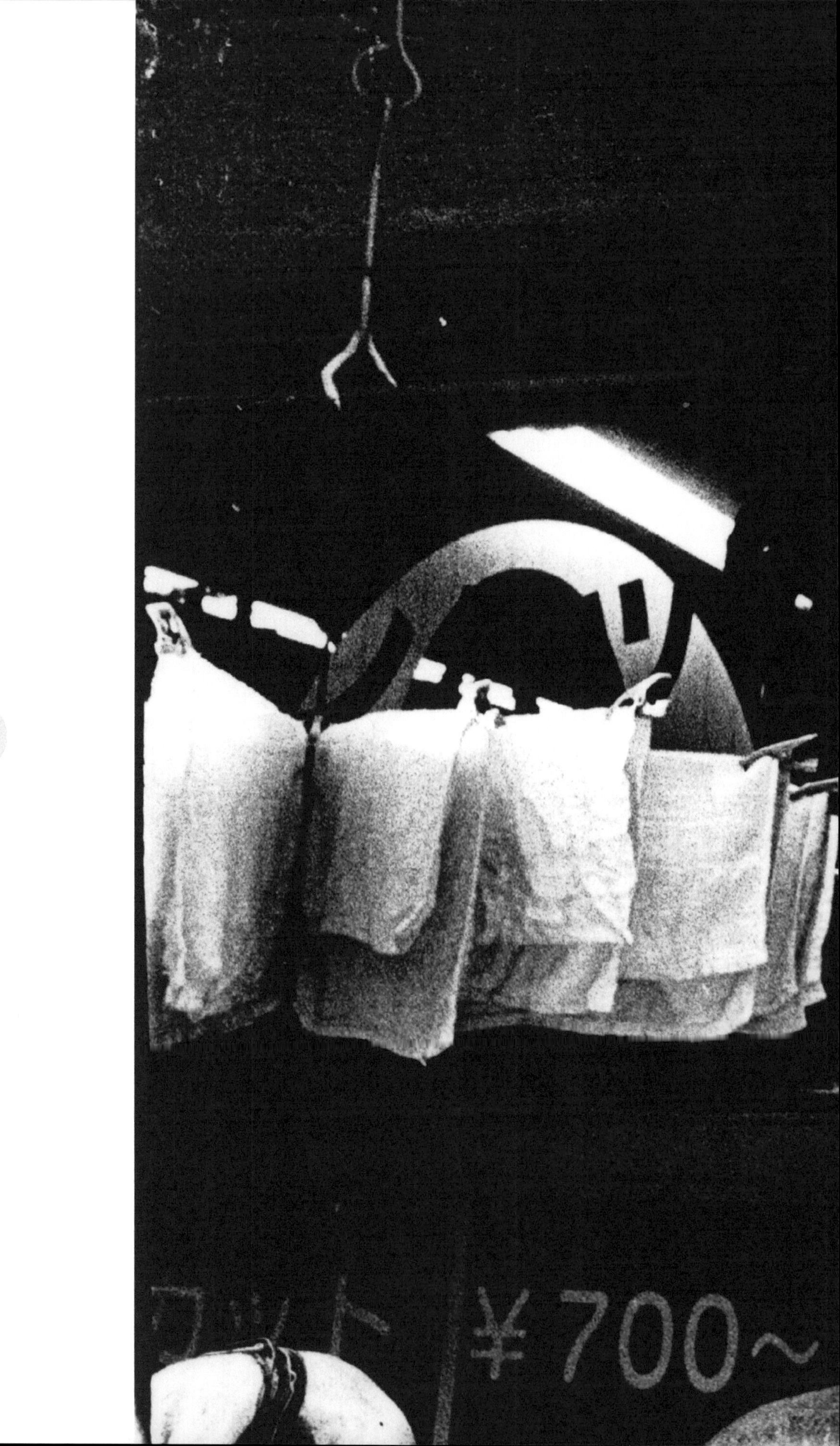

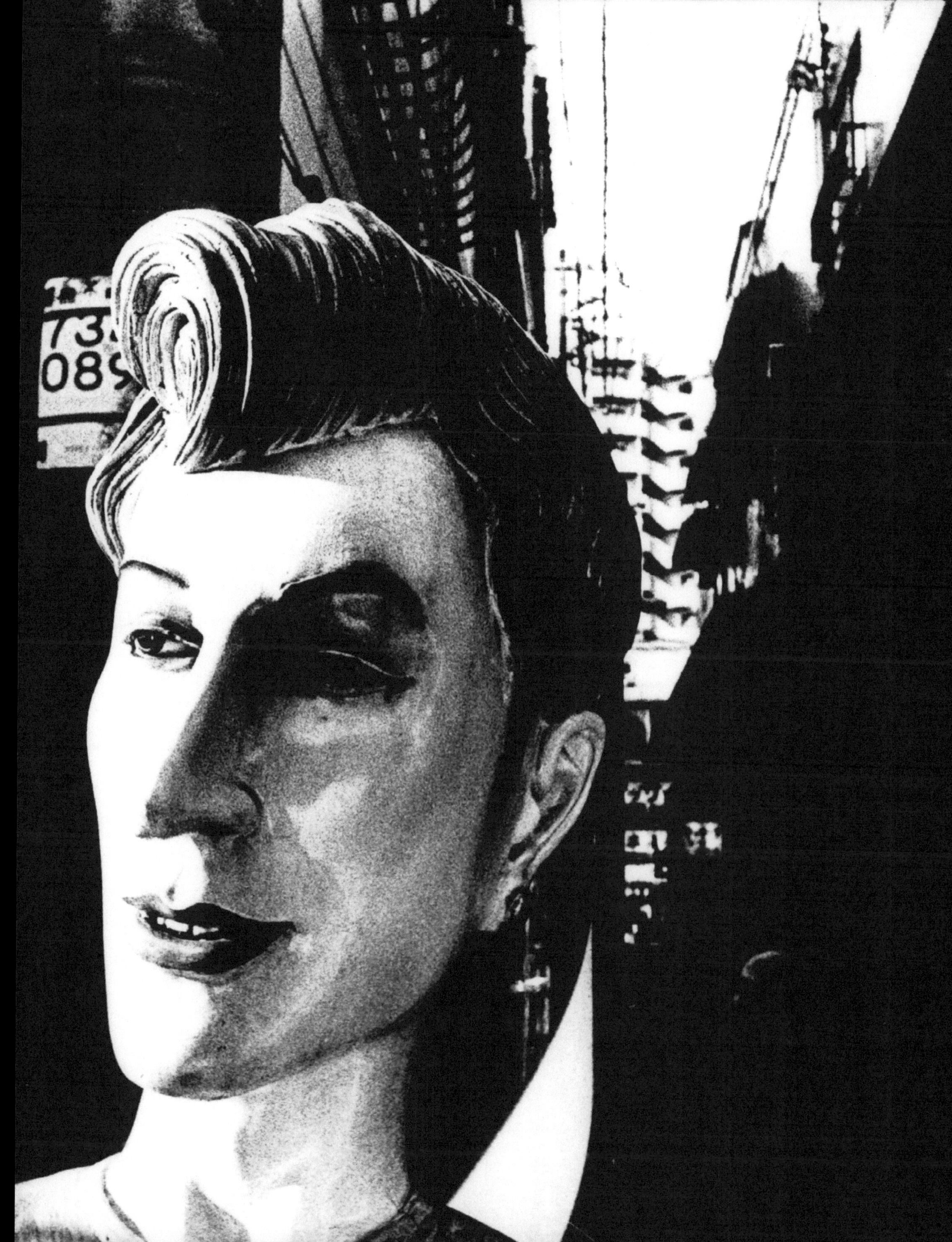

21

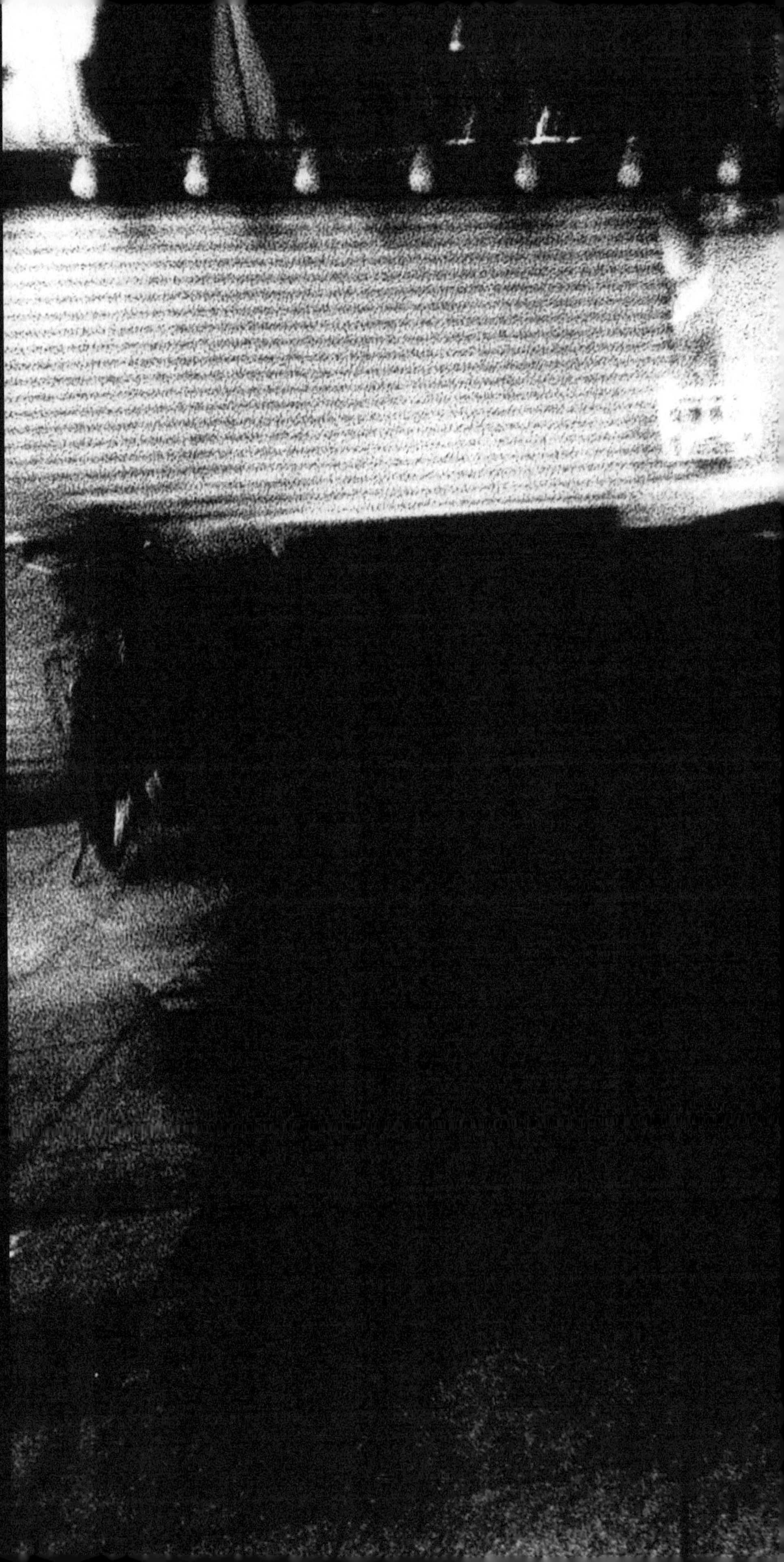

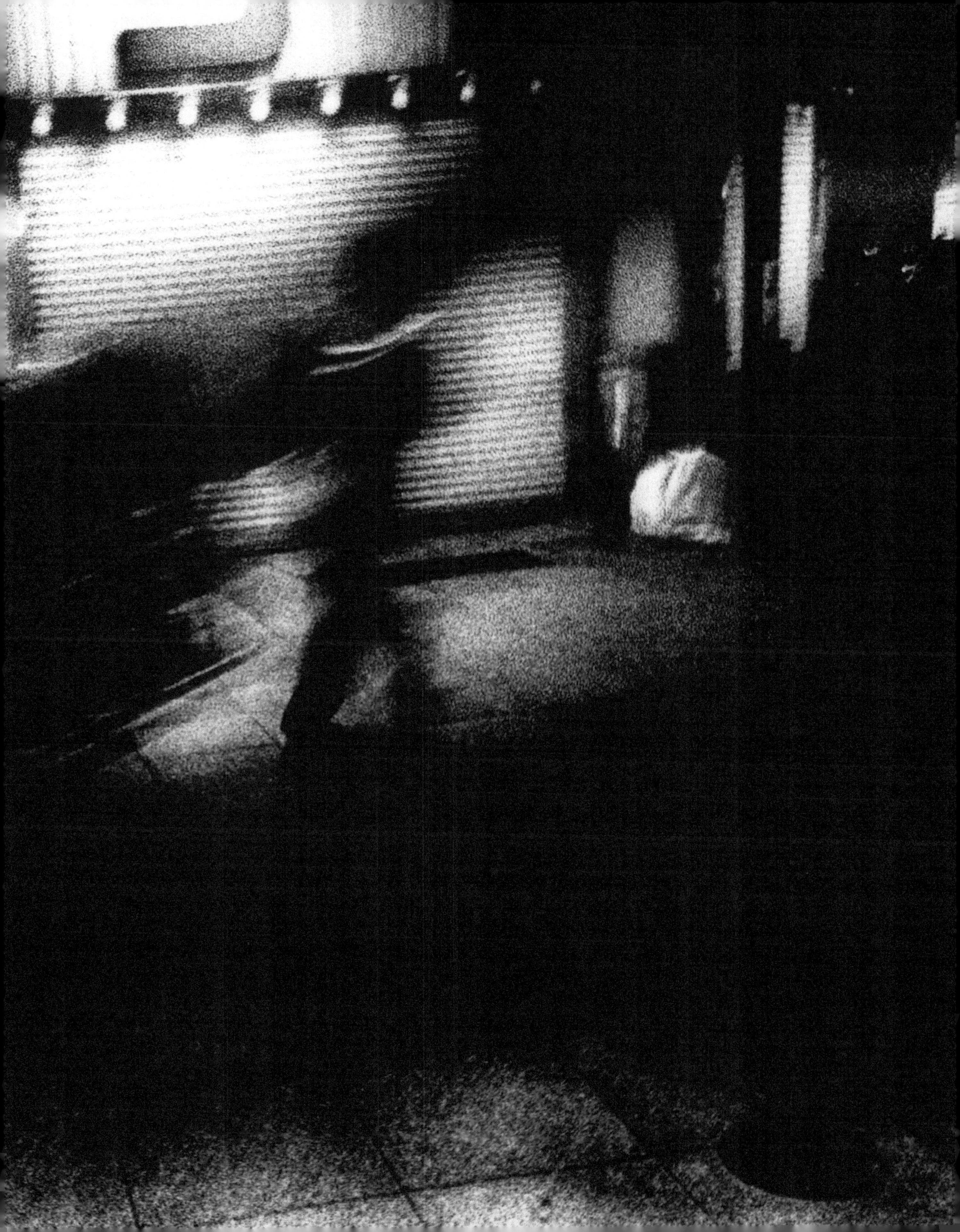

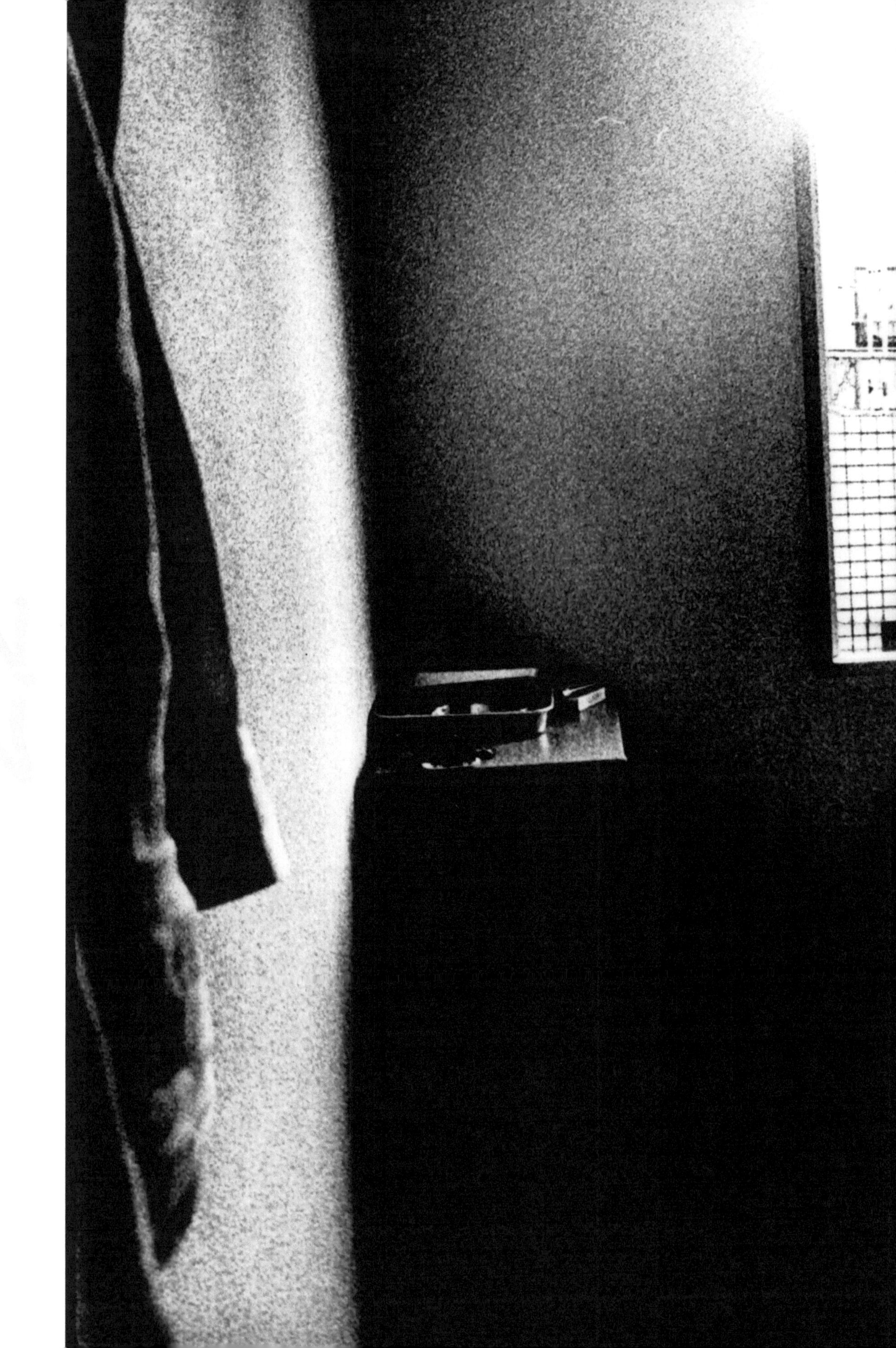

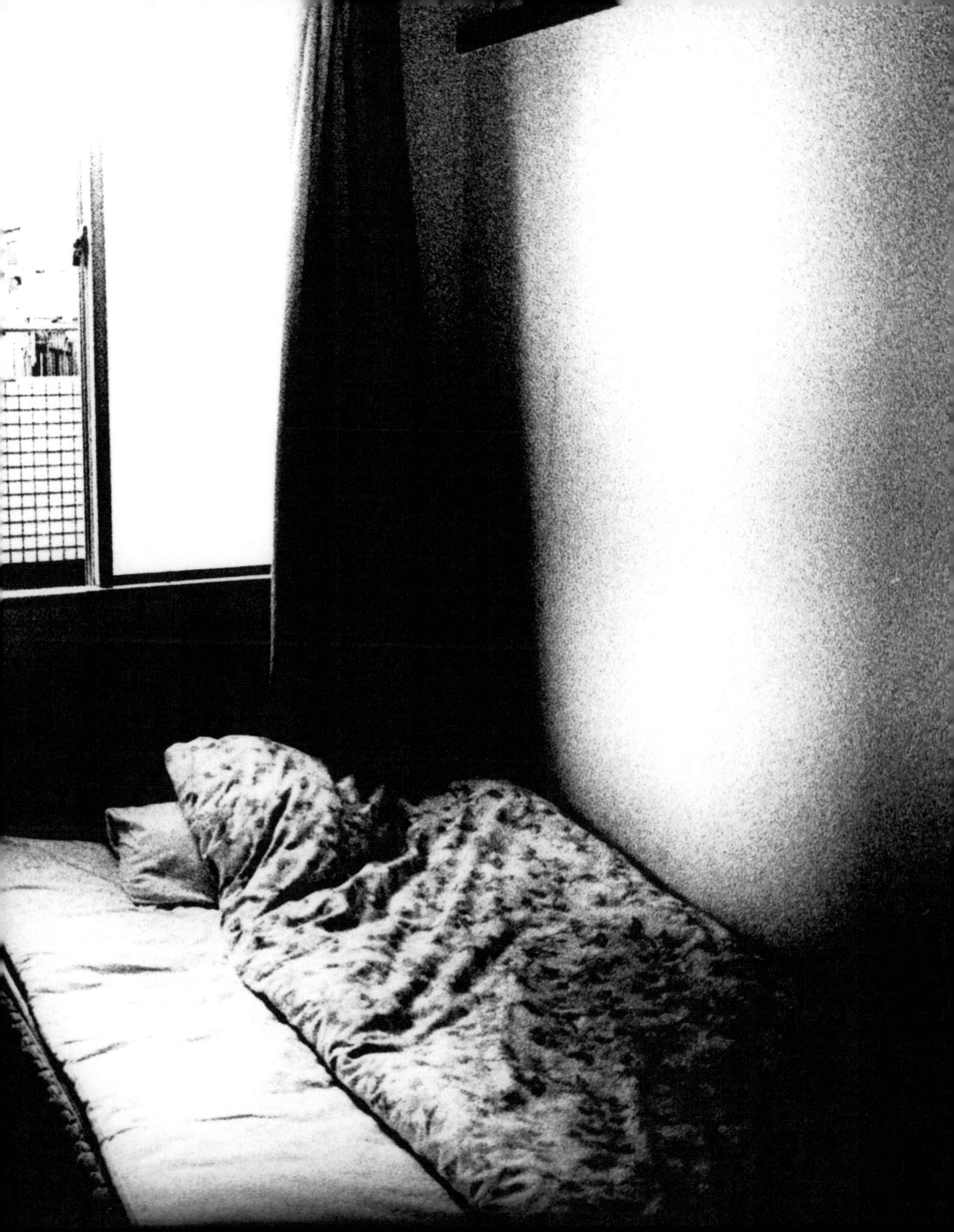

23

↑ 御堂筋線
Midosuji Line

24

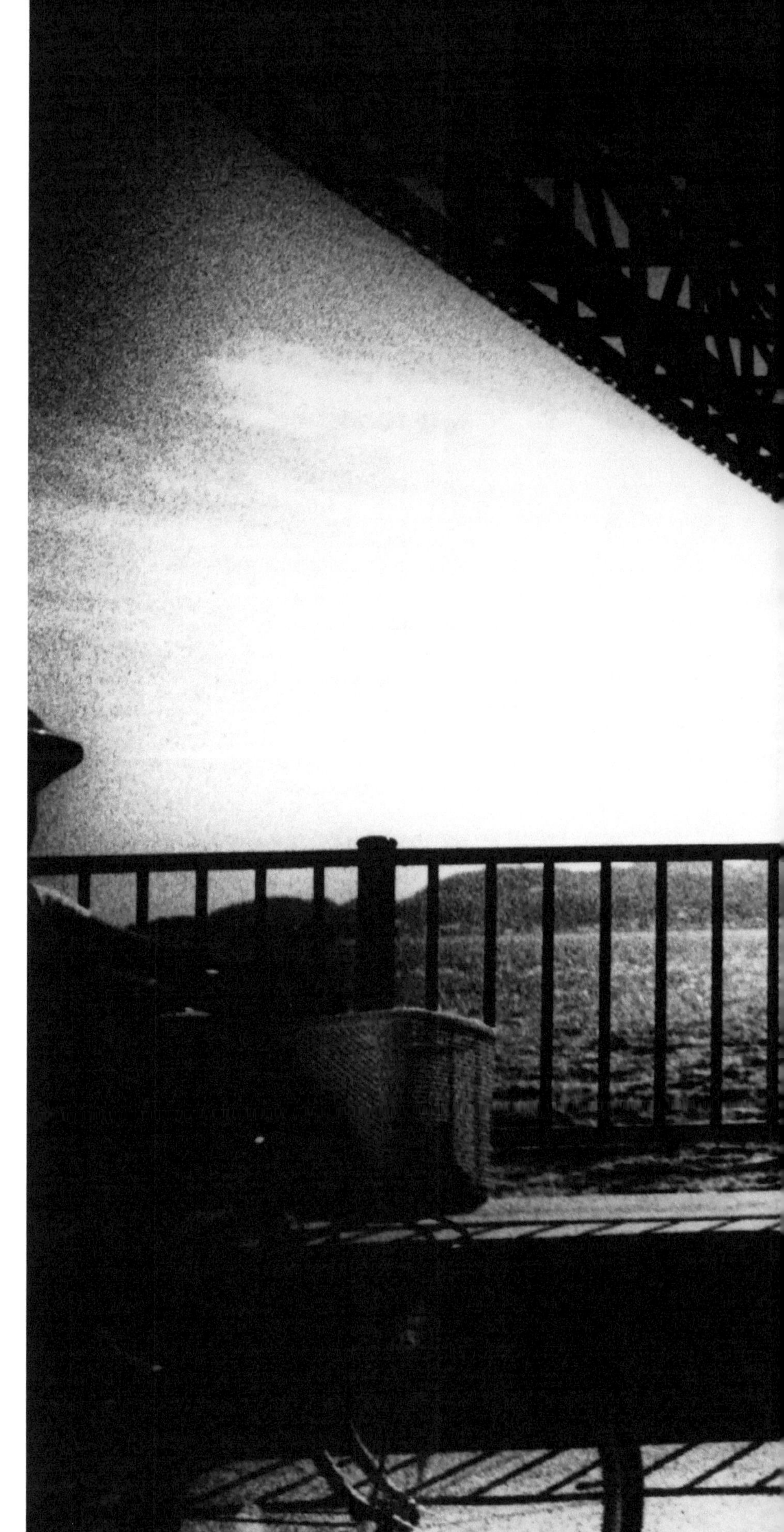

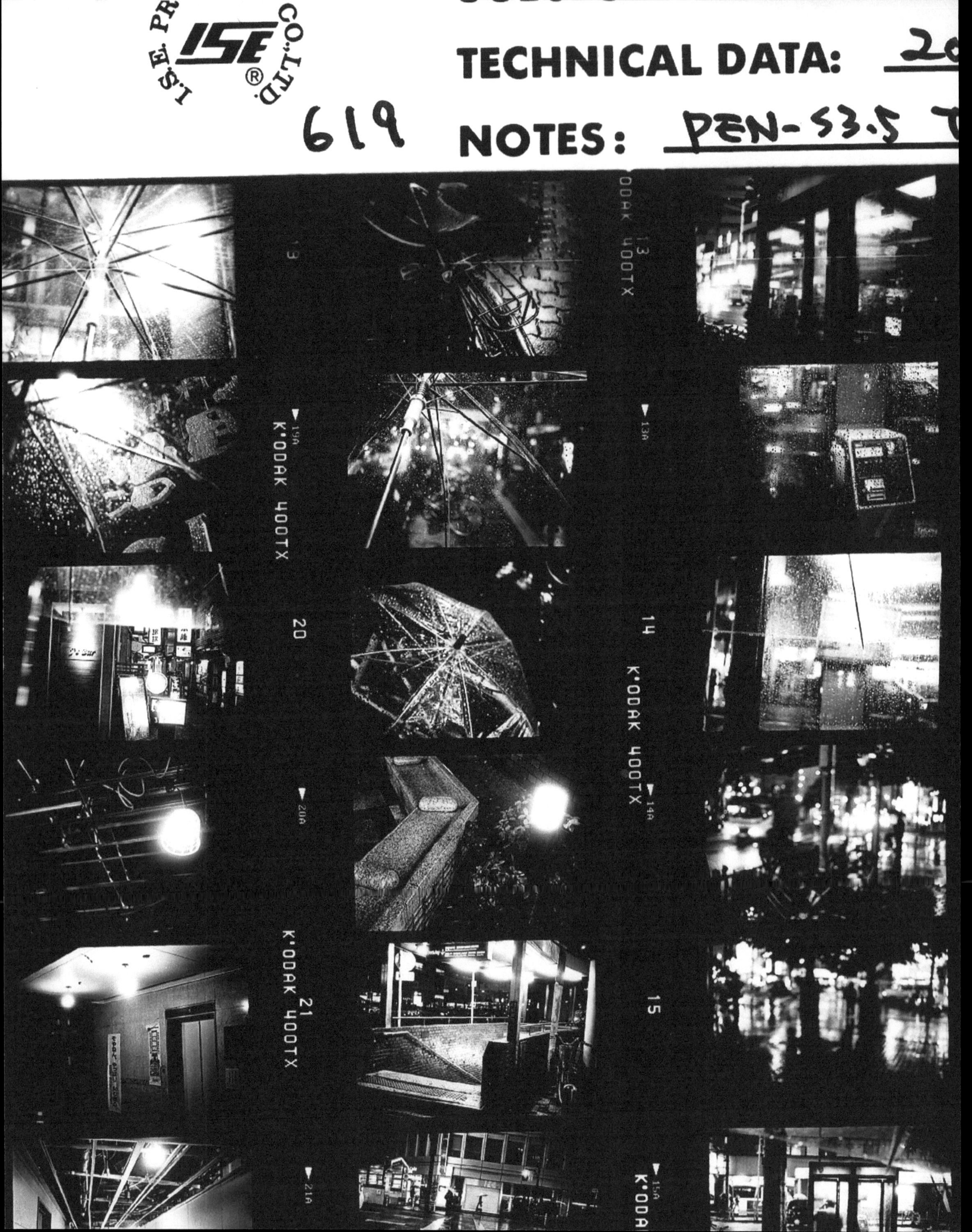

TECHNICAL DATA: 2

NOTES: PEN-53.5

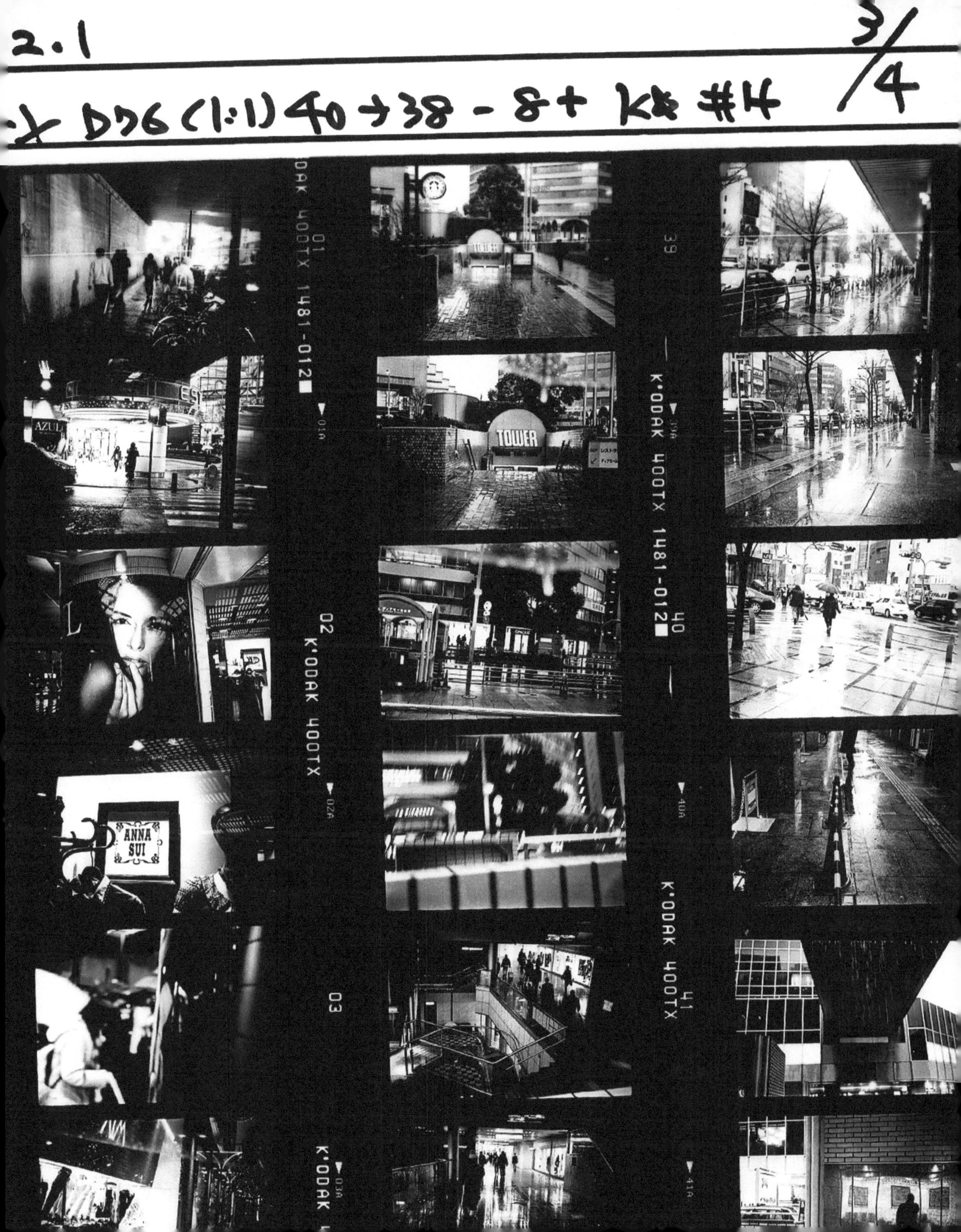

2.1

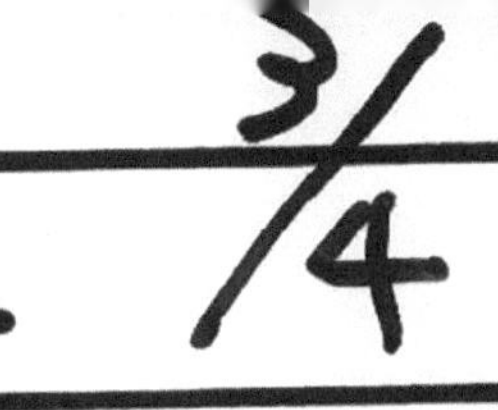

3/4

↓ D76 (1:1) 40→38 - 8+ K# #4

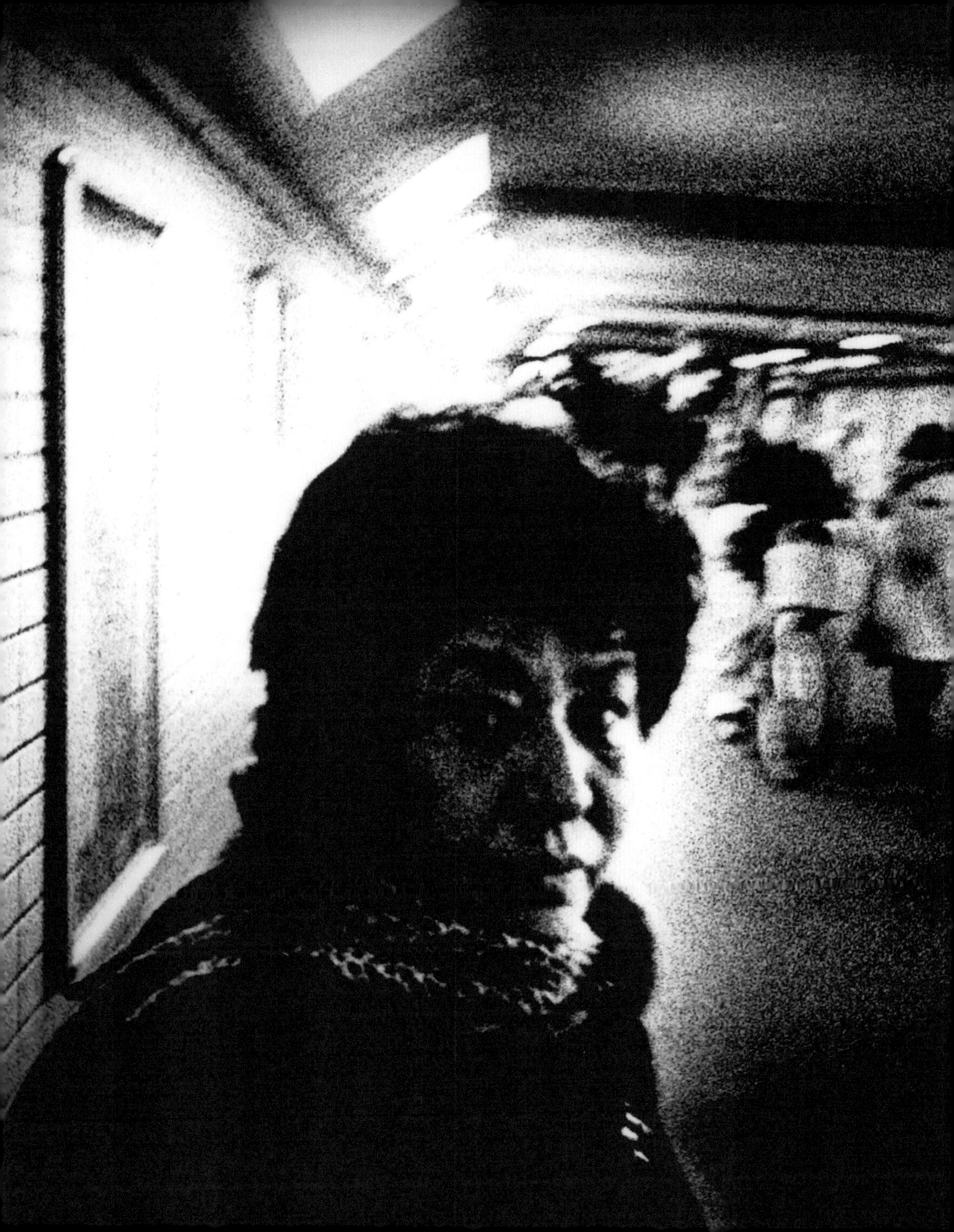

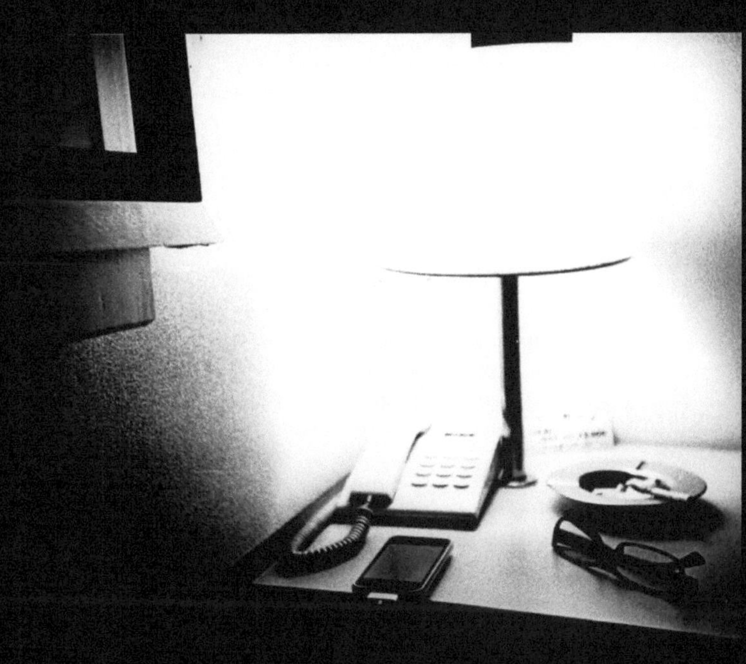

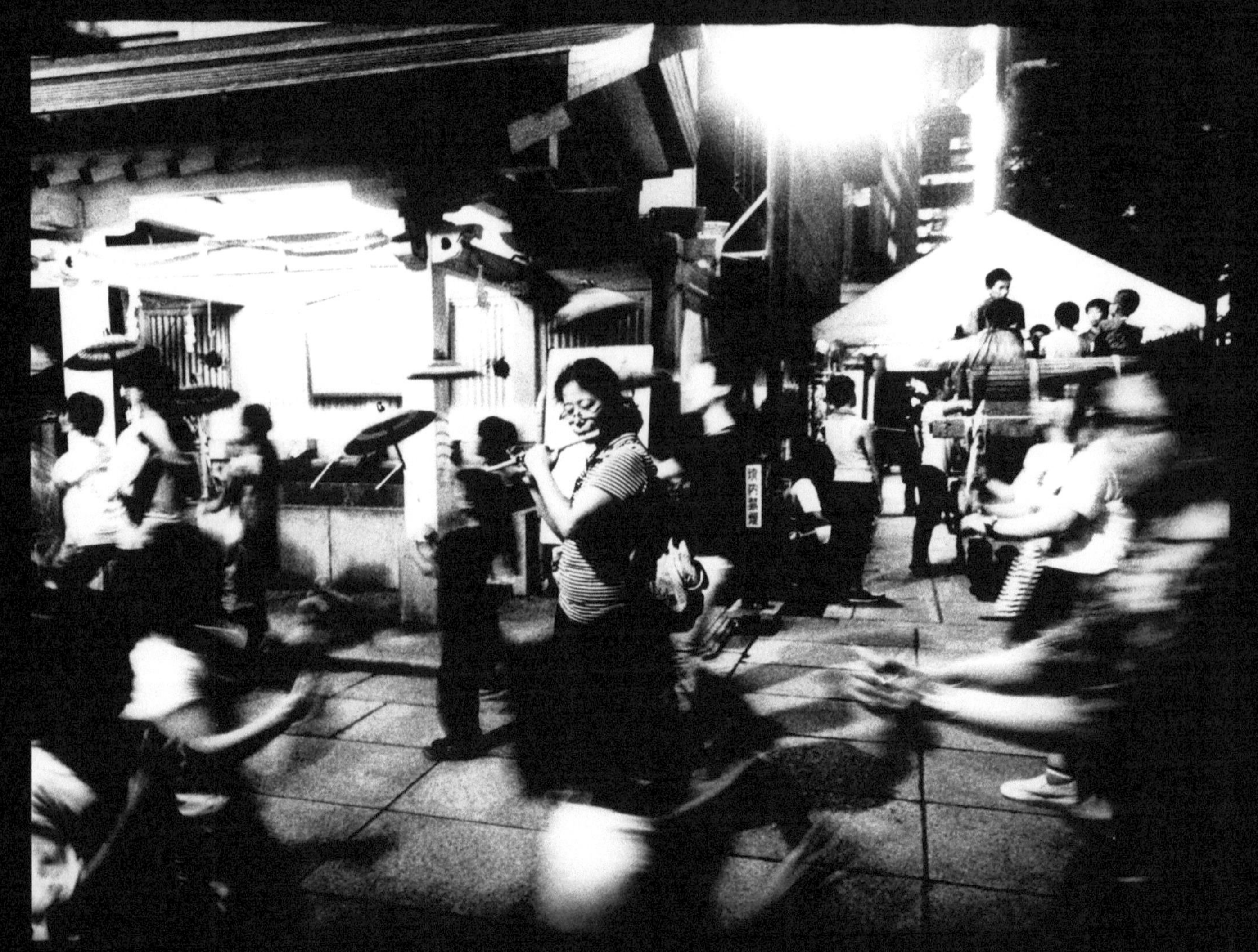

27

28

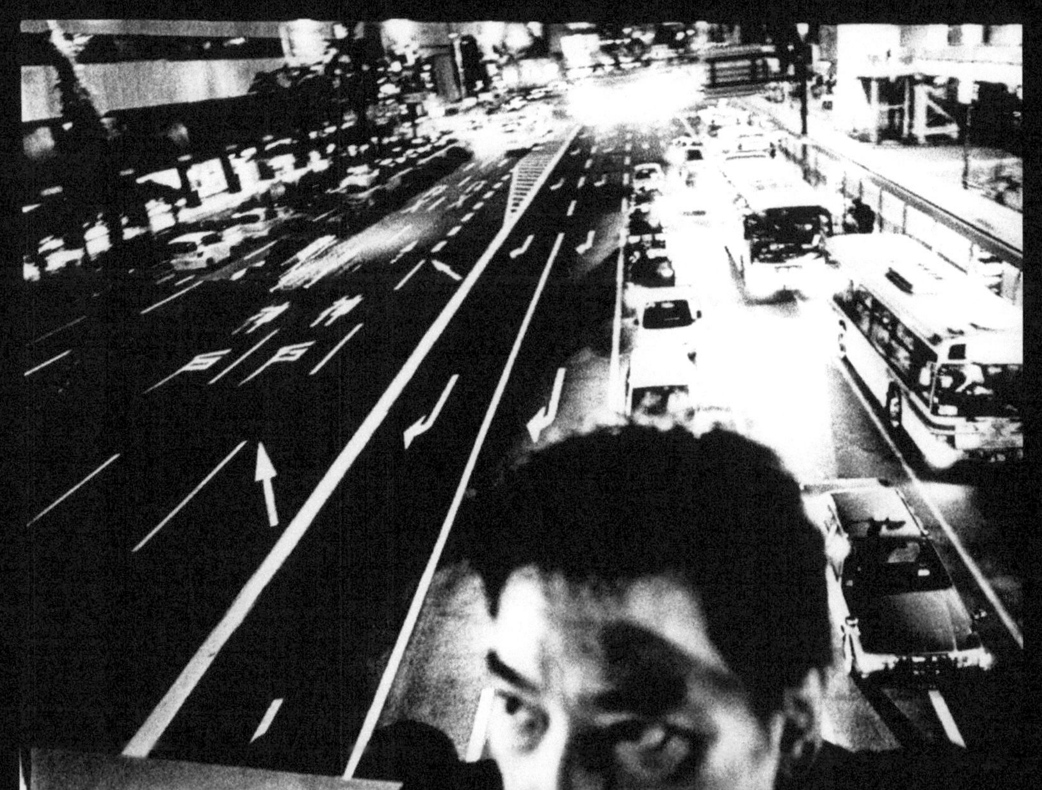

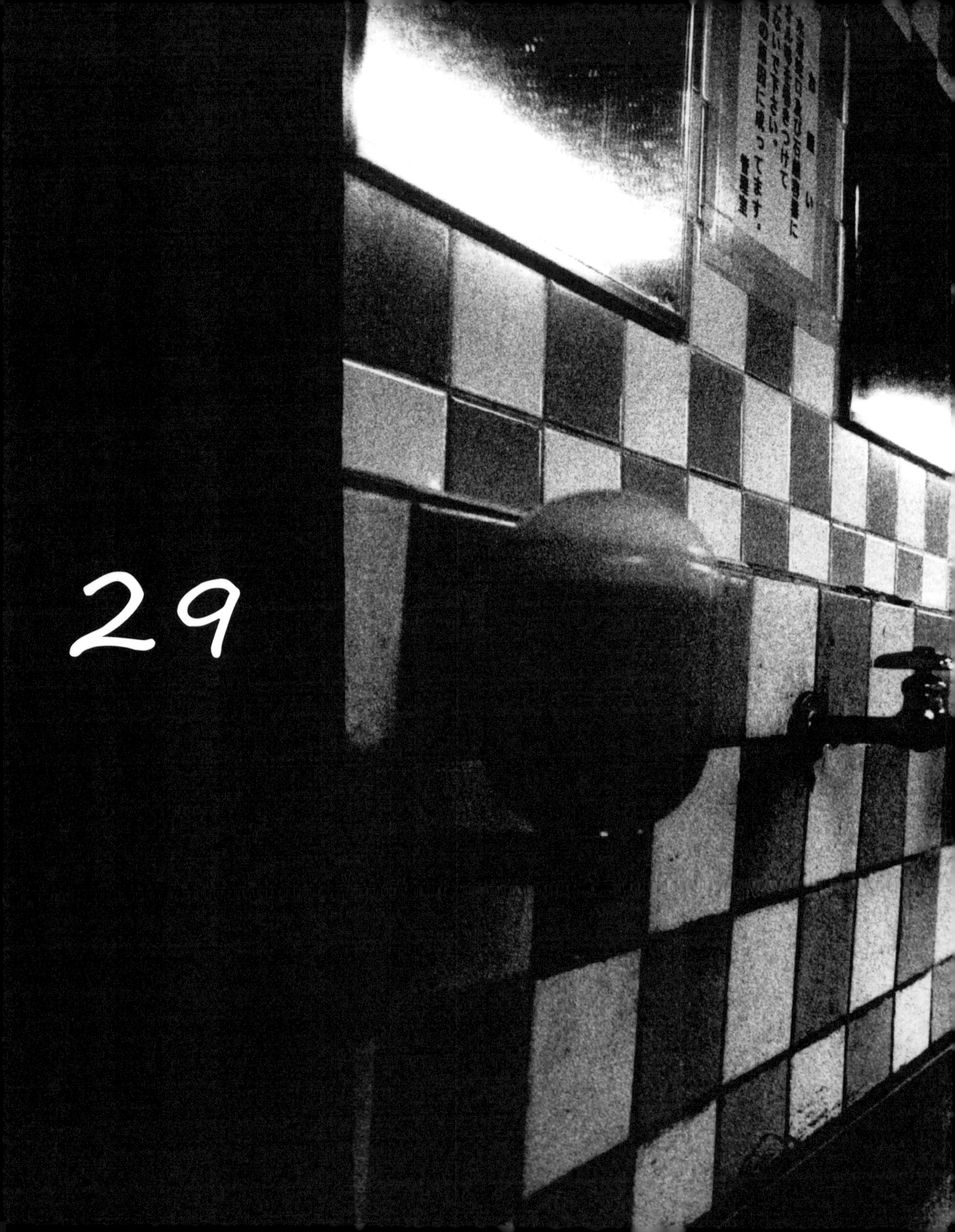

29

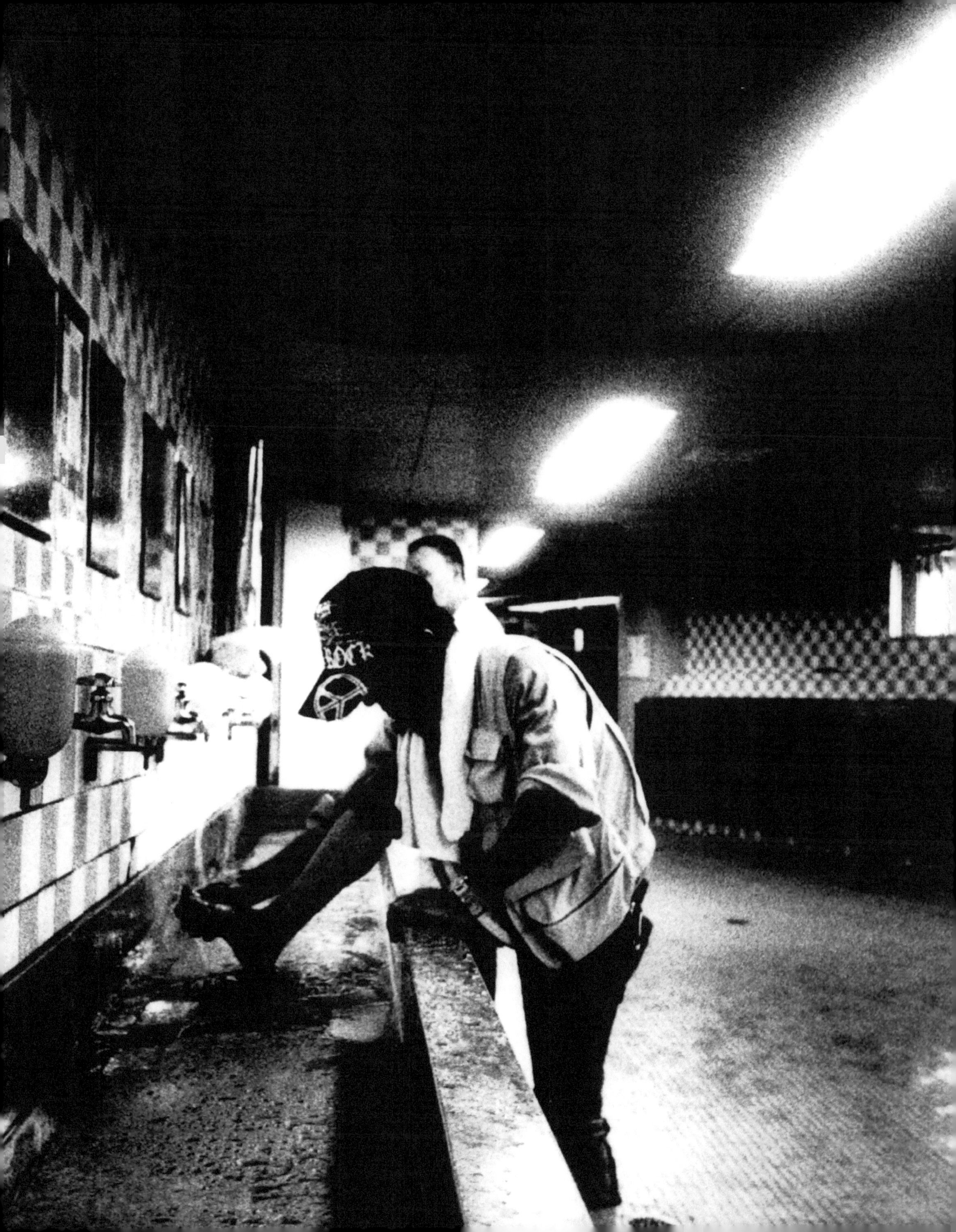

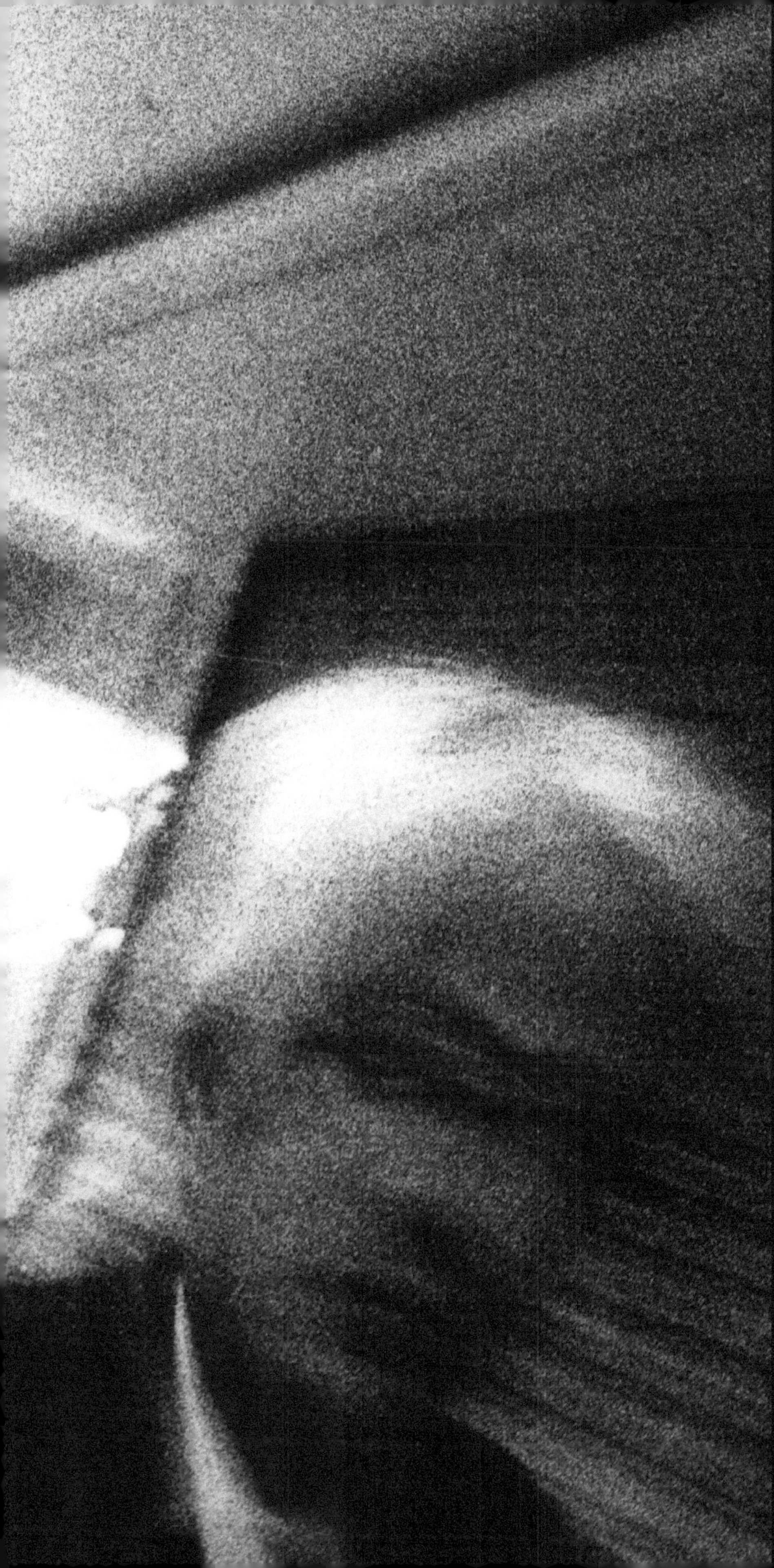

30

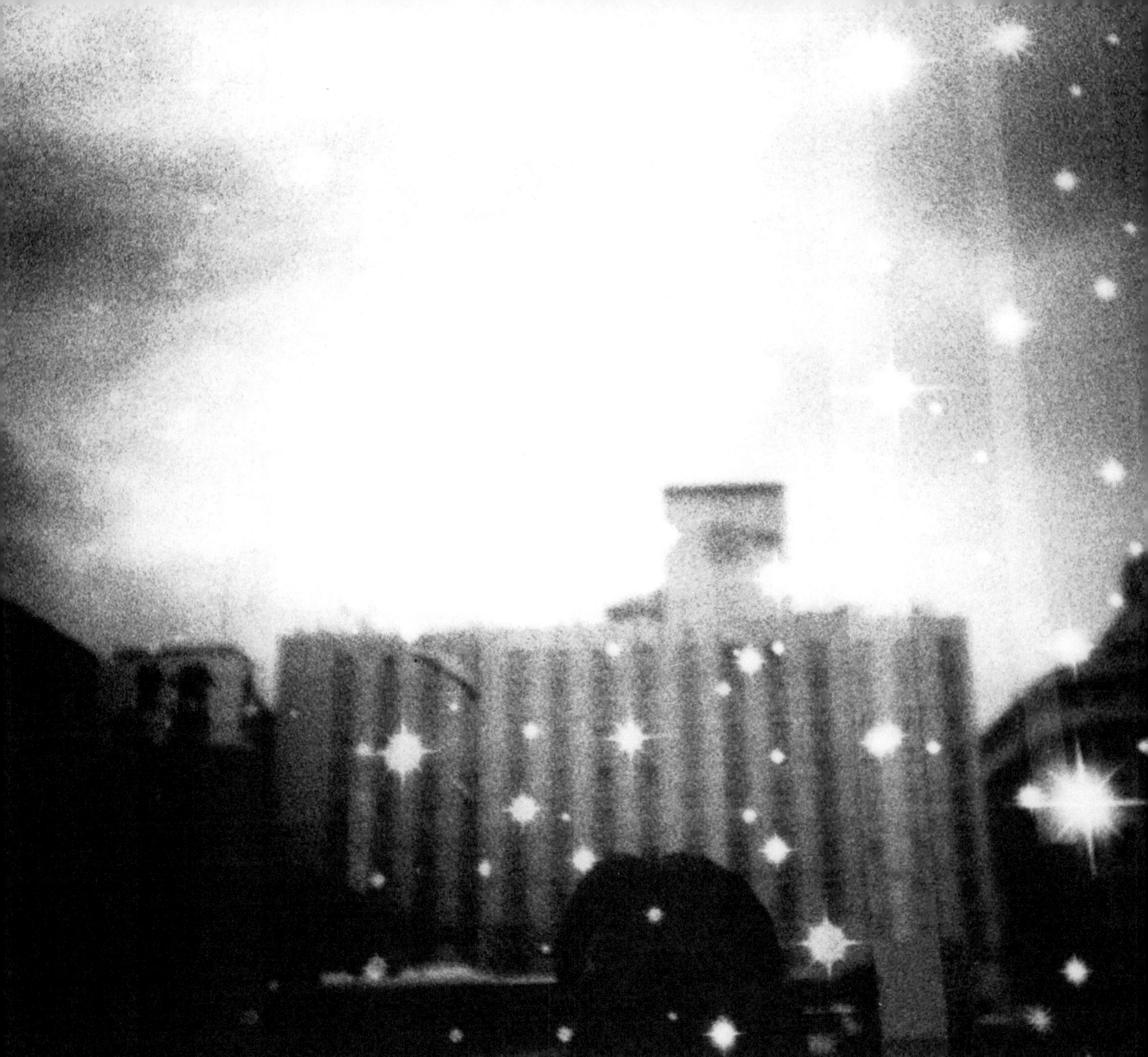

31

32

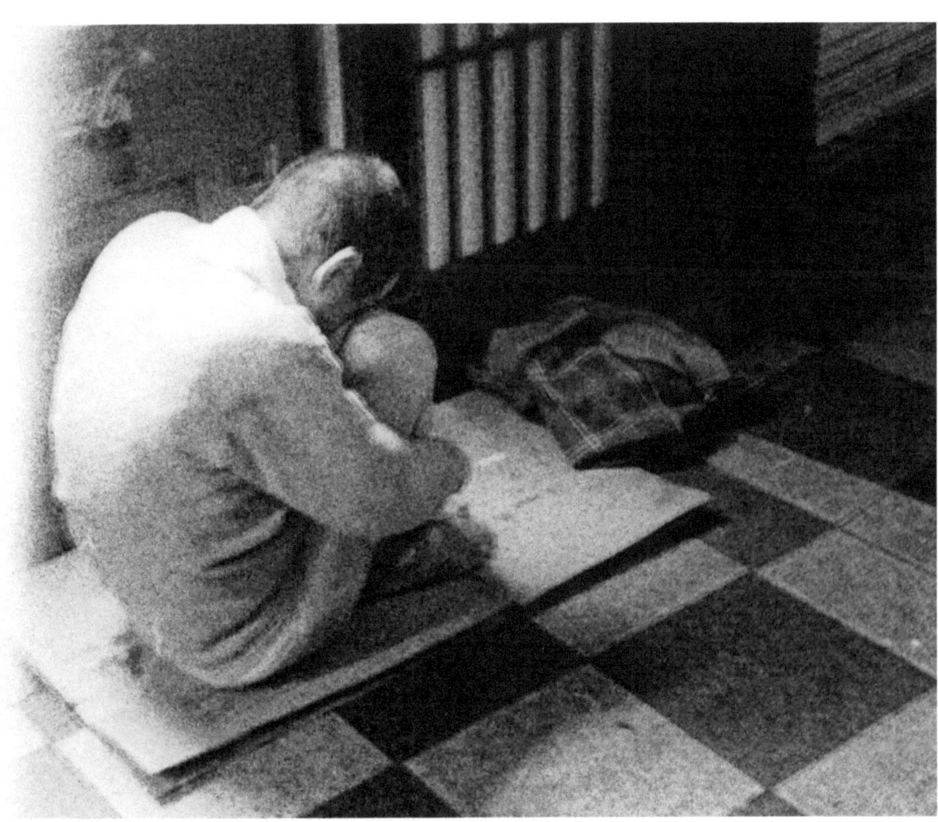

33

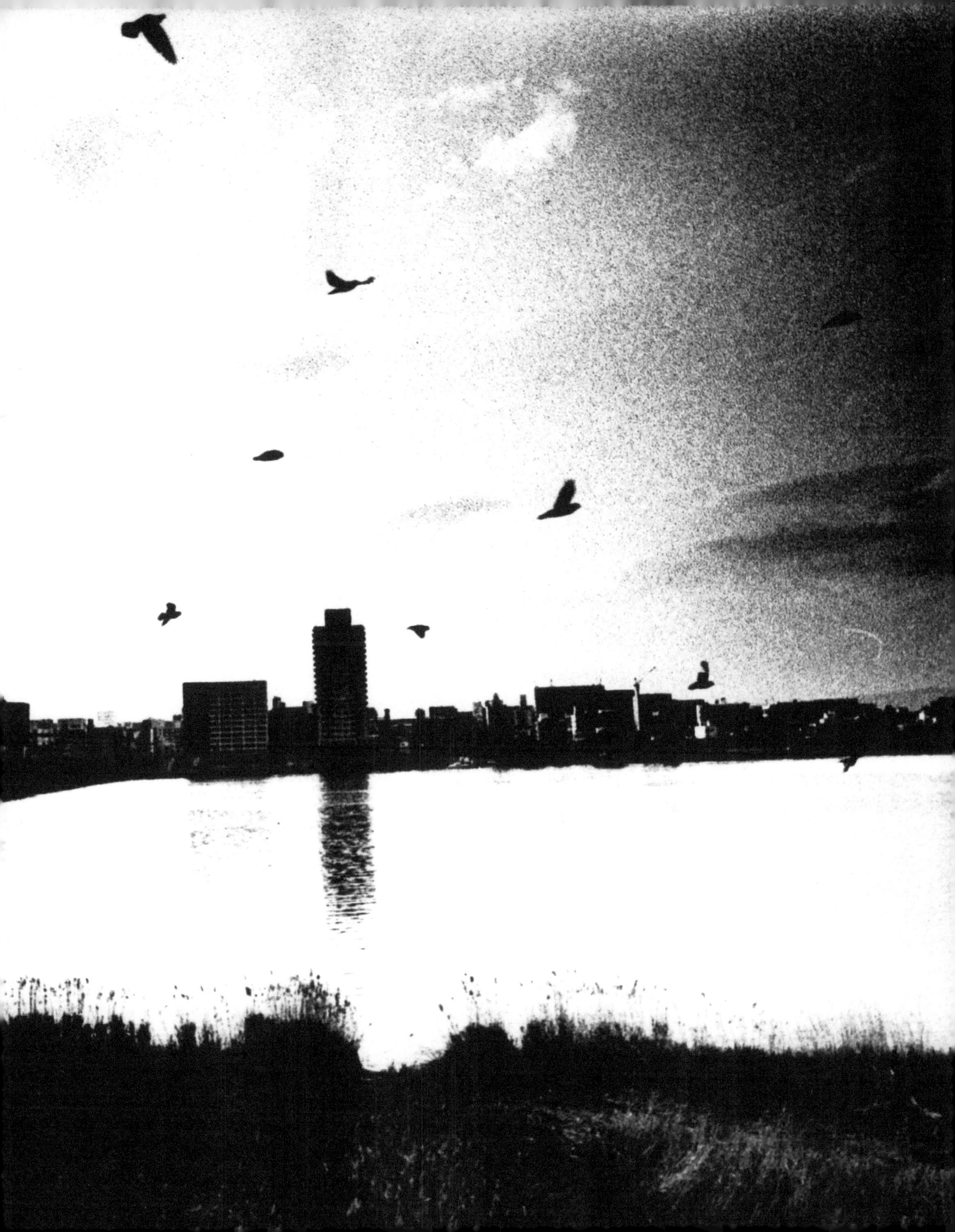

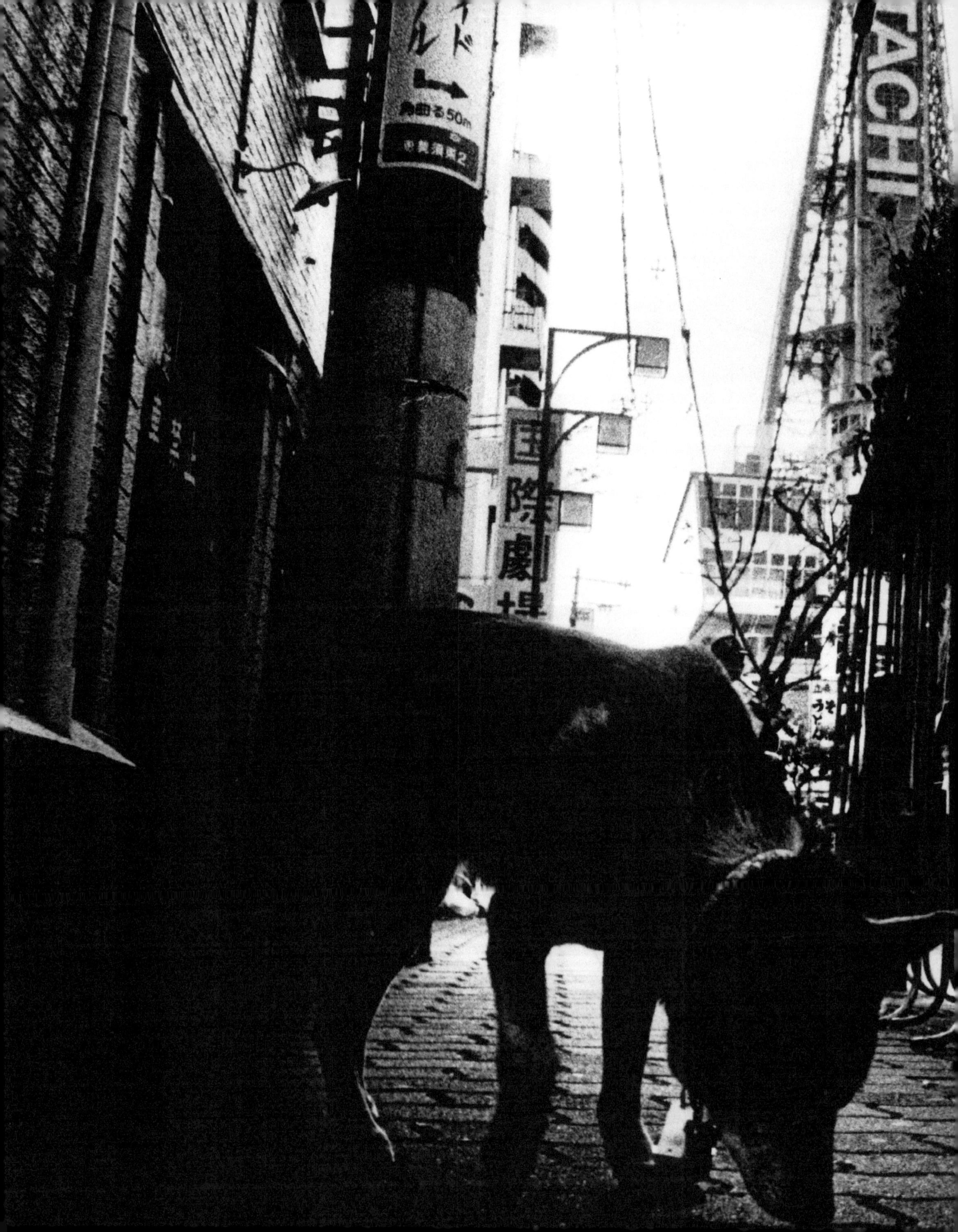
HITACHI
ルド
↑
角田る50m
国際劇場
そ
うどん

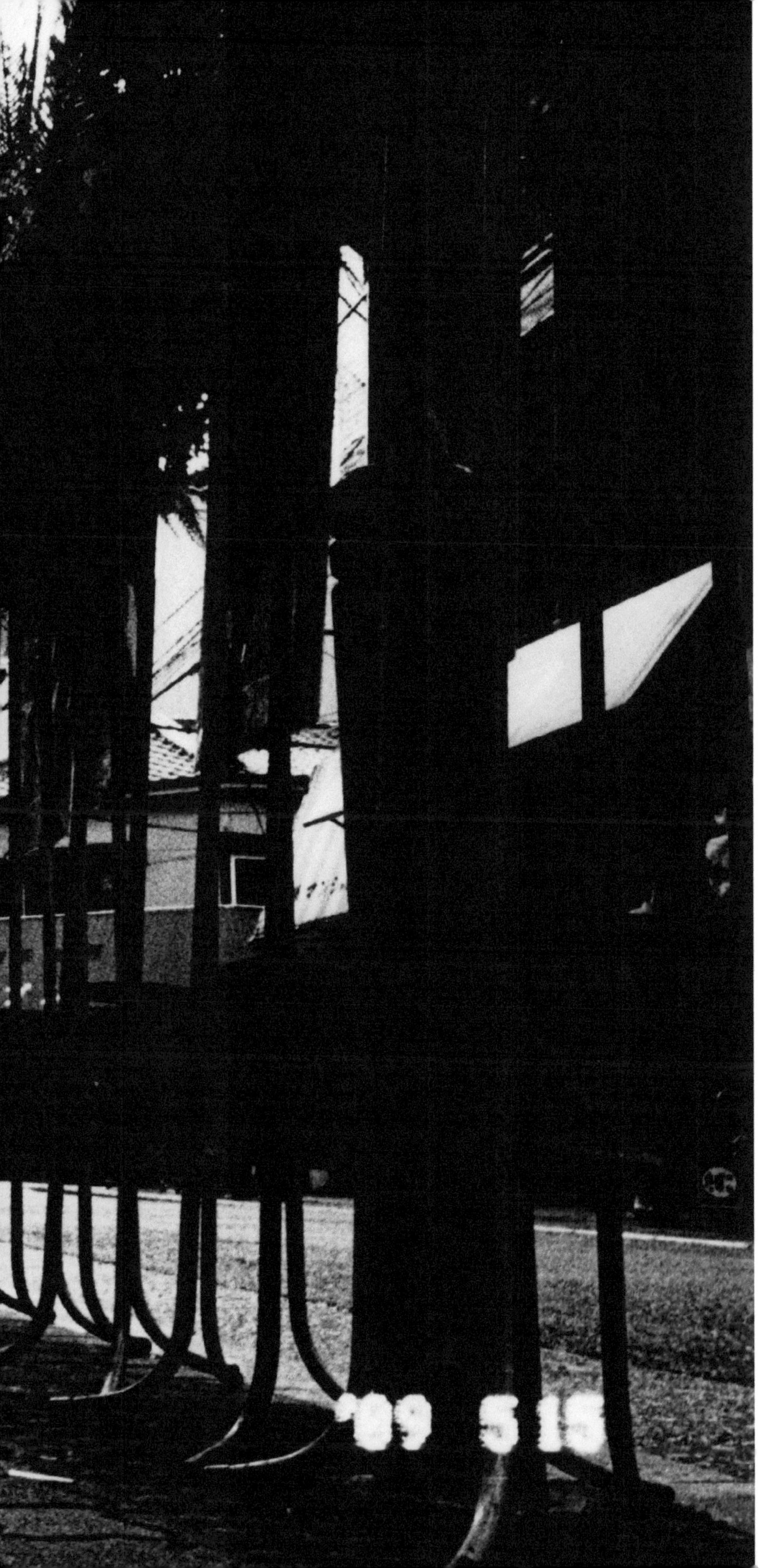

34

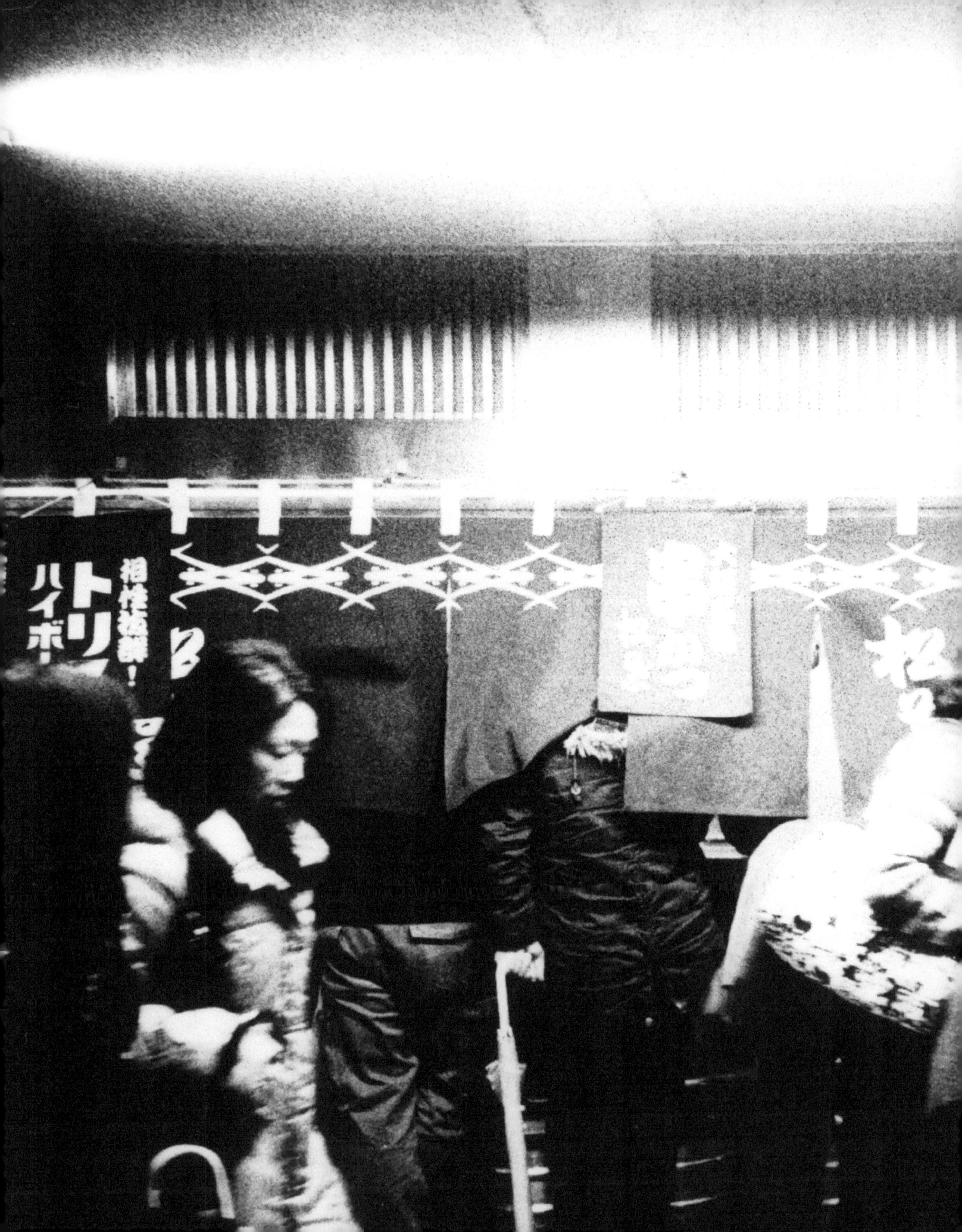
トリ
ハイボー
相性抜群！

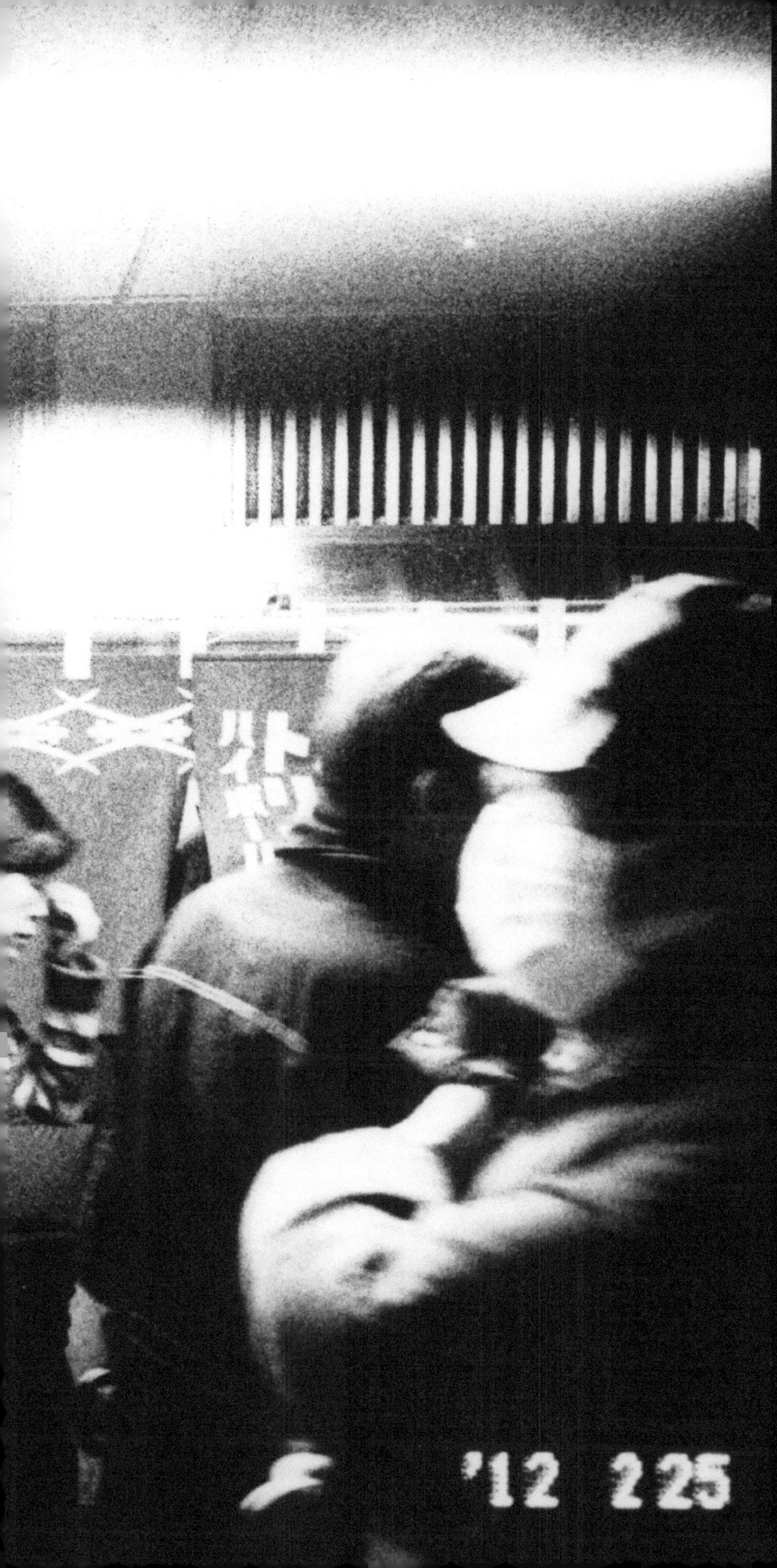

35
'12 2 25

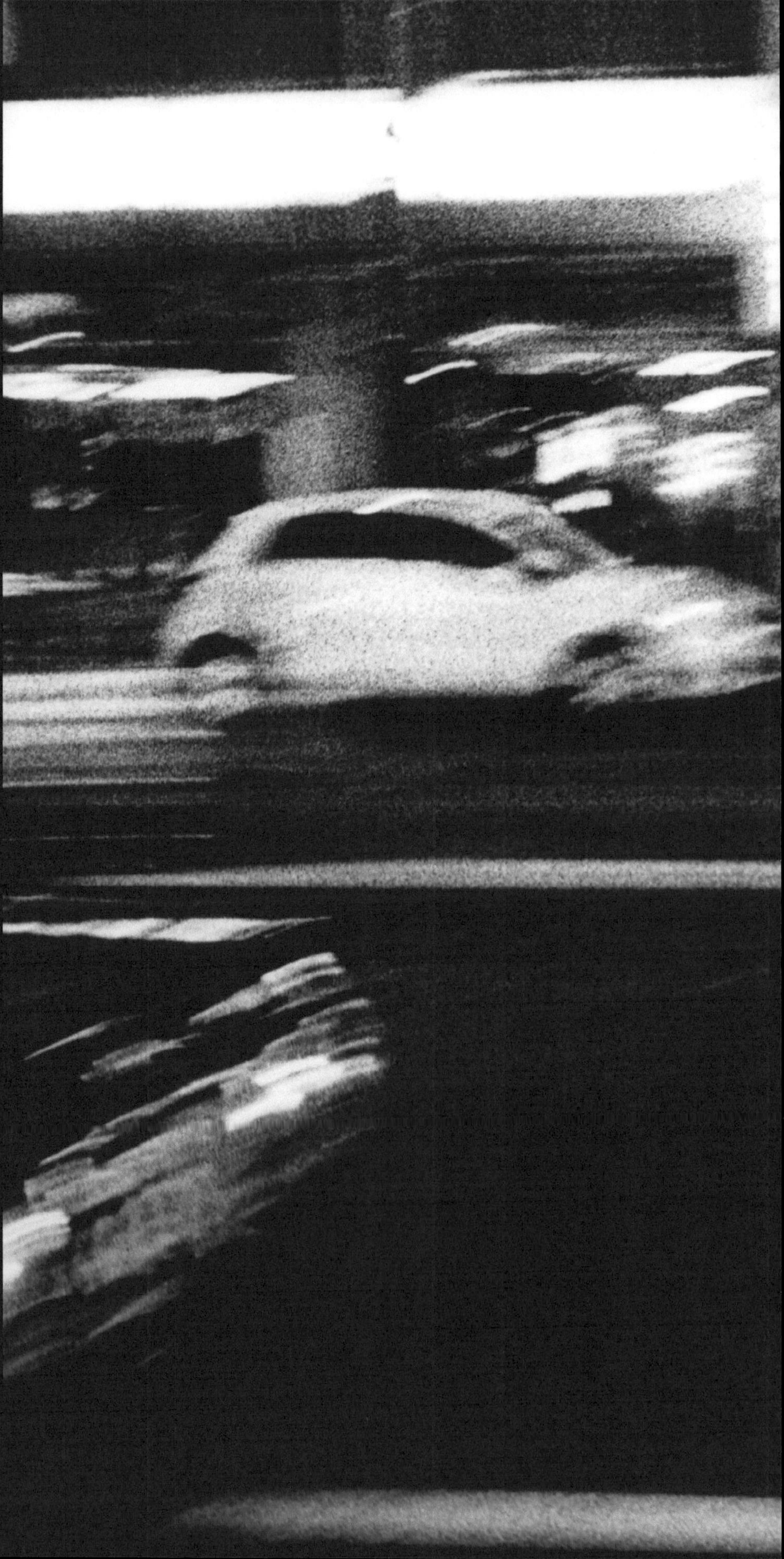

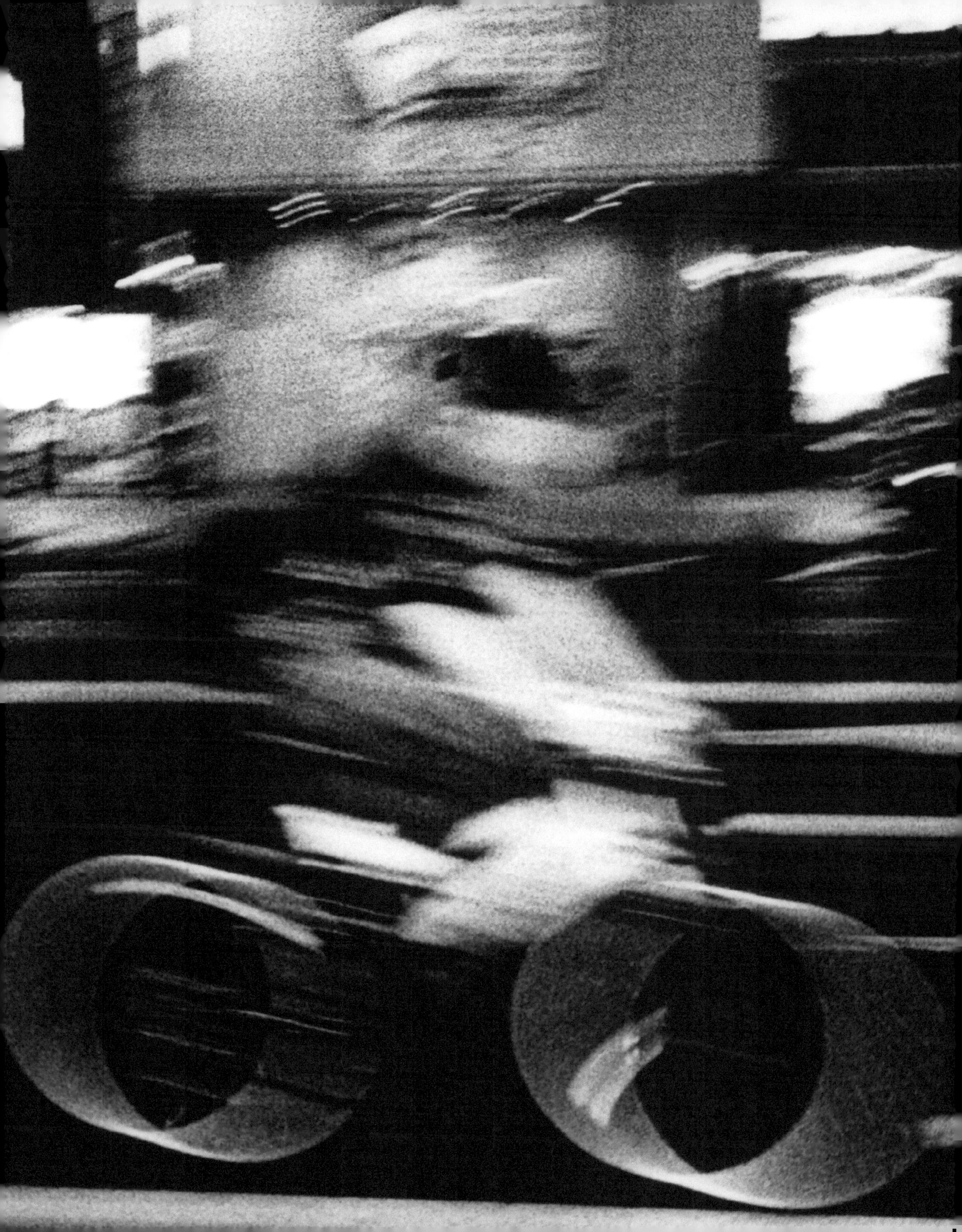

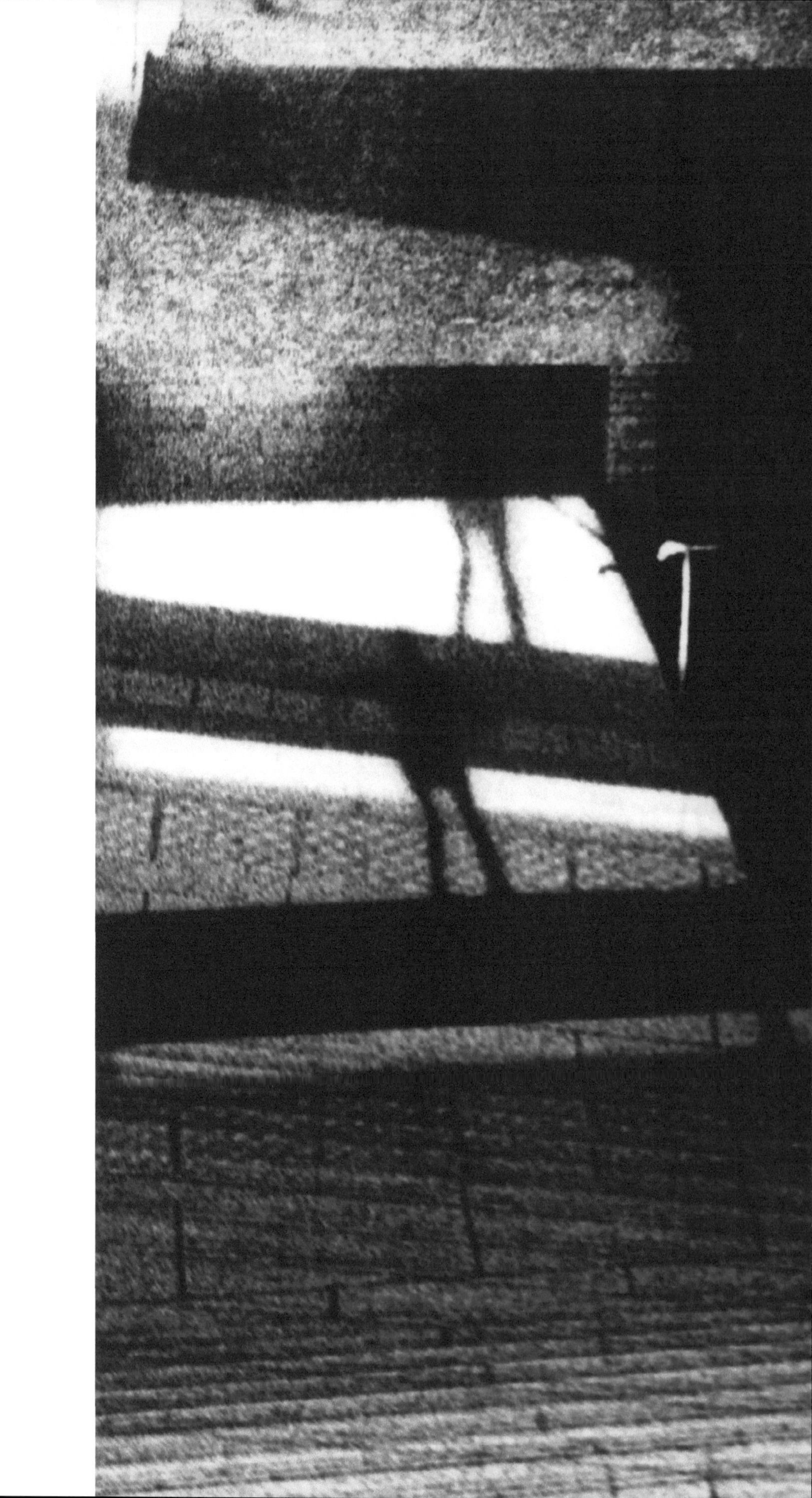

37

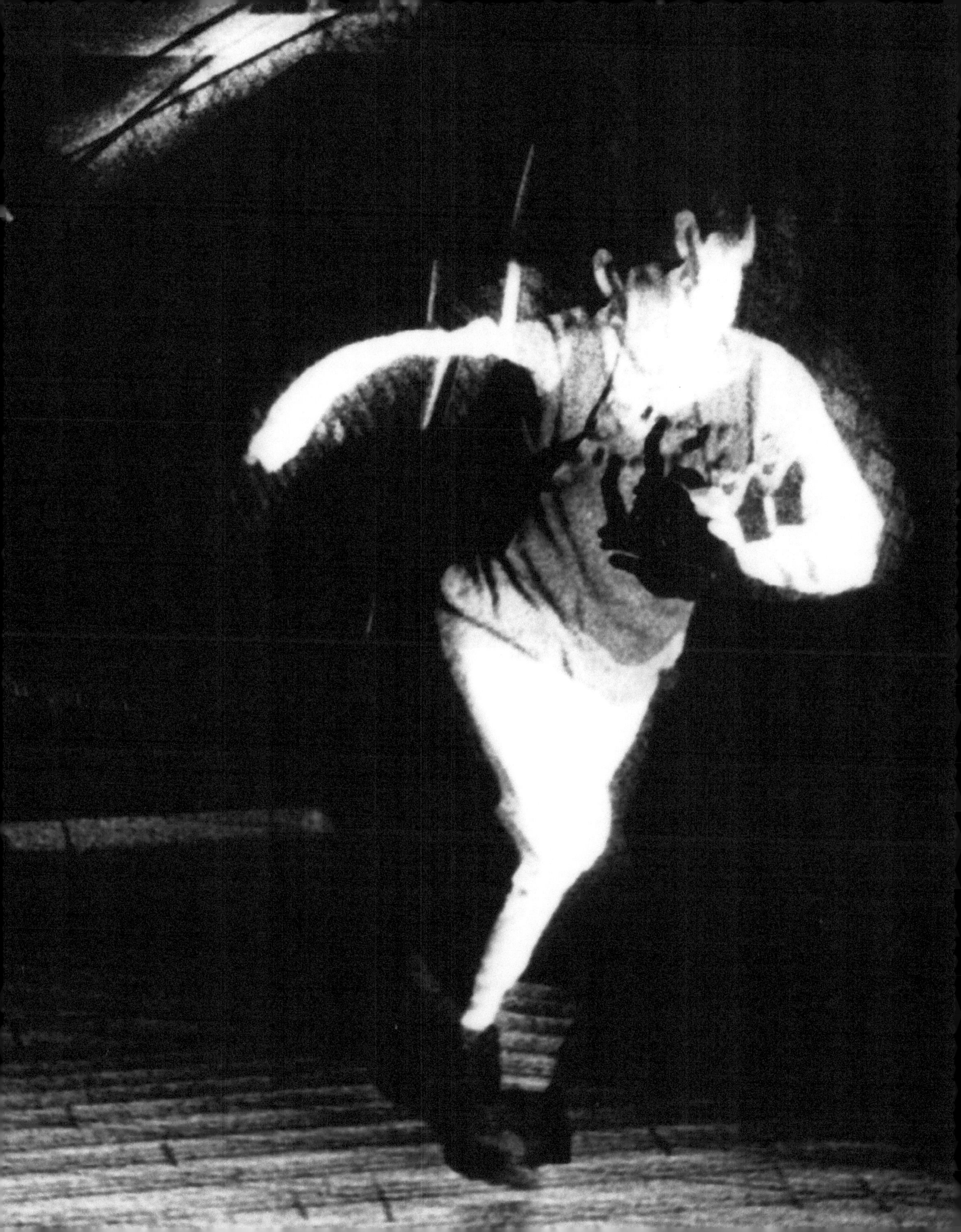

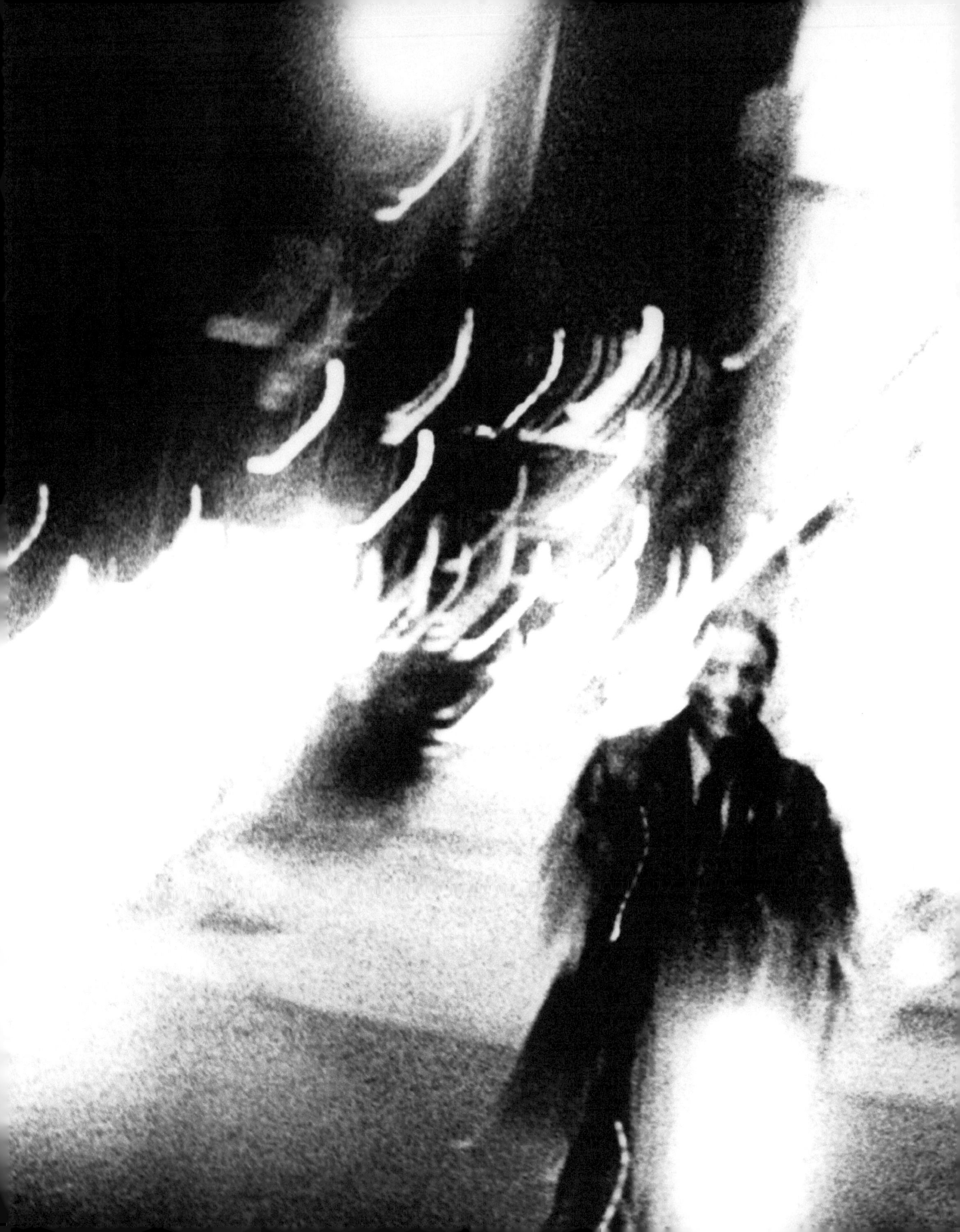

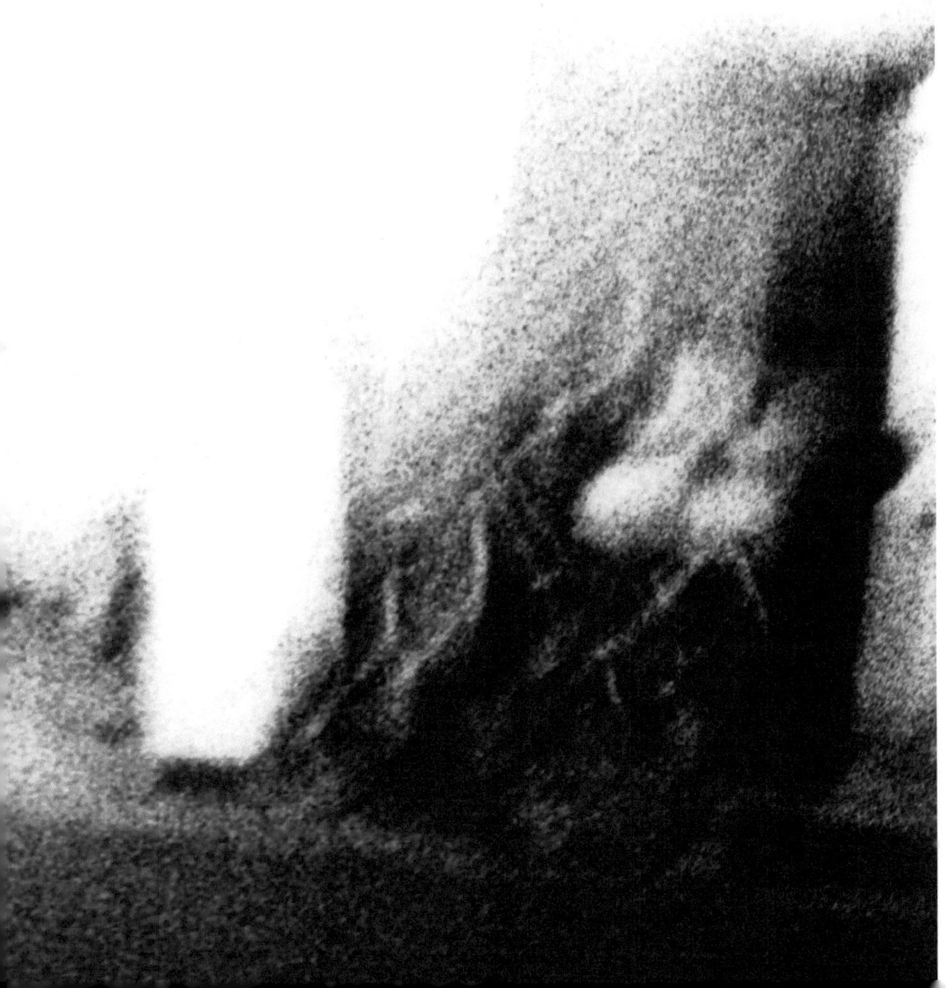

38

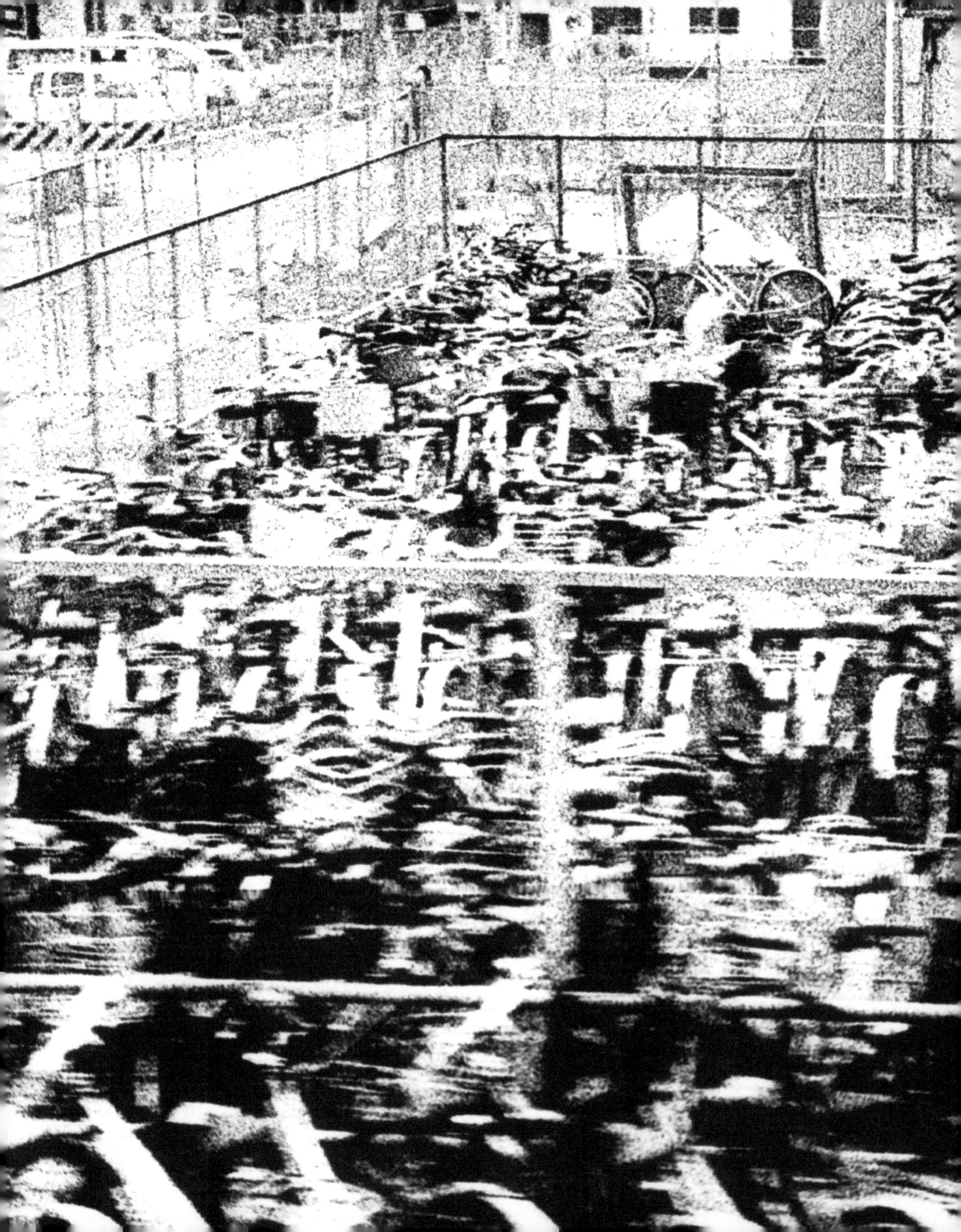

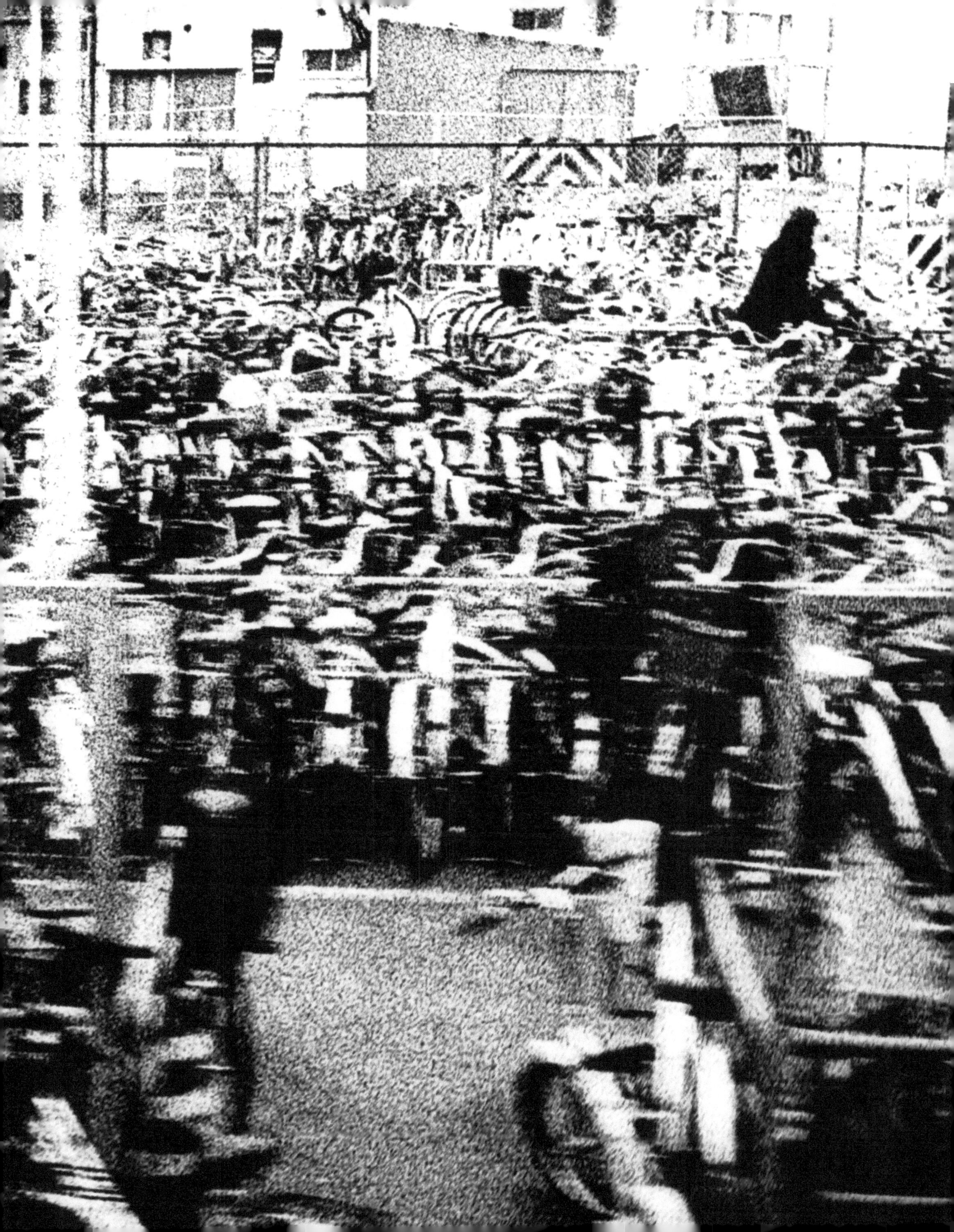

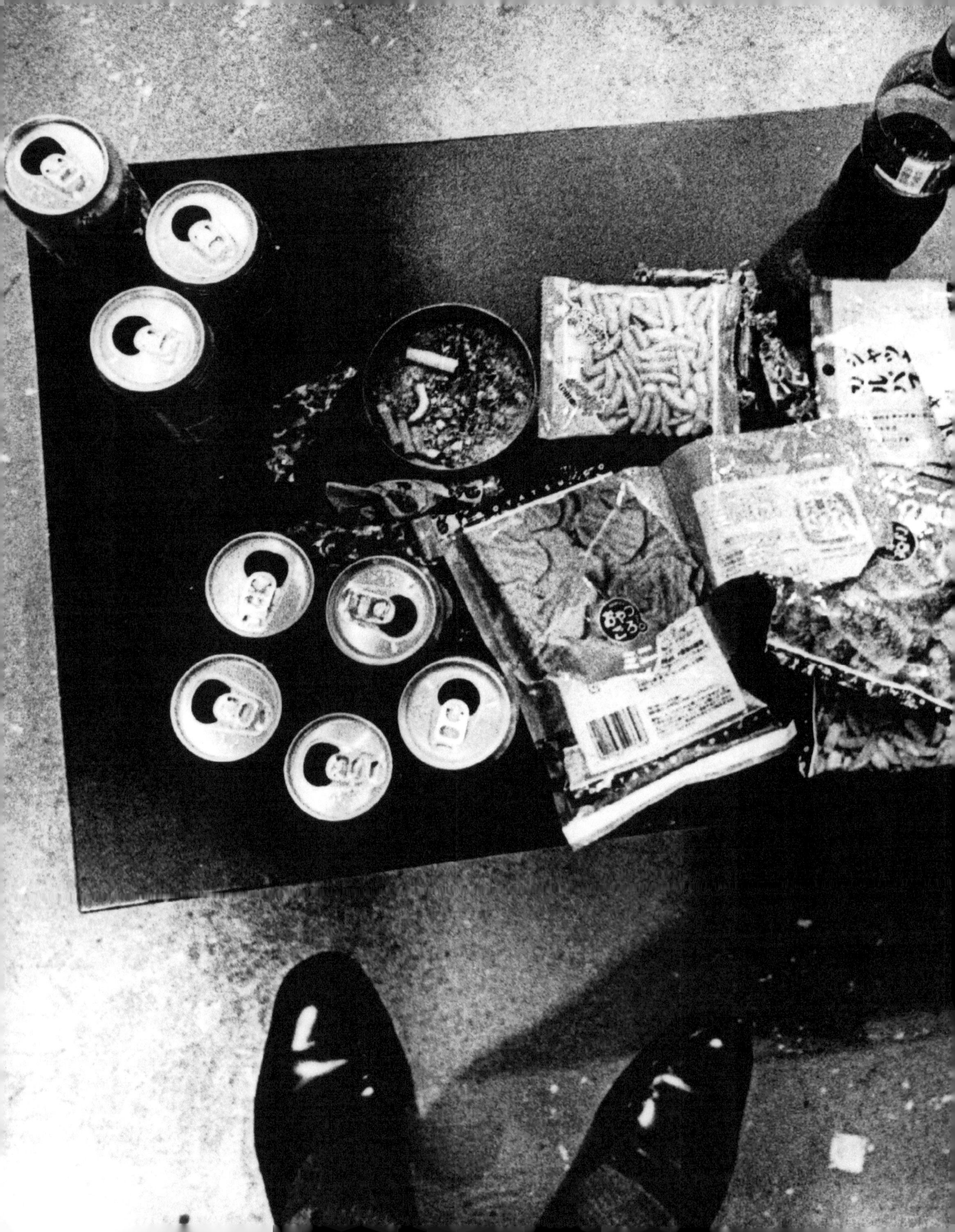

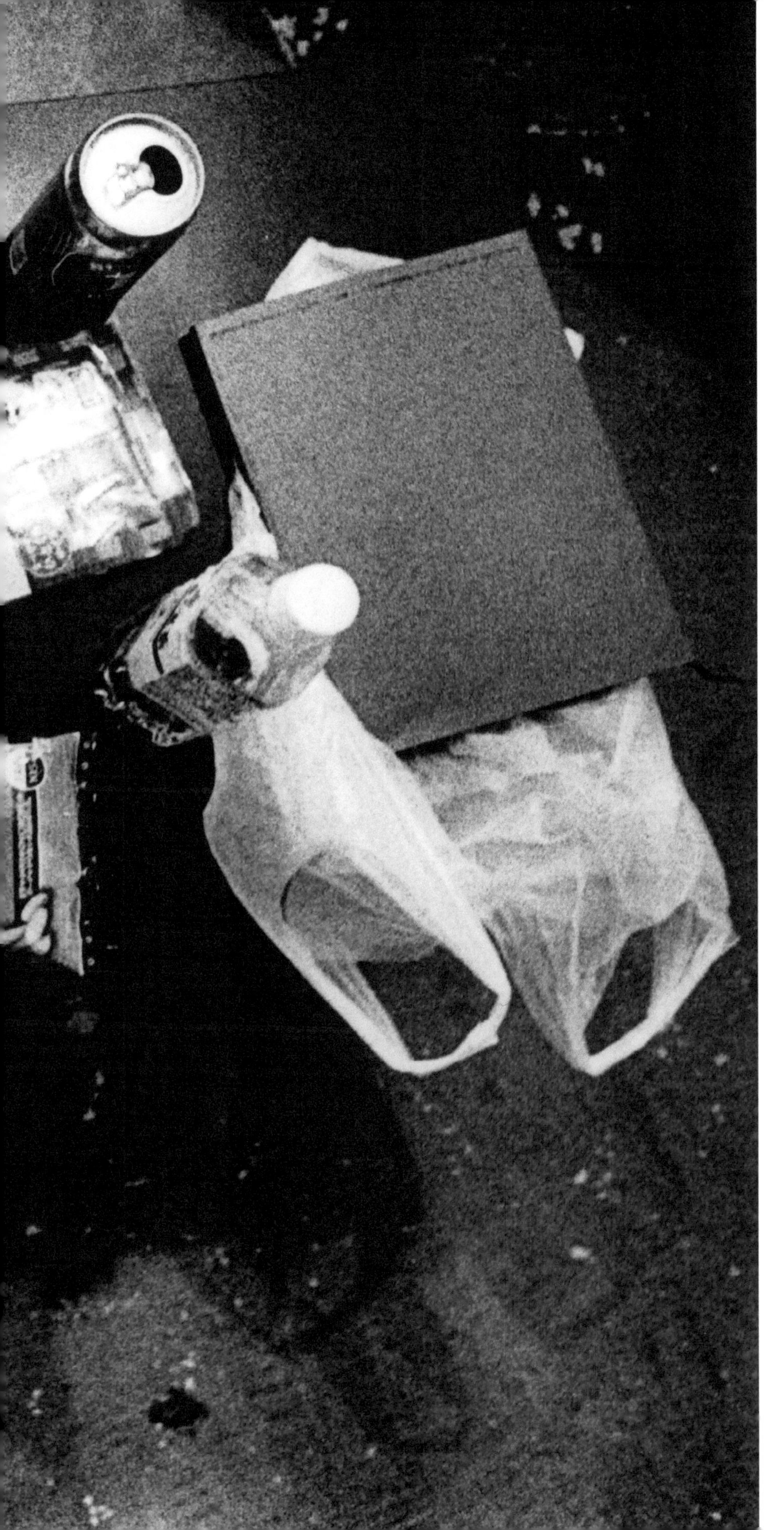

40

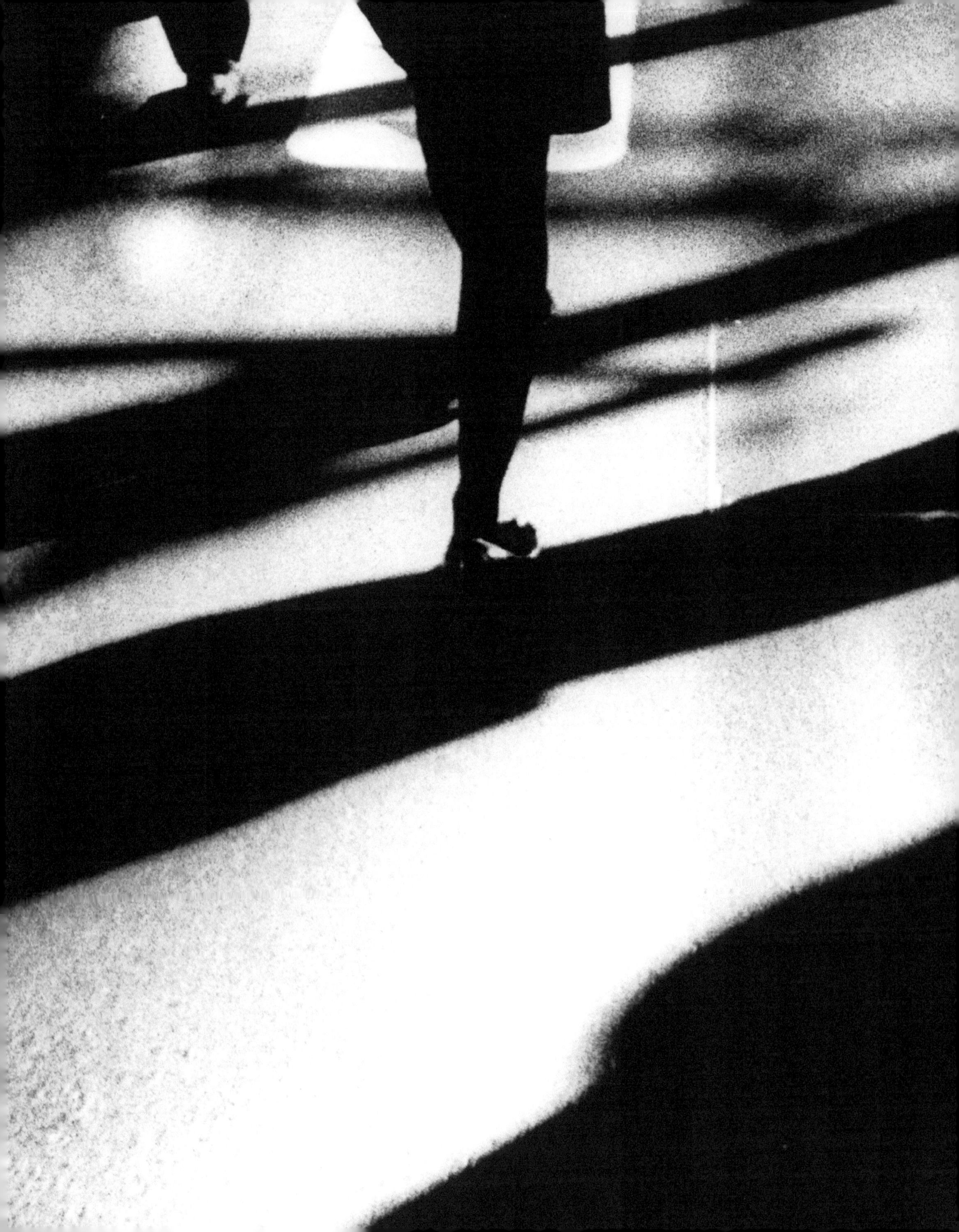

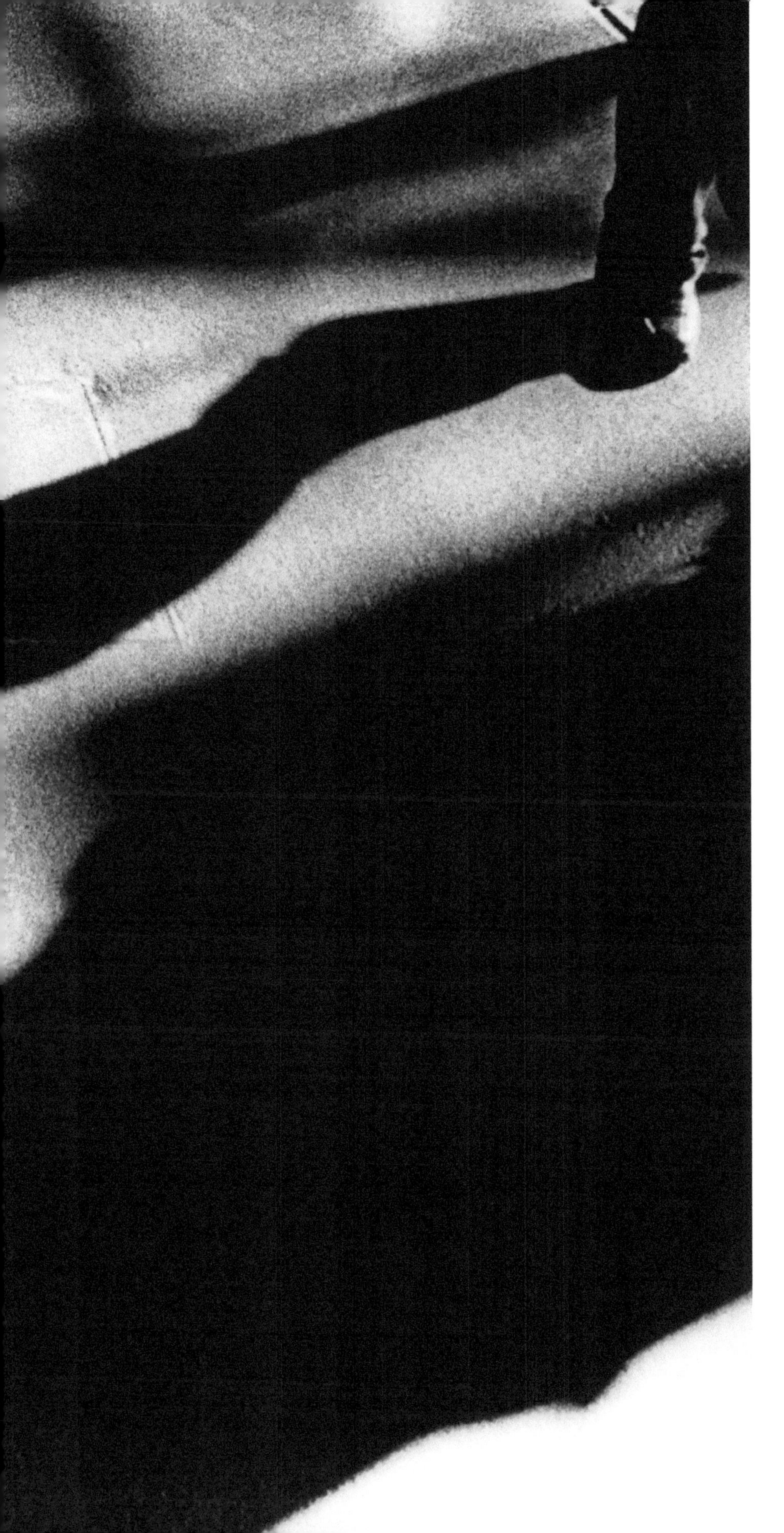

41

HoTEL

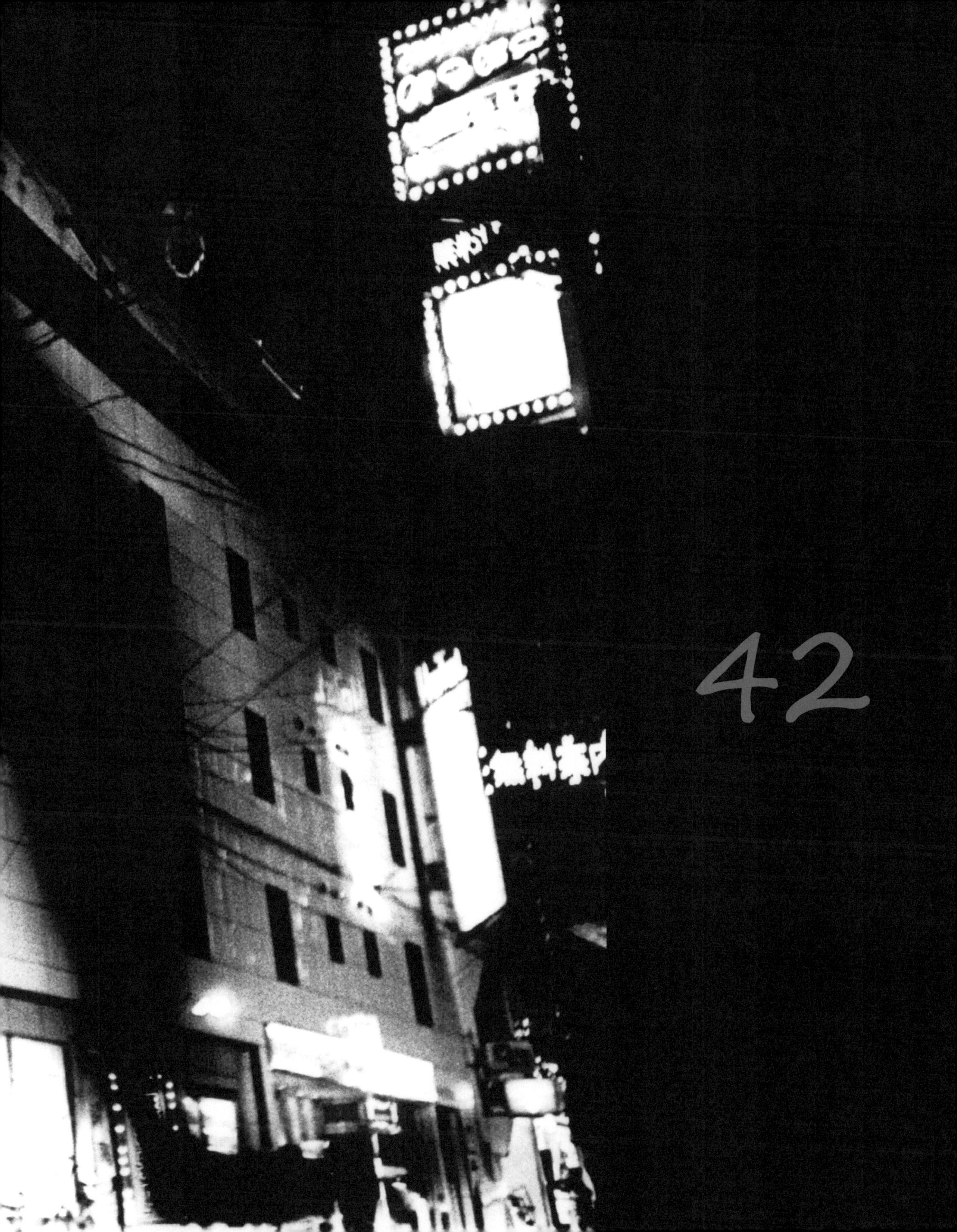

42

43

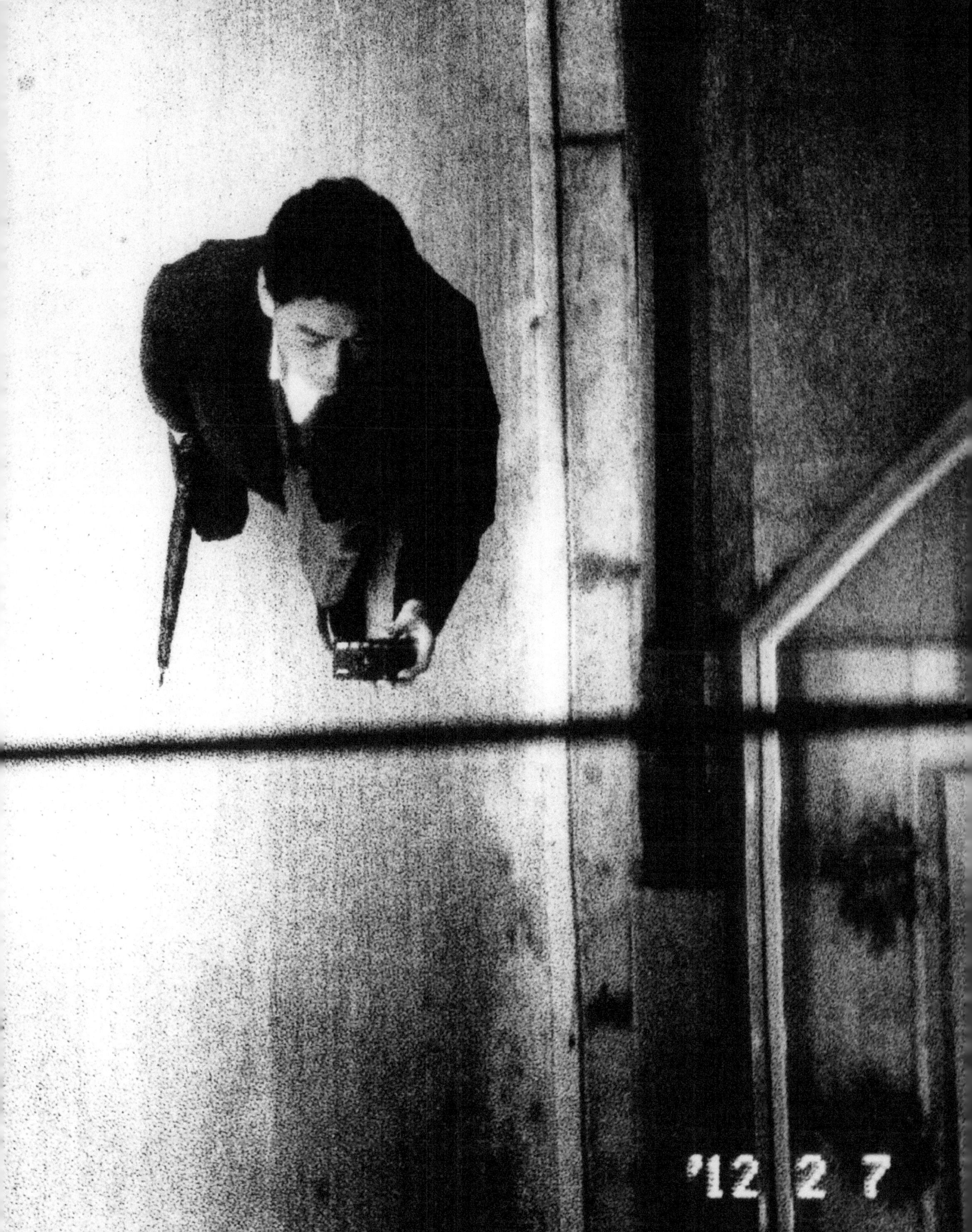
'12 2 7

44

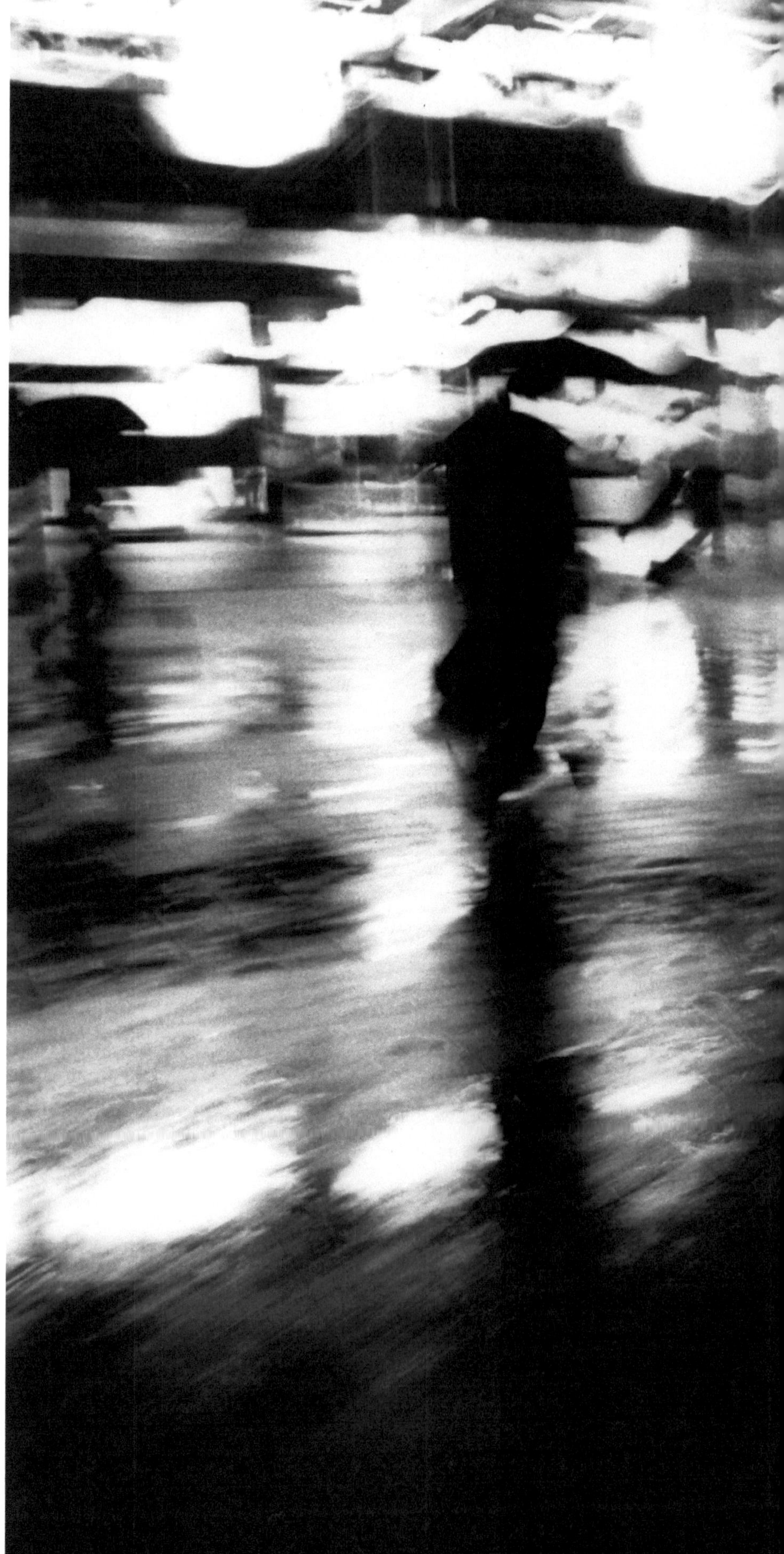

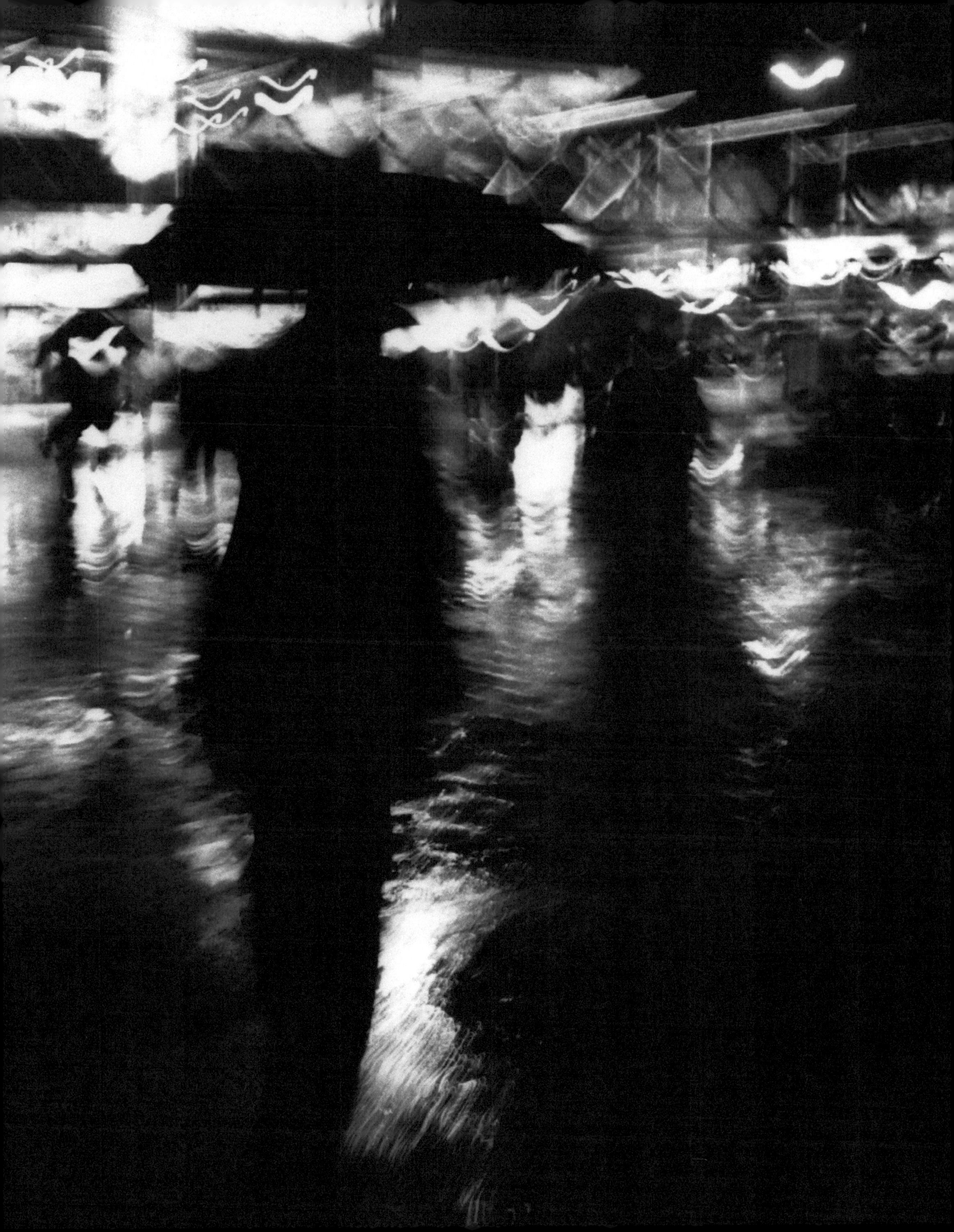

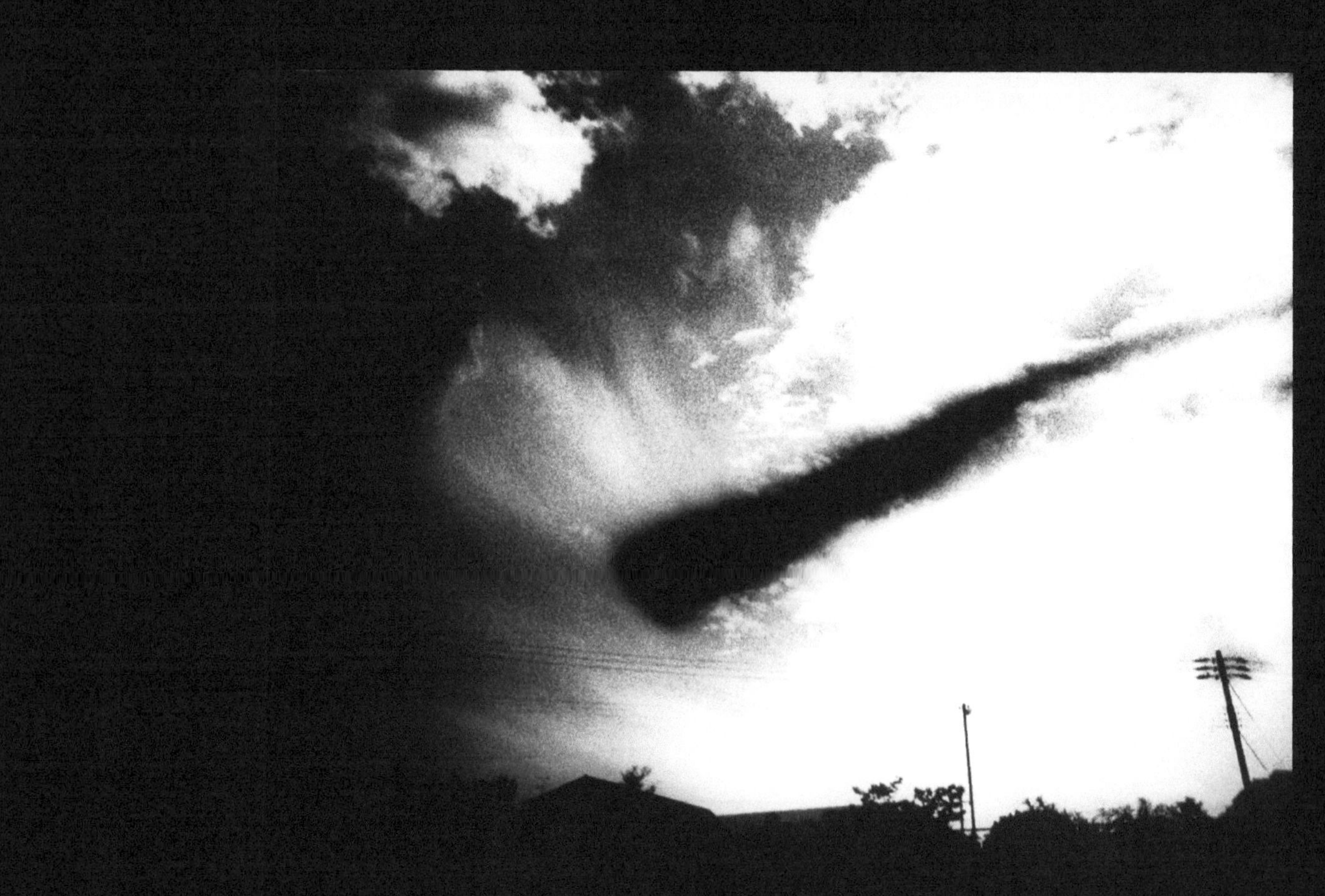

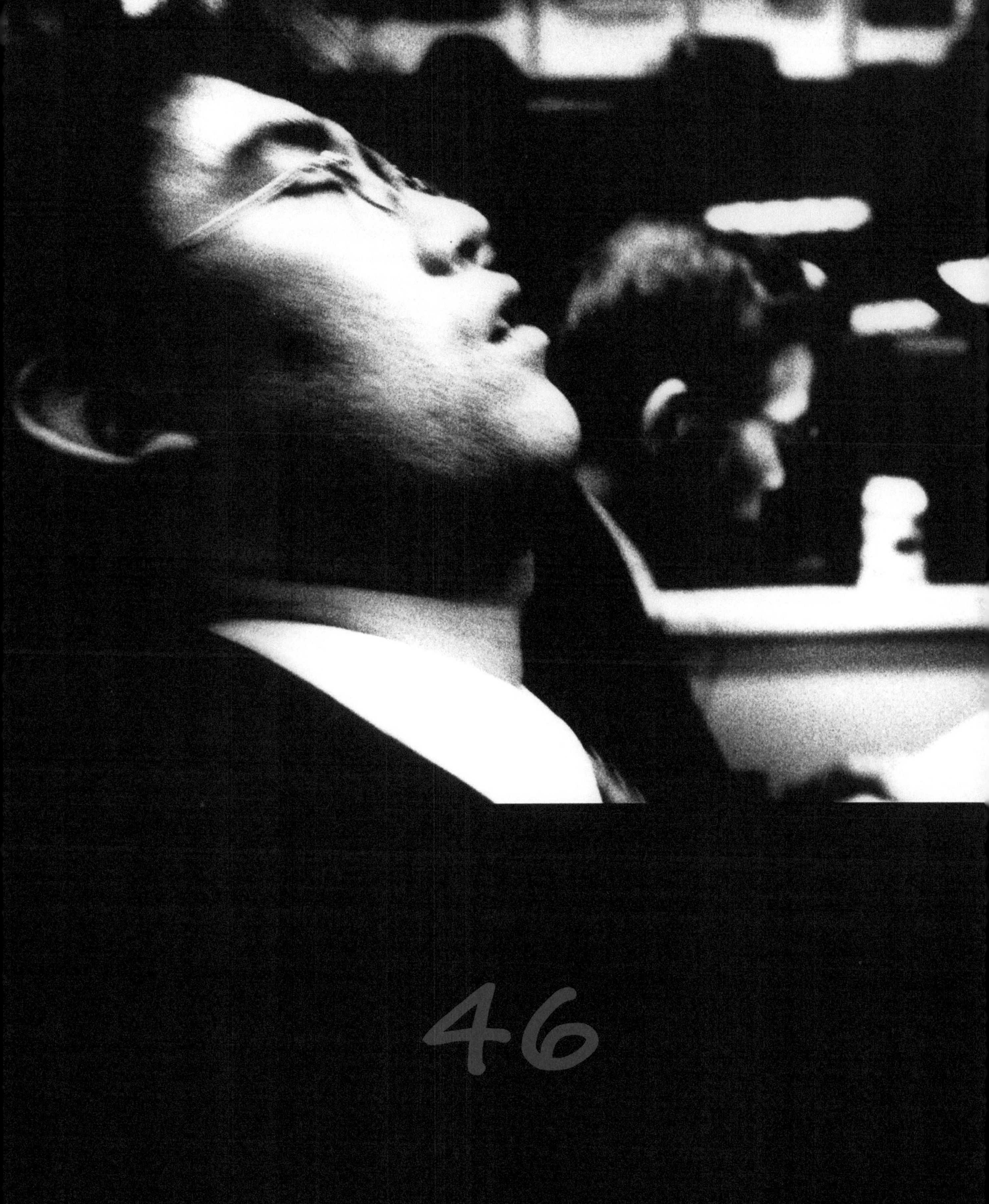

46

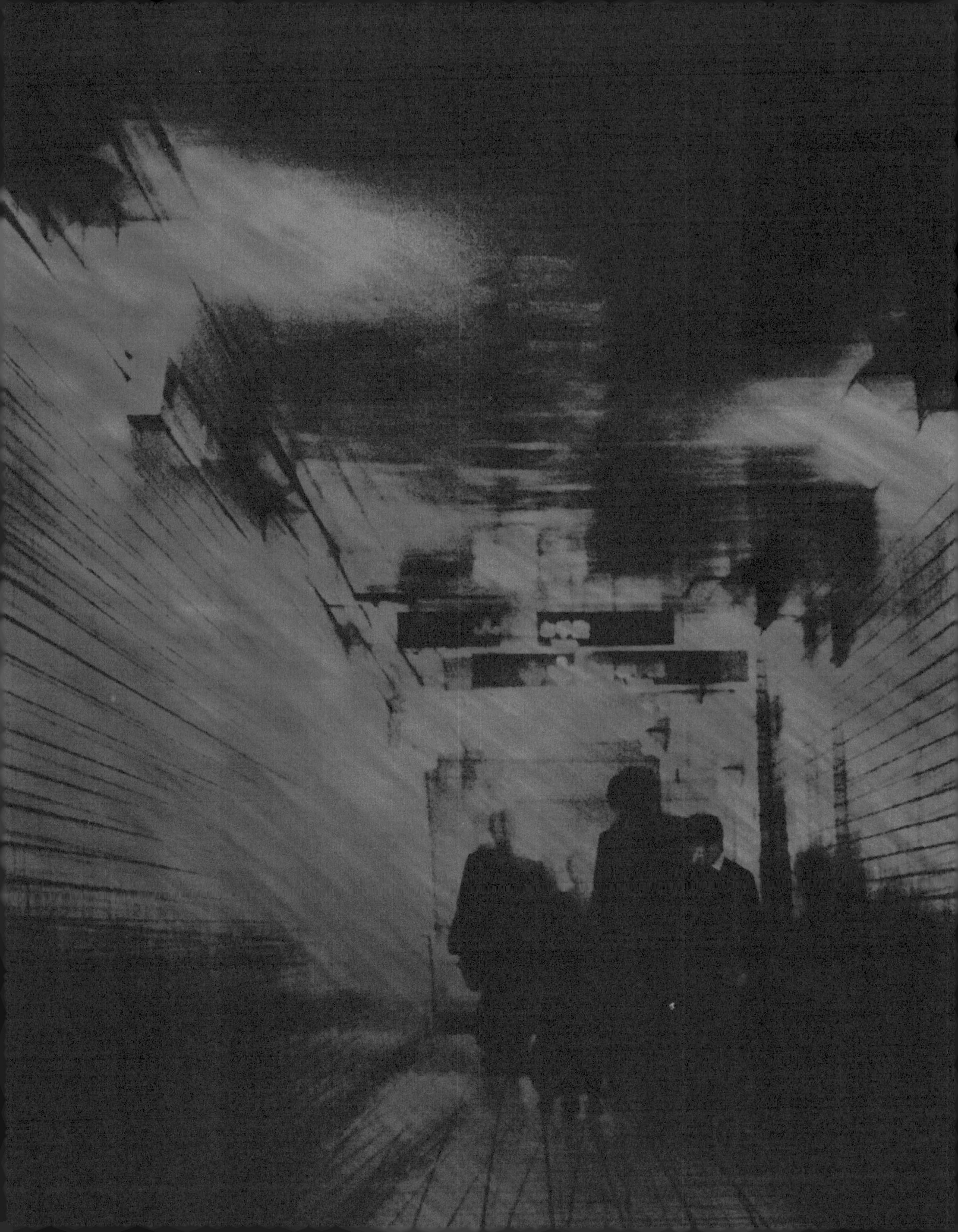

禁
NO SMO
NO SM

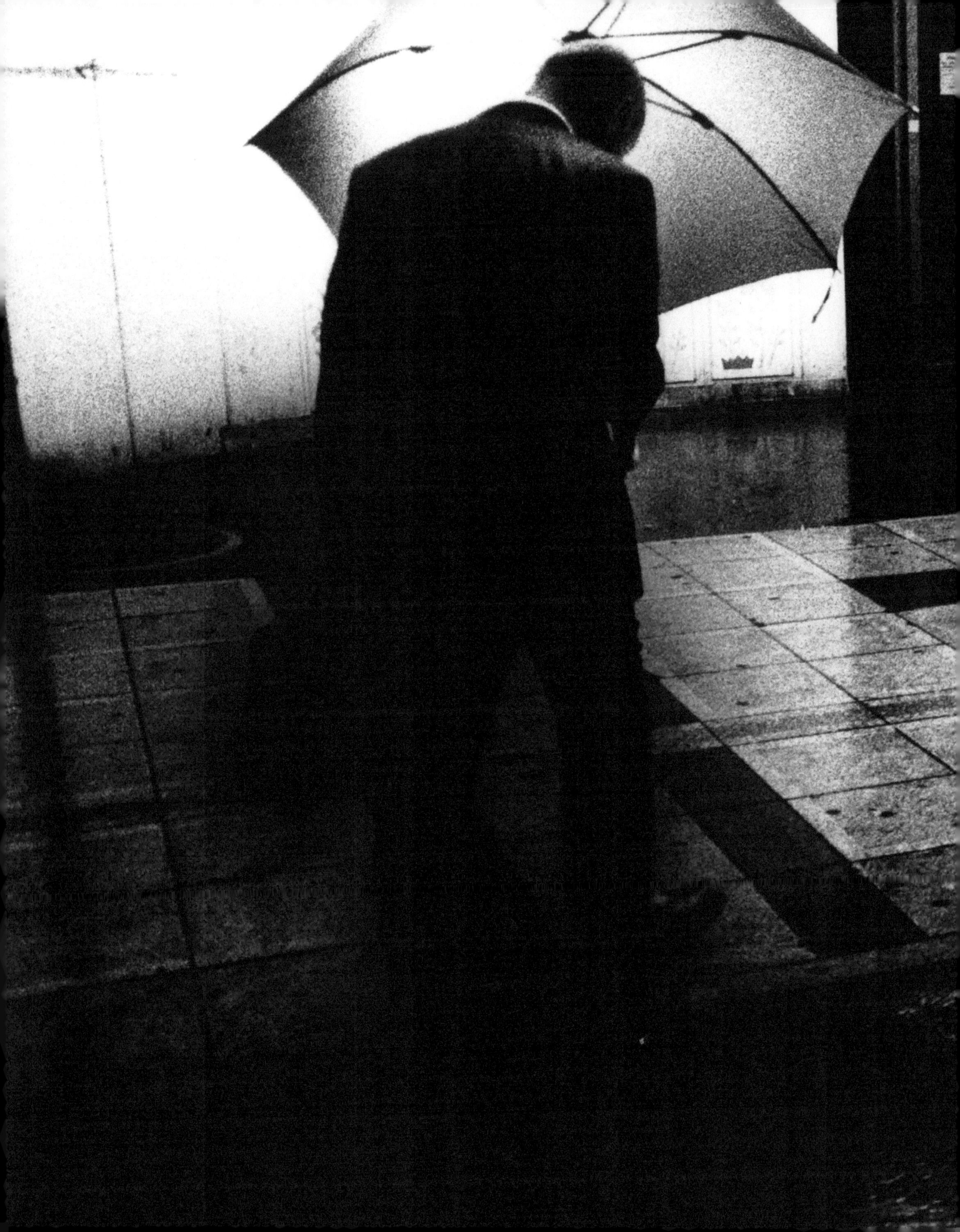

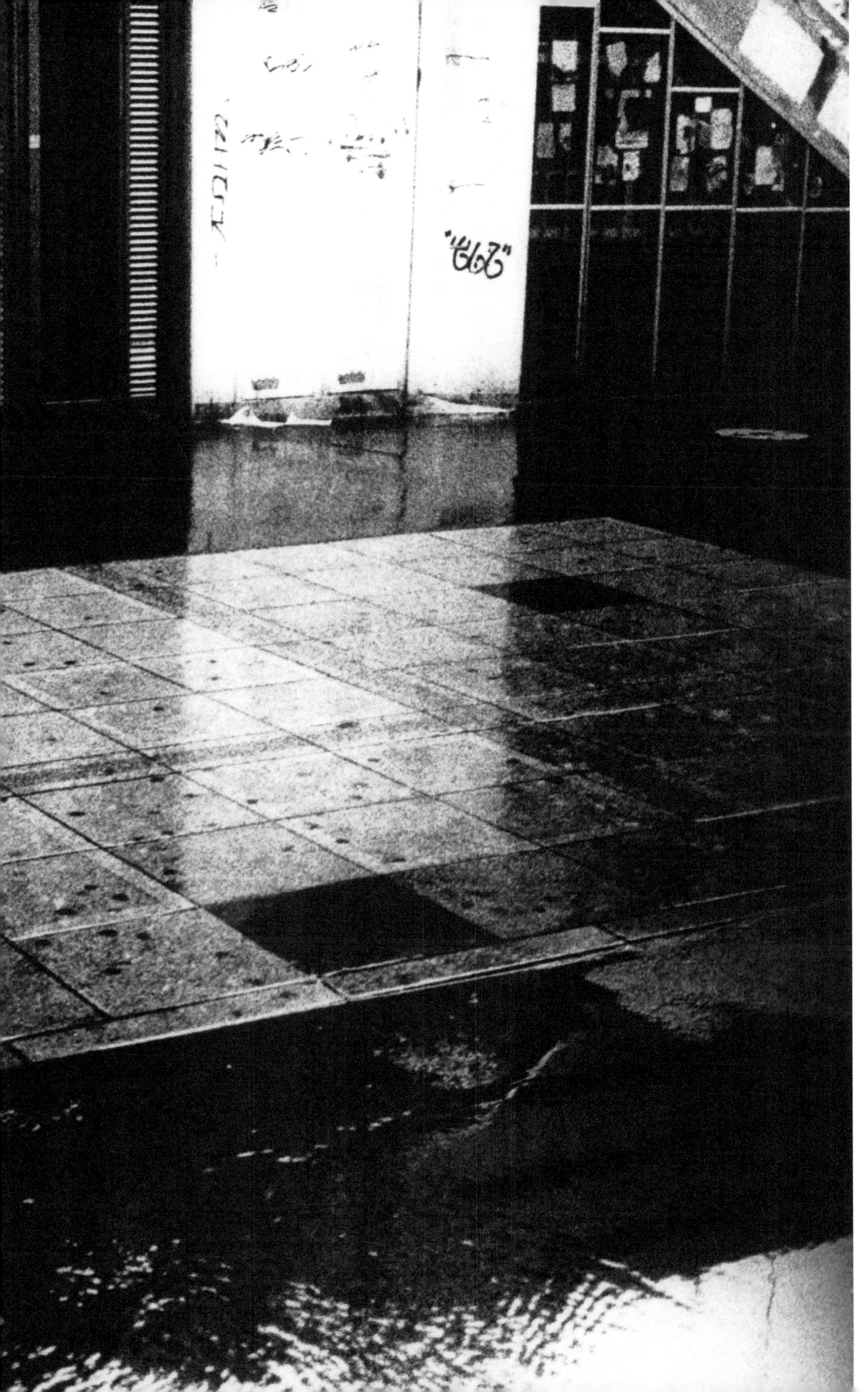

48

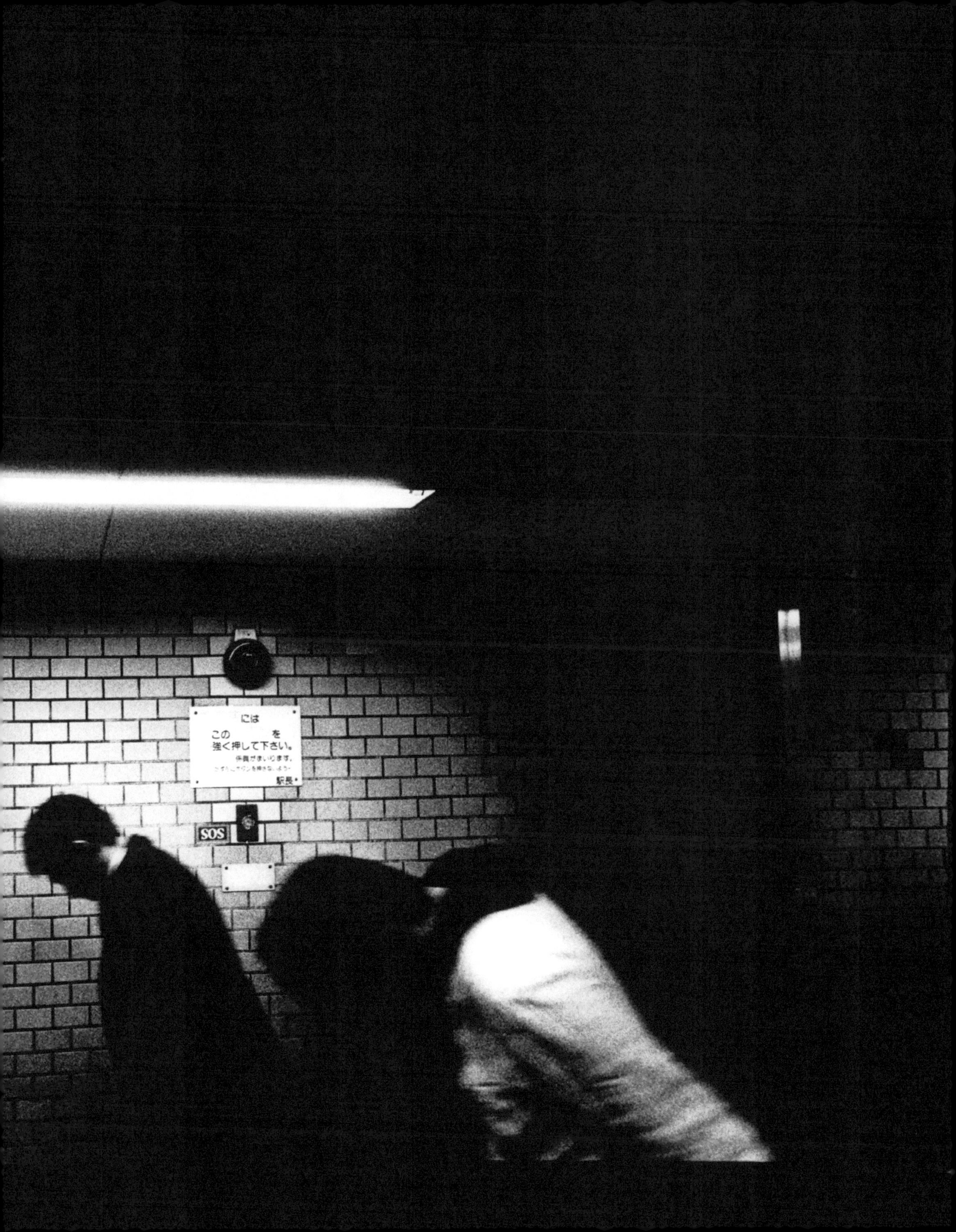
には
この　　　　　を
強く押して下さい。
係員がまいります。
SOS
駅長

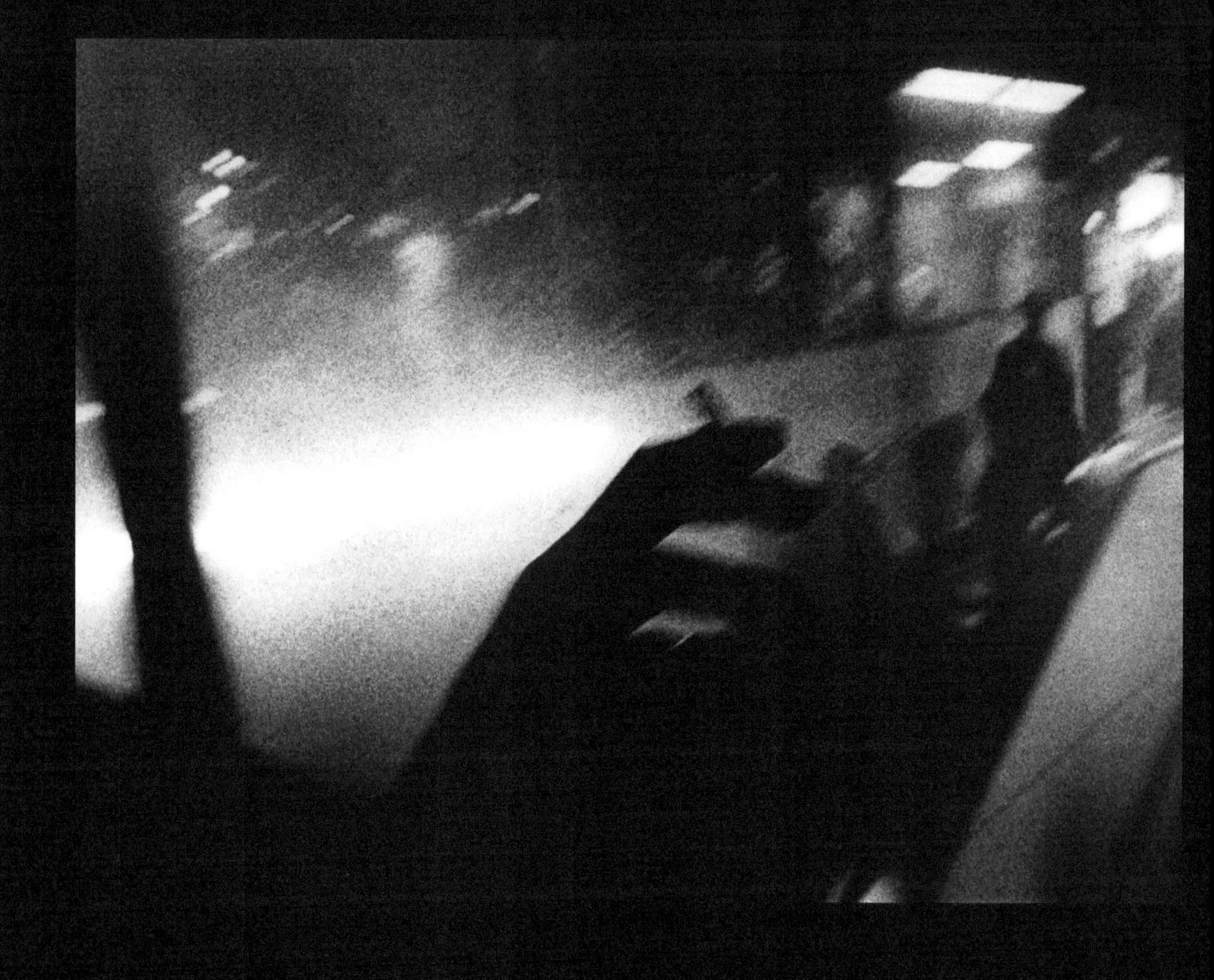

50

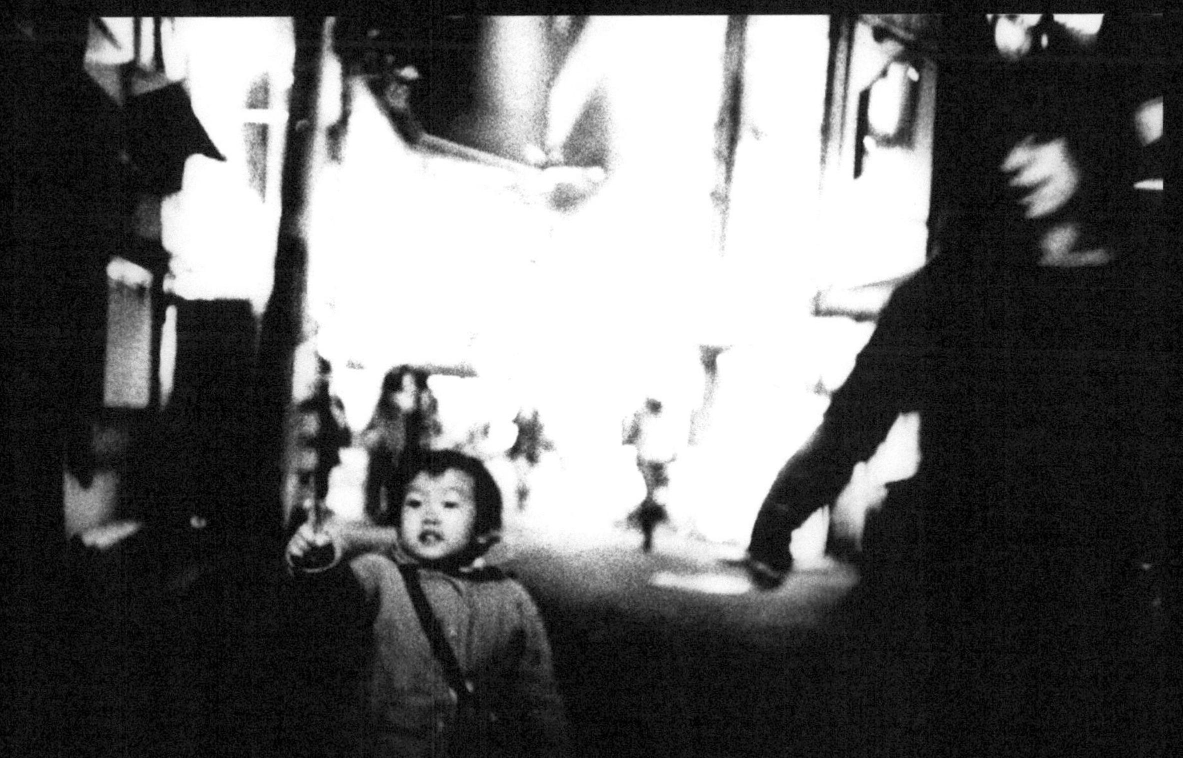

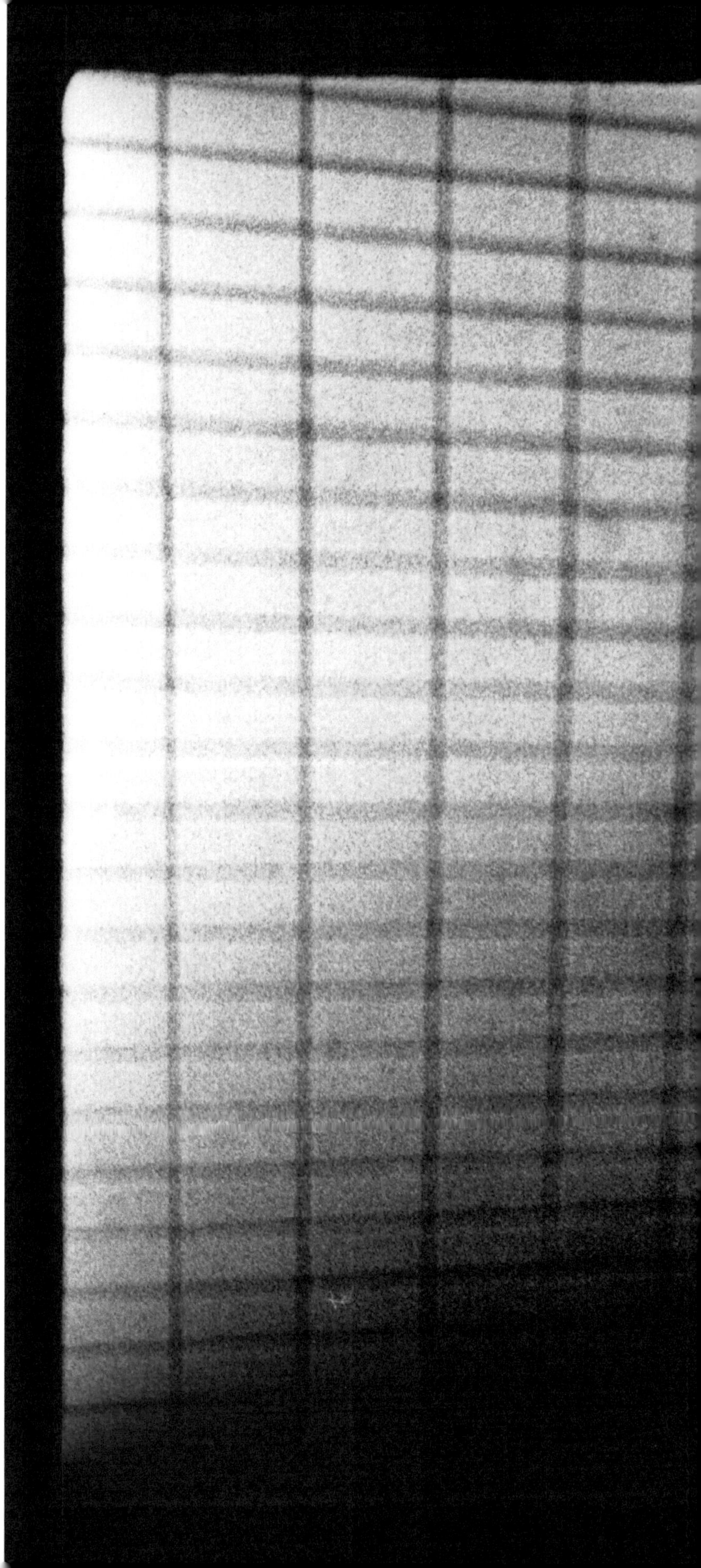

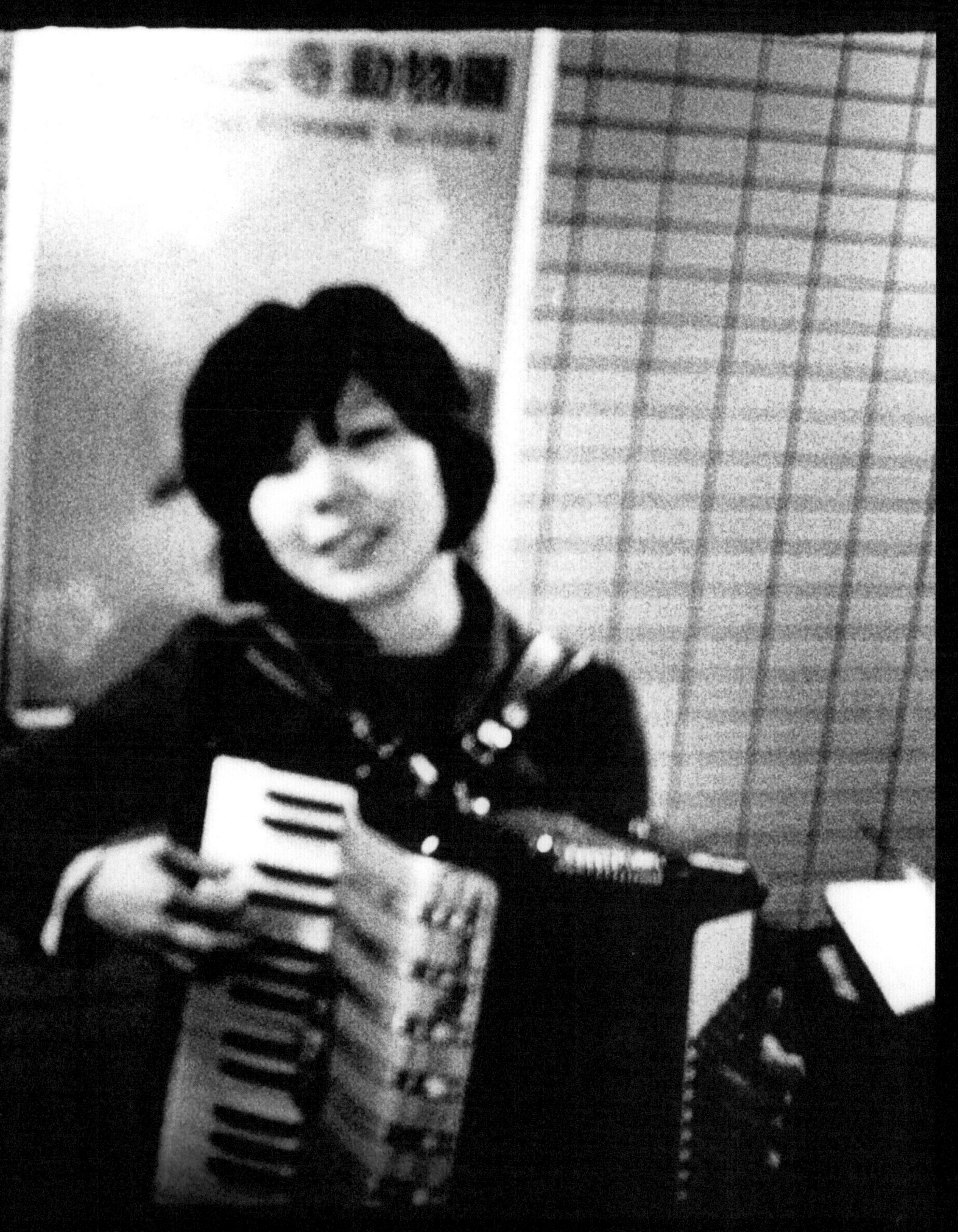

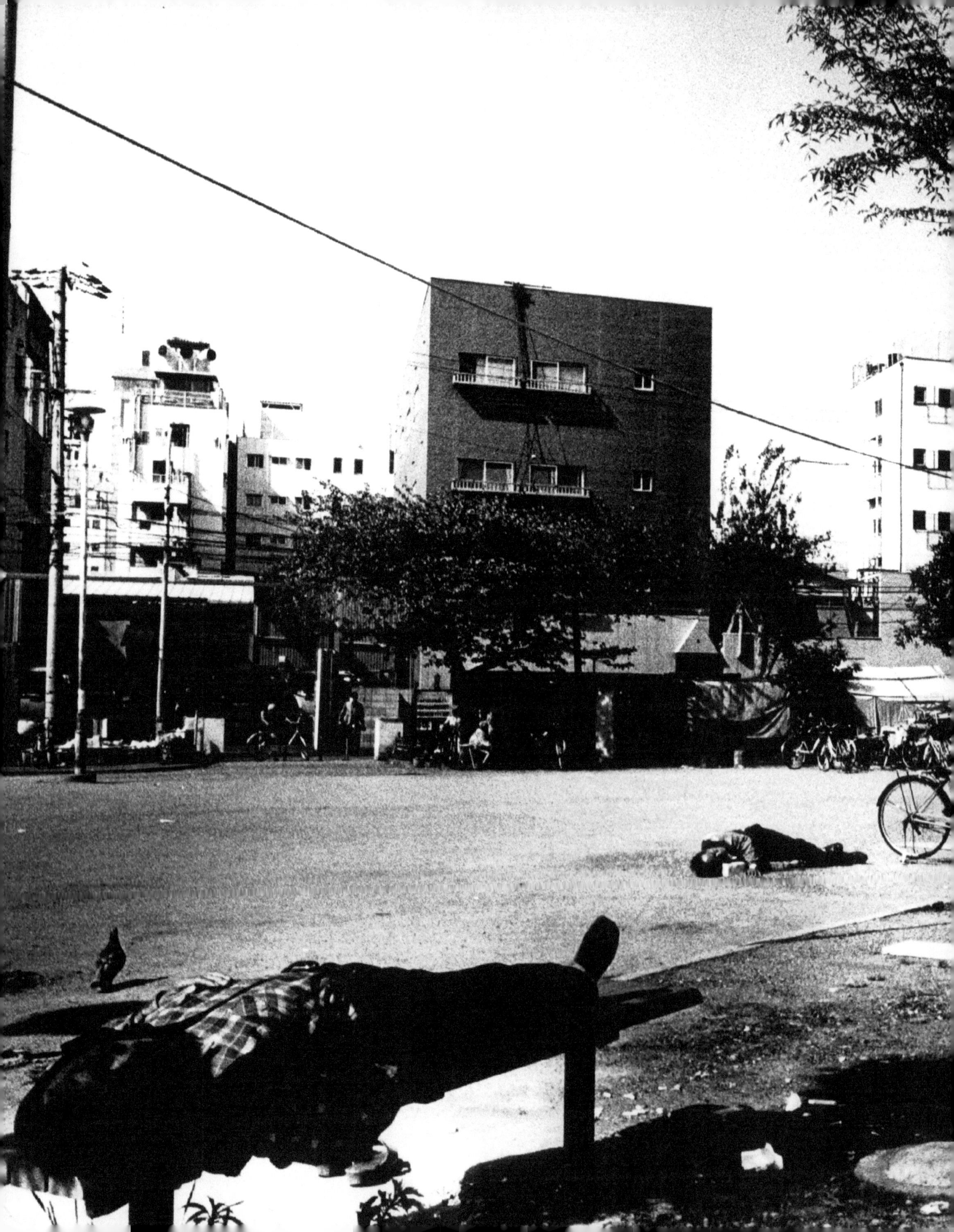

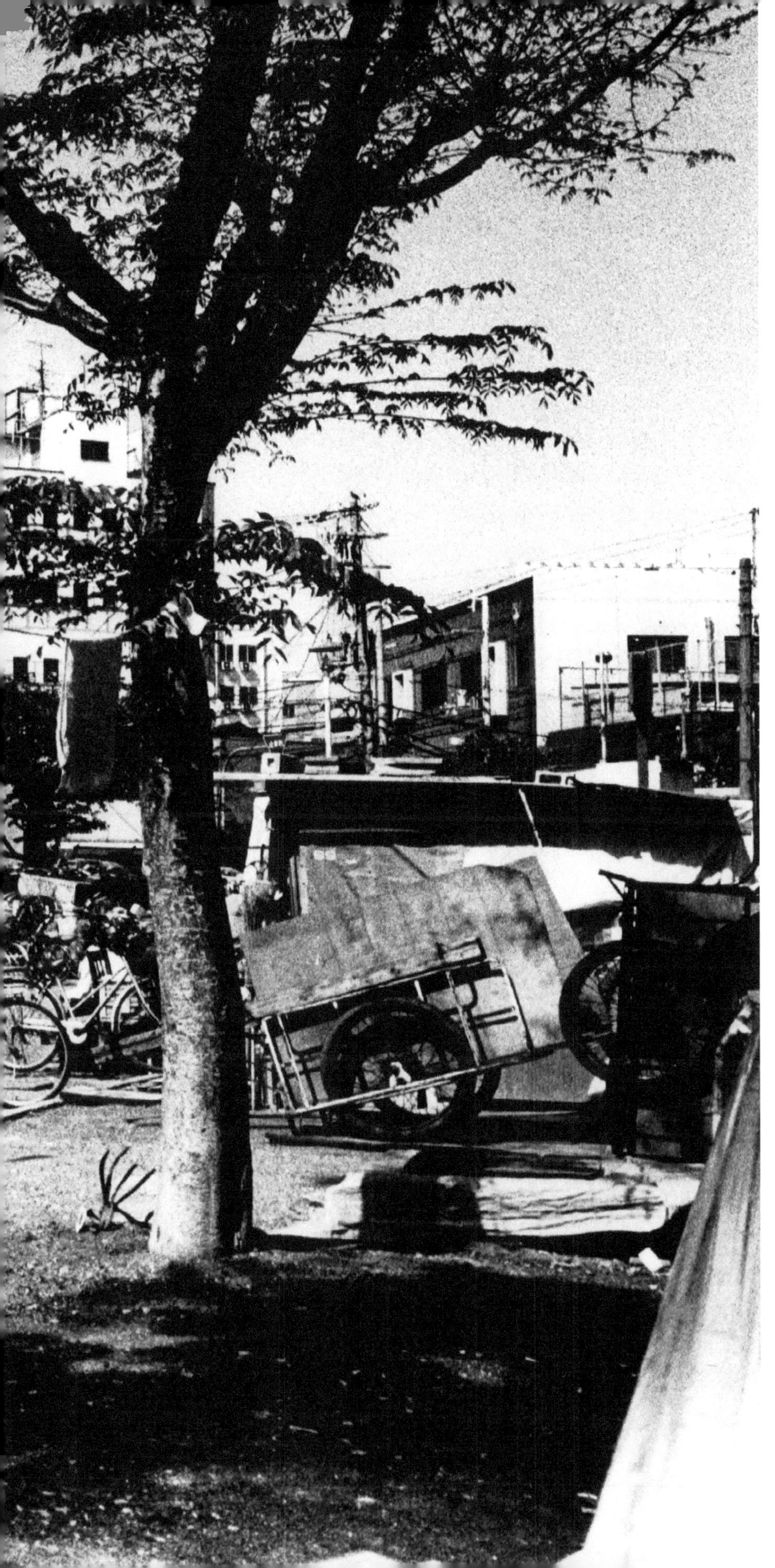

53

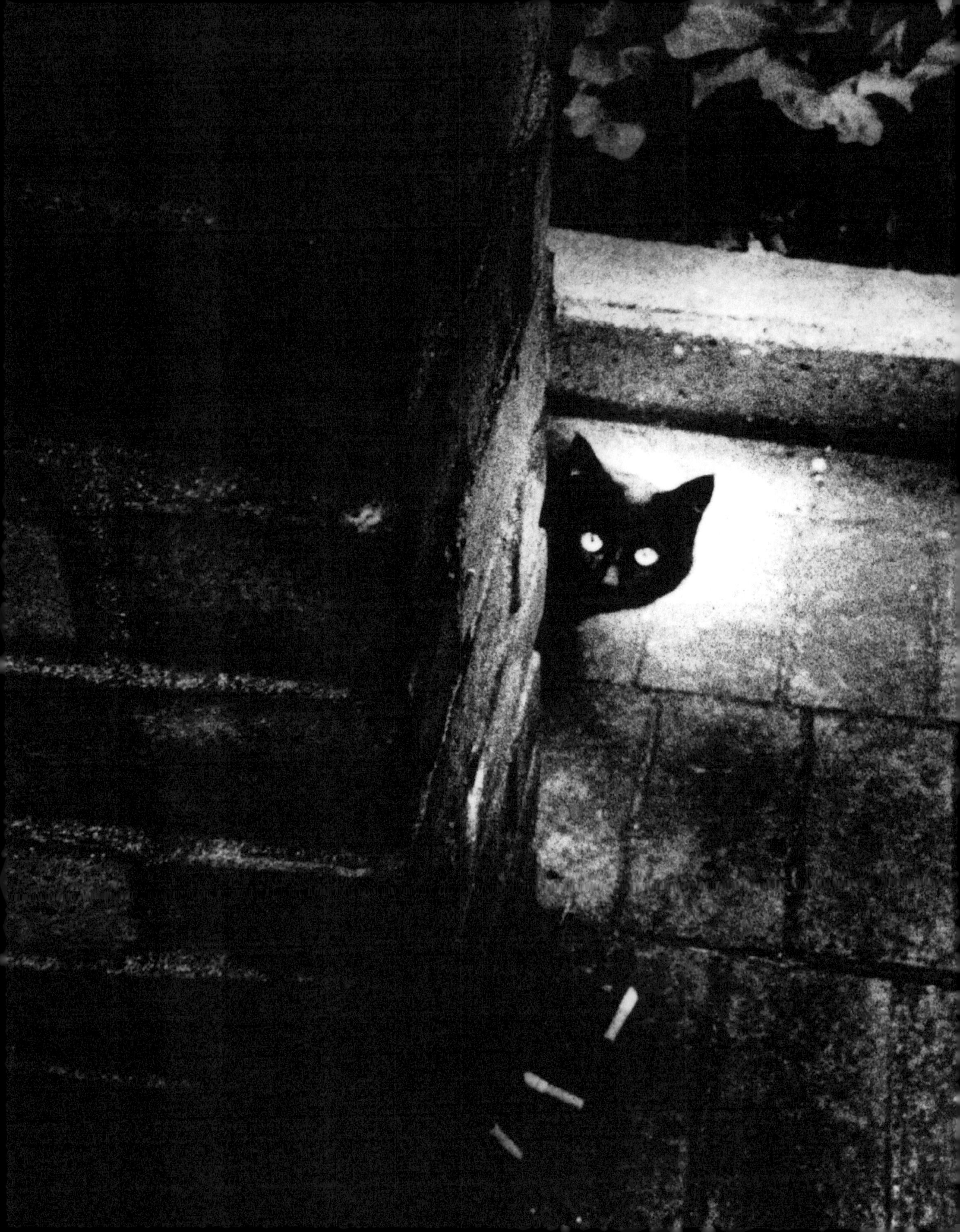

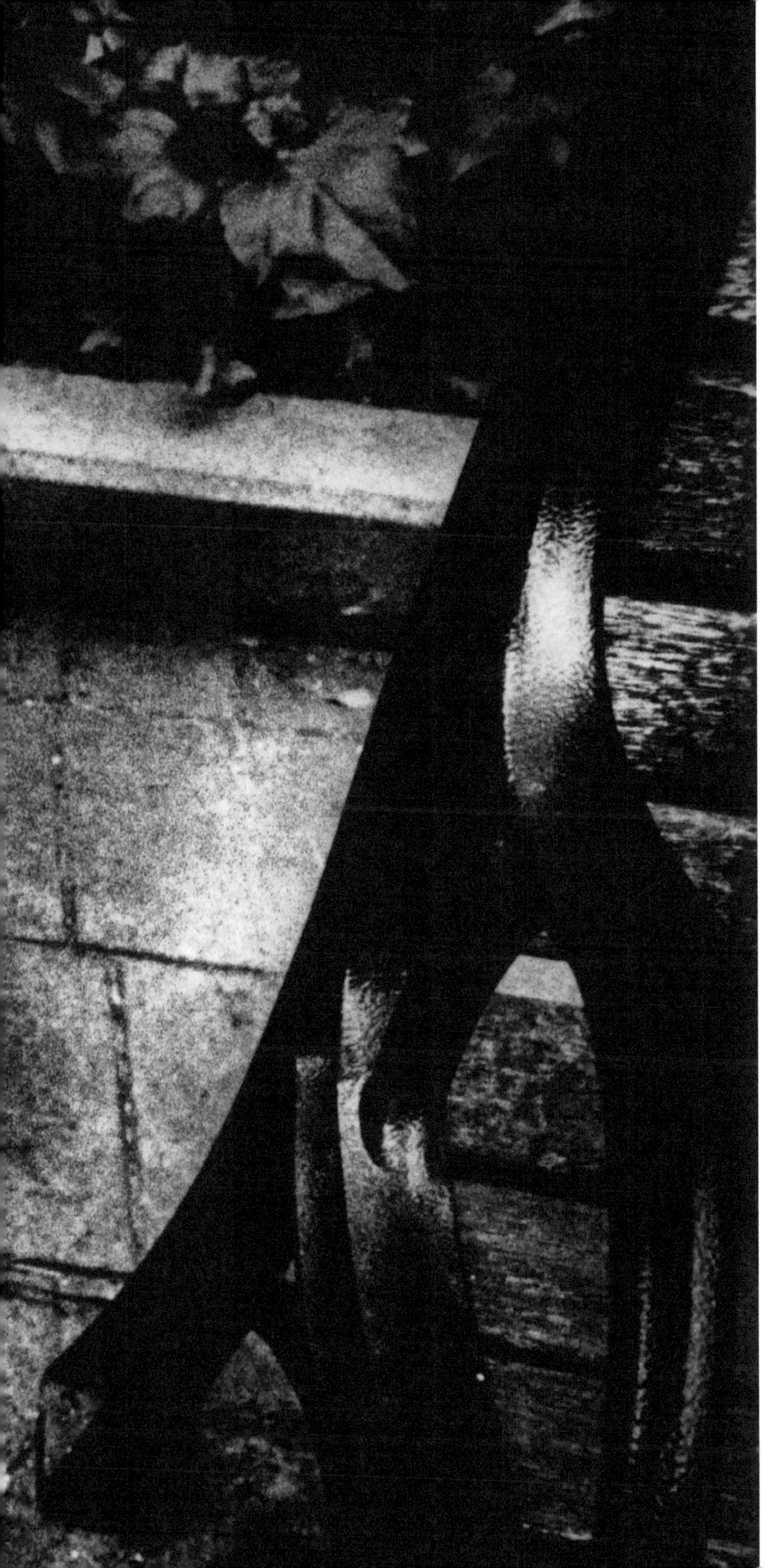

54

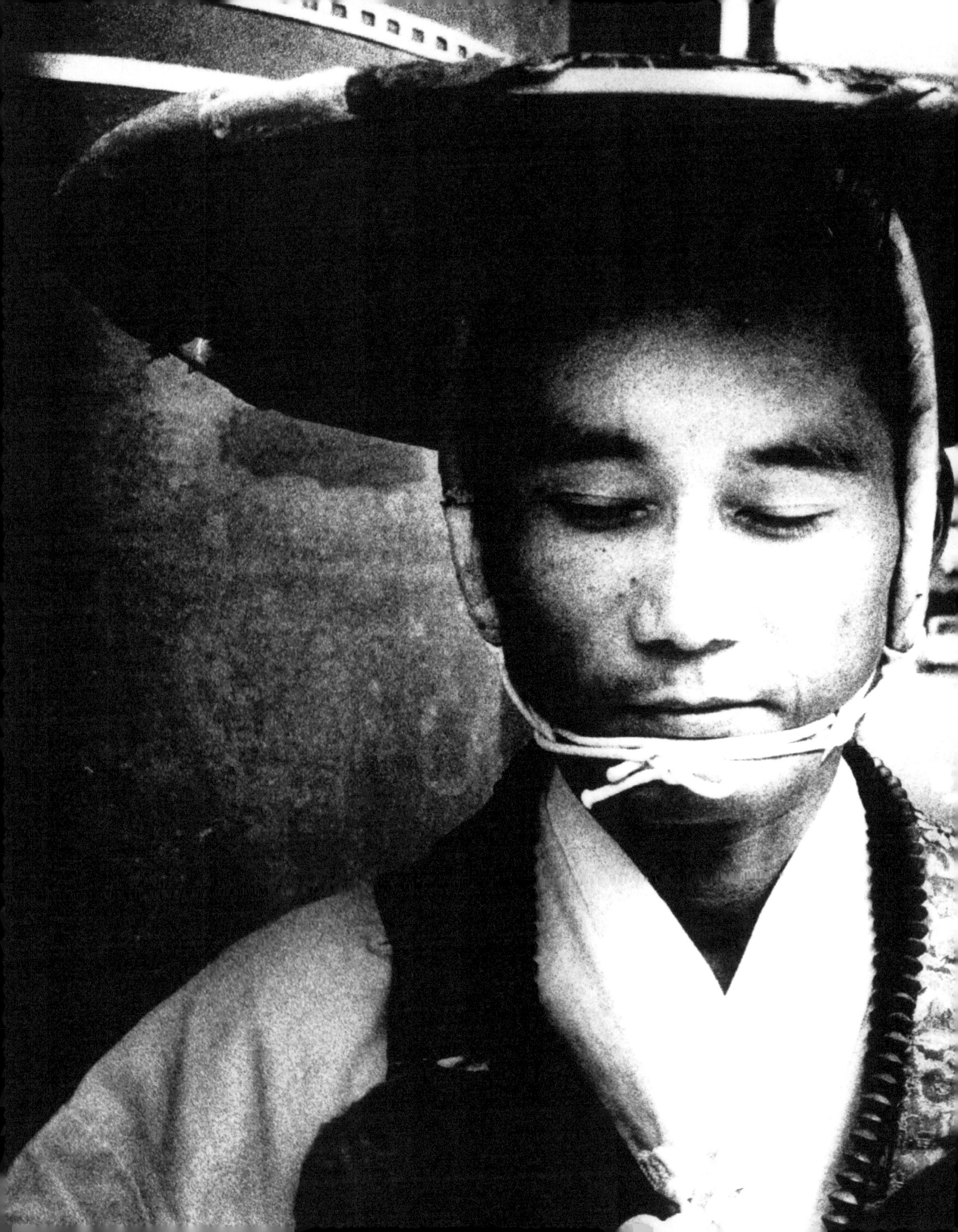

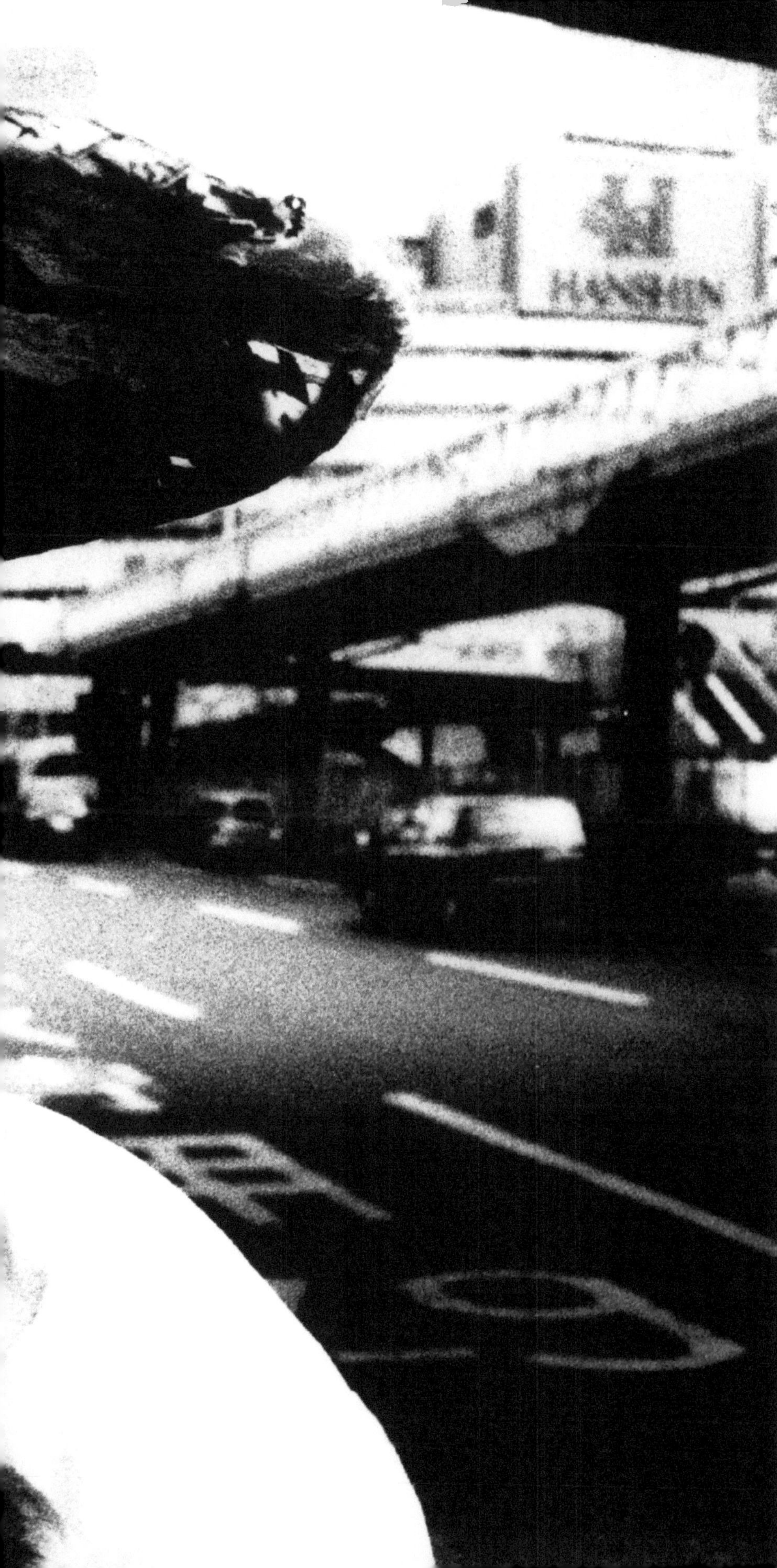

HANSHIN

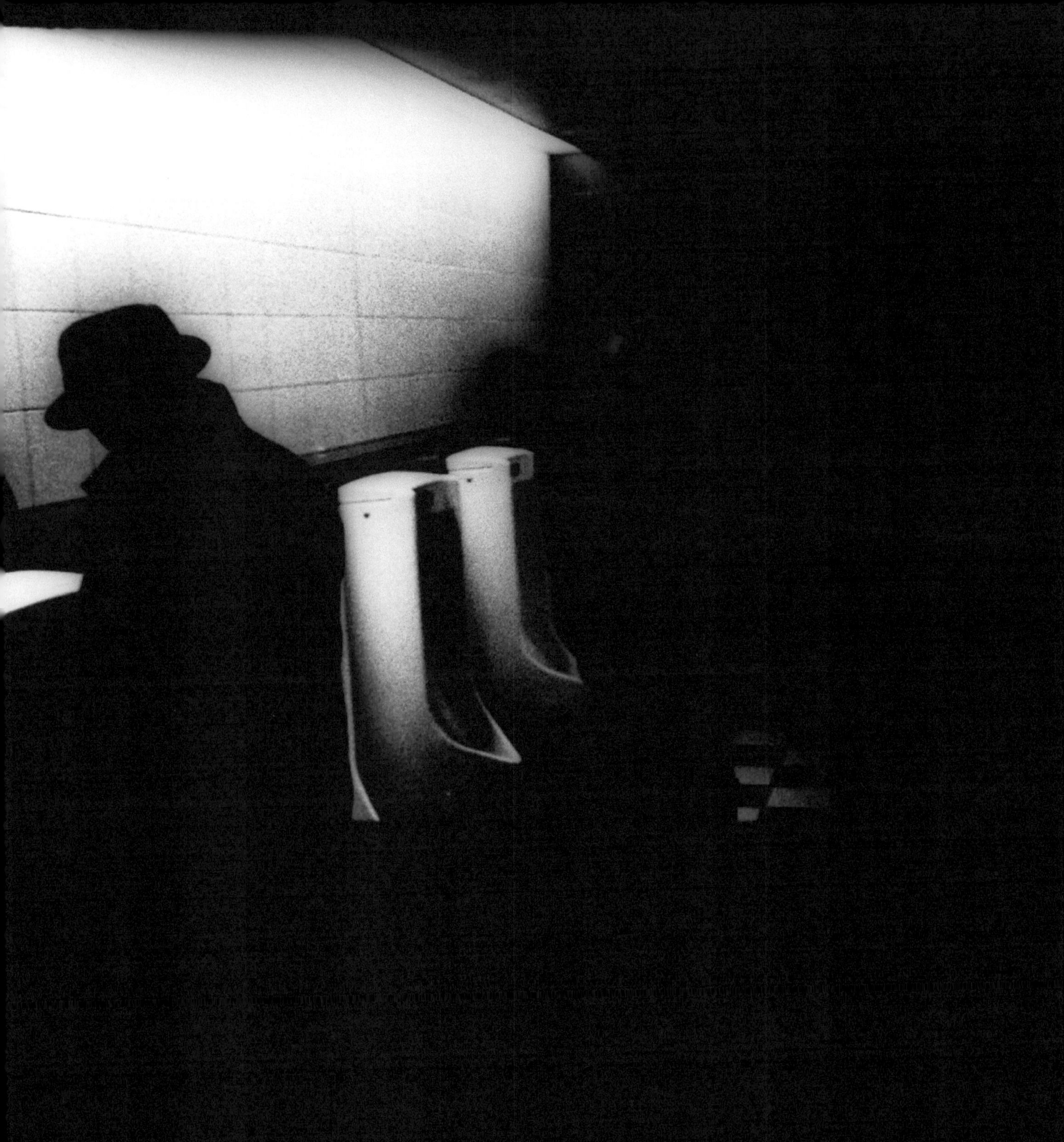

56

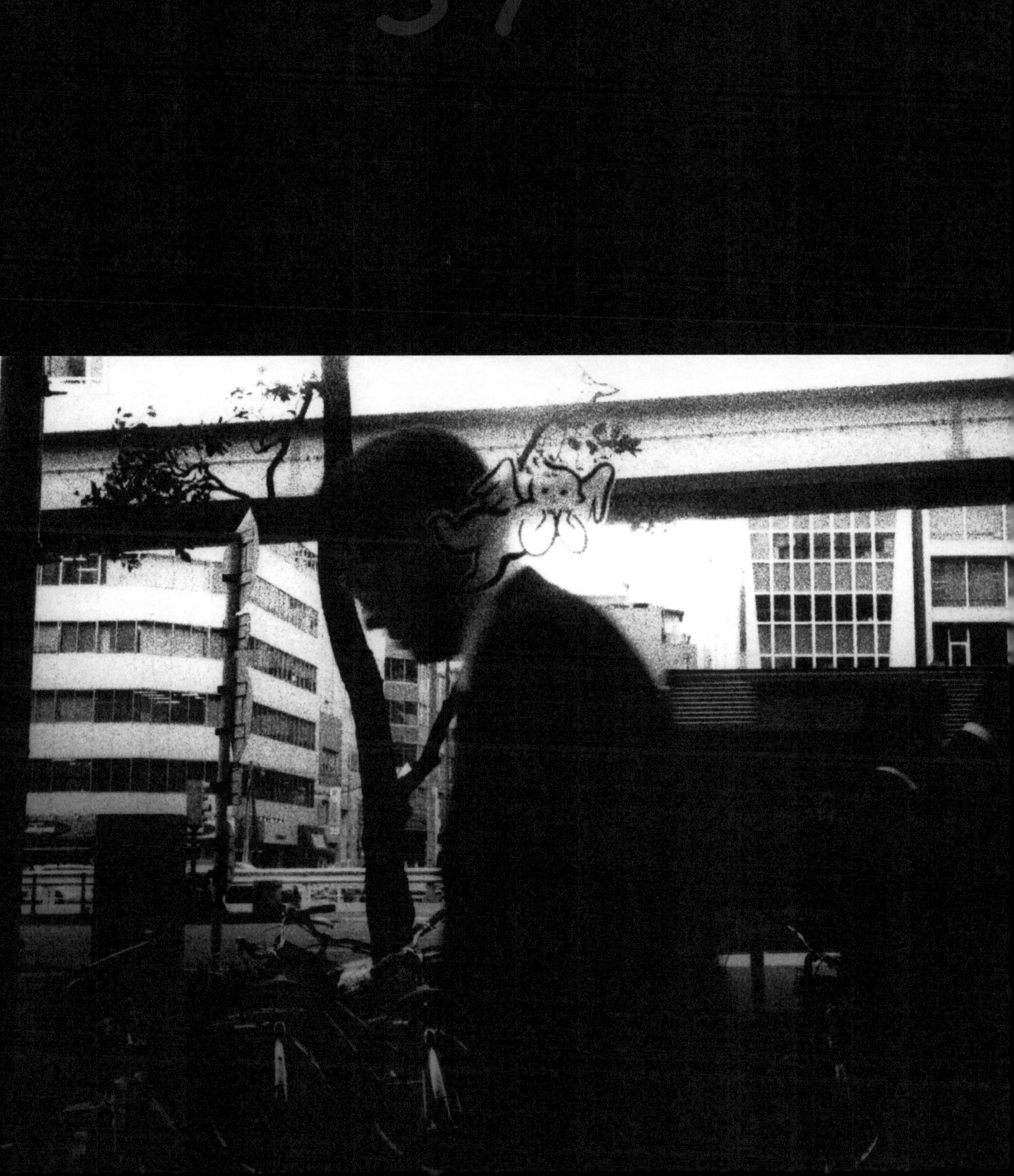

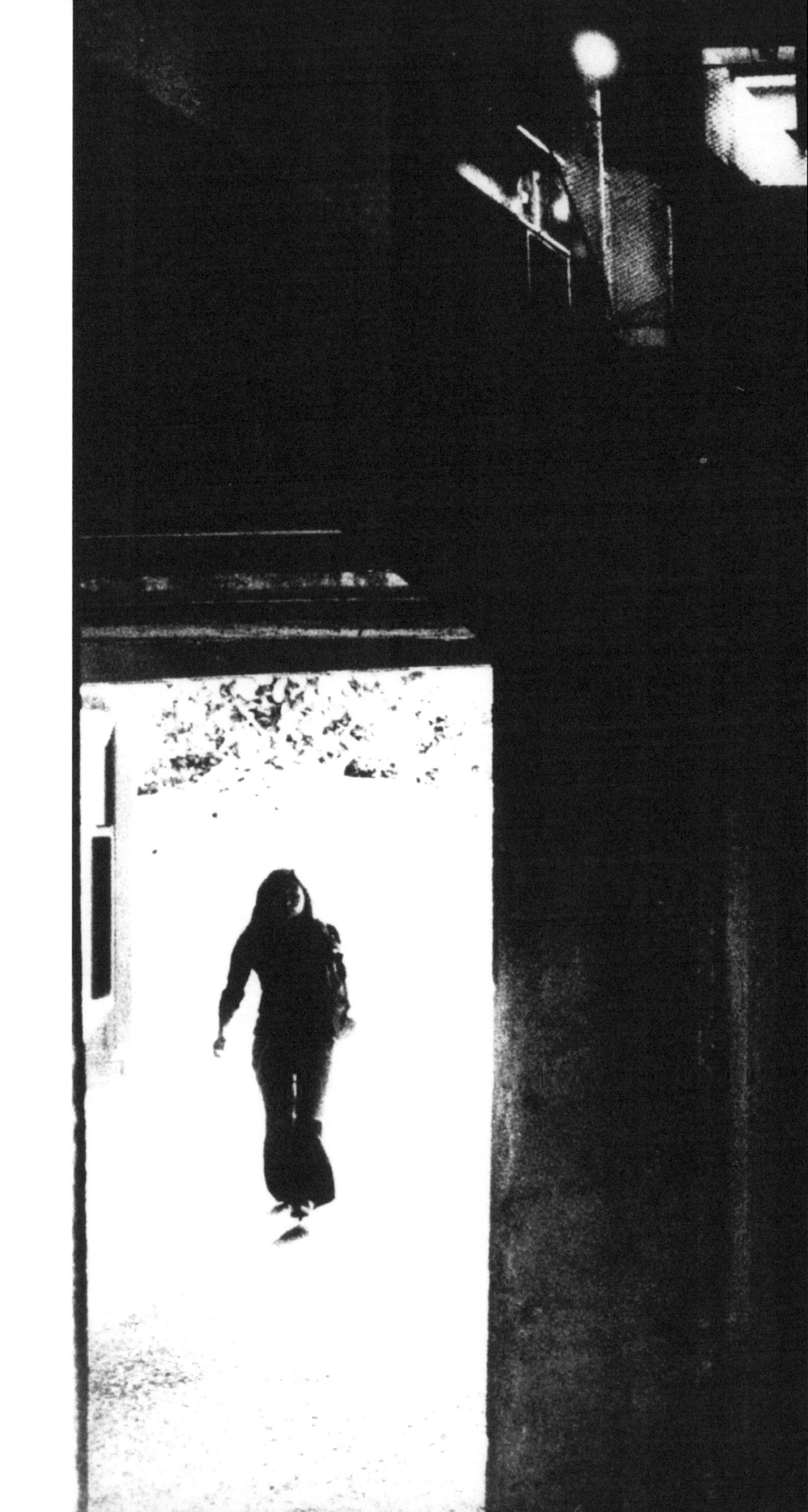

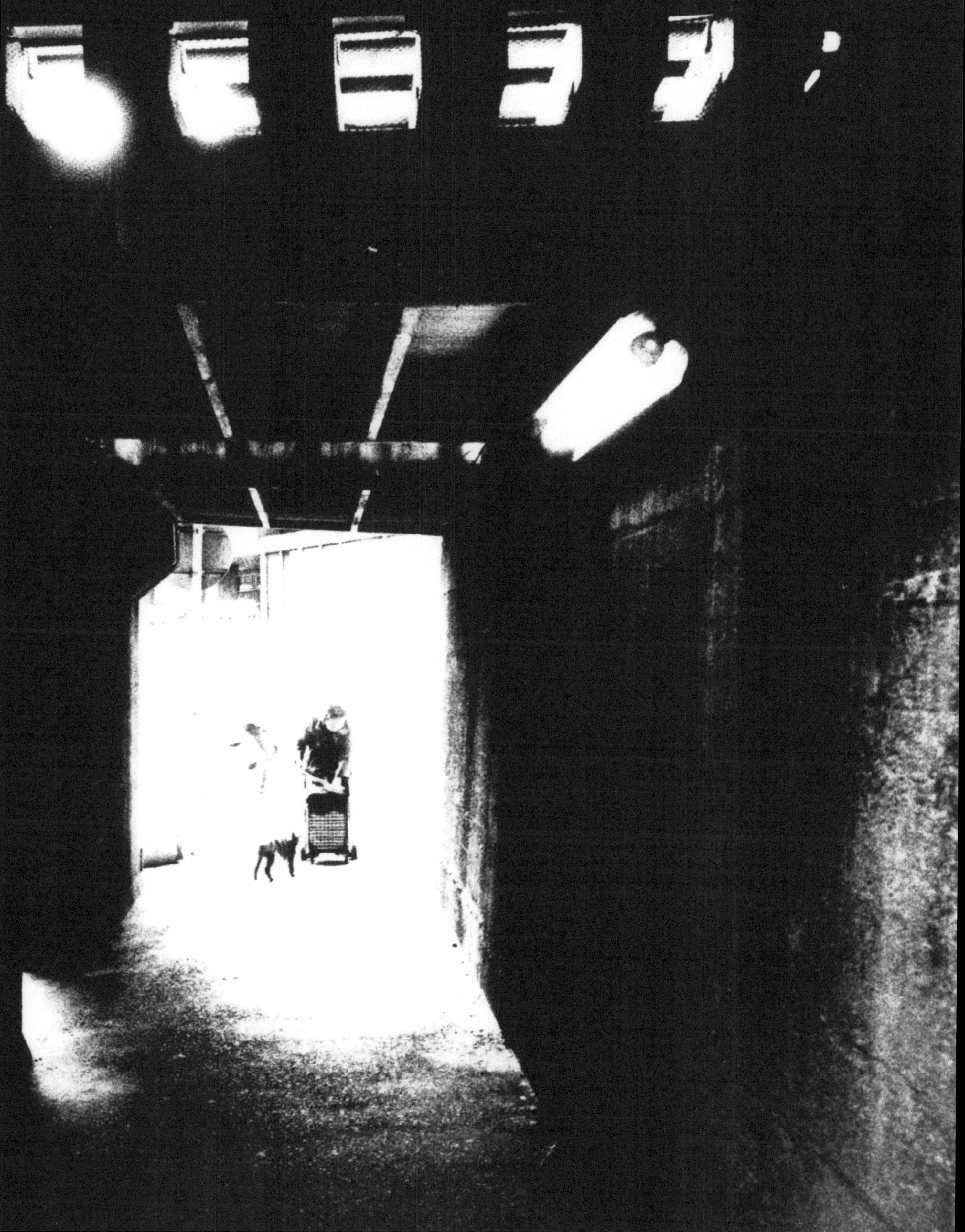

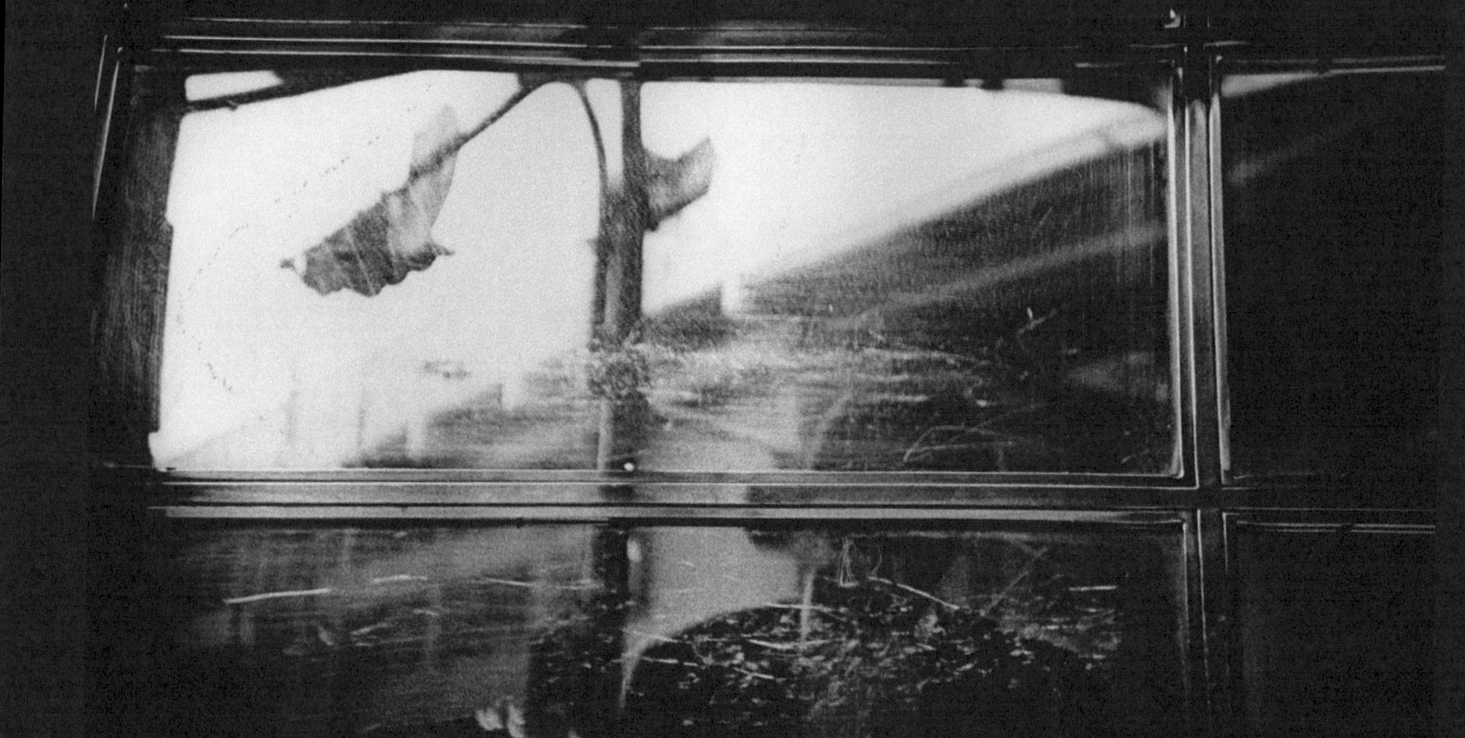

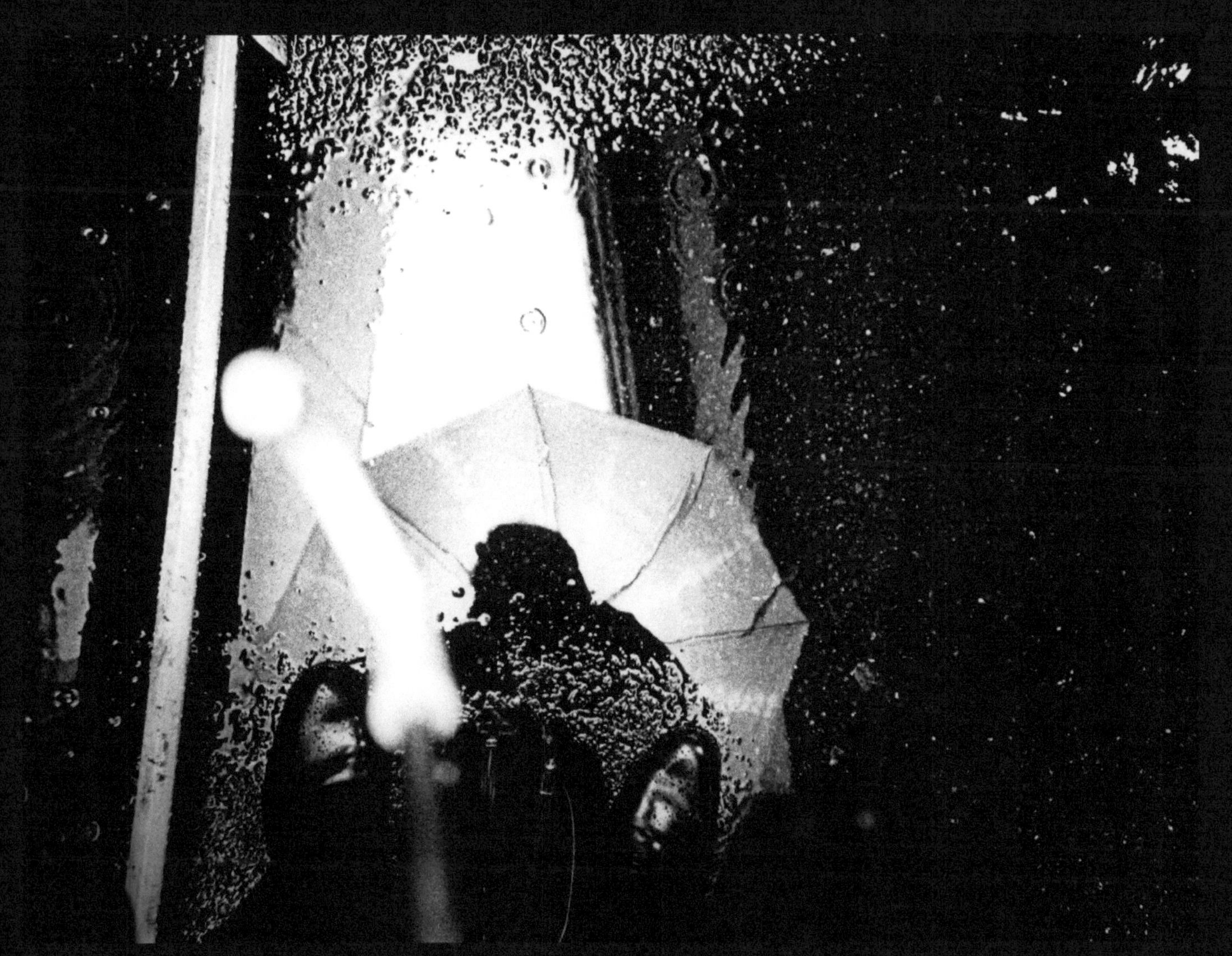

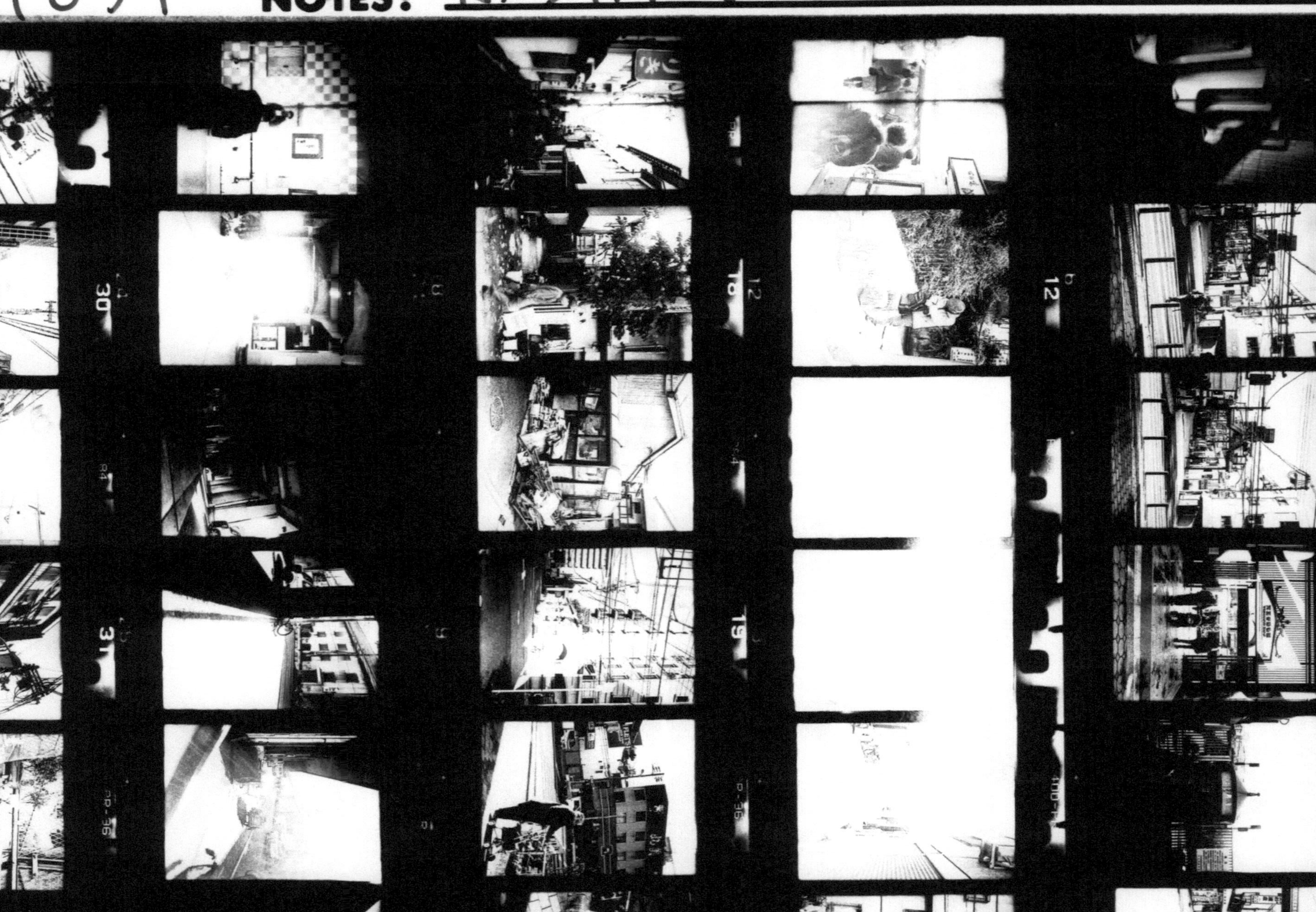
SUBJECT:
DATE:
TECHNICAL DATA: 2013.12.13
NOTES: PEN-S PR400 D76 (1:1) 40-7.30 K& T5KIP2M
ISE PR
ISE CO.,LTD
1054

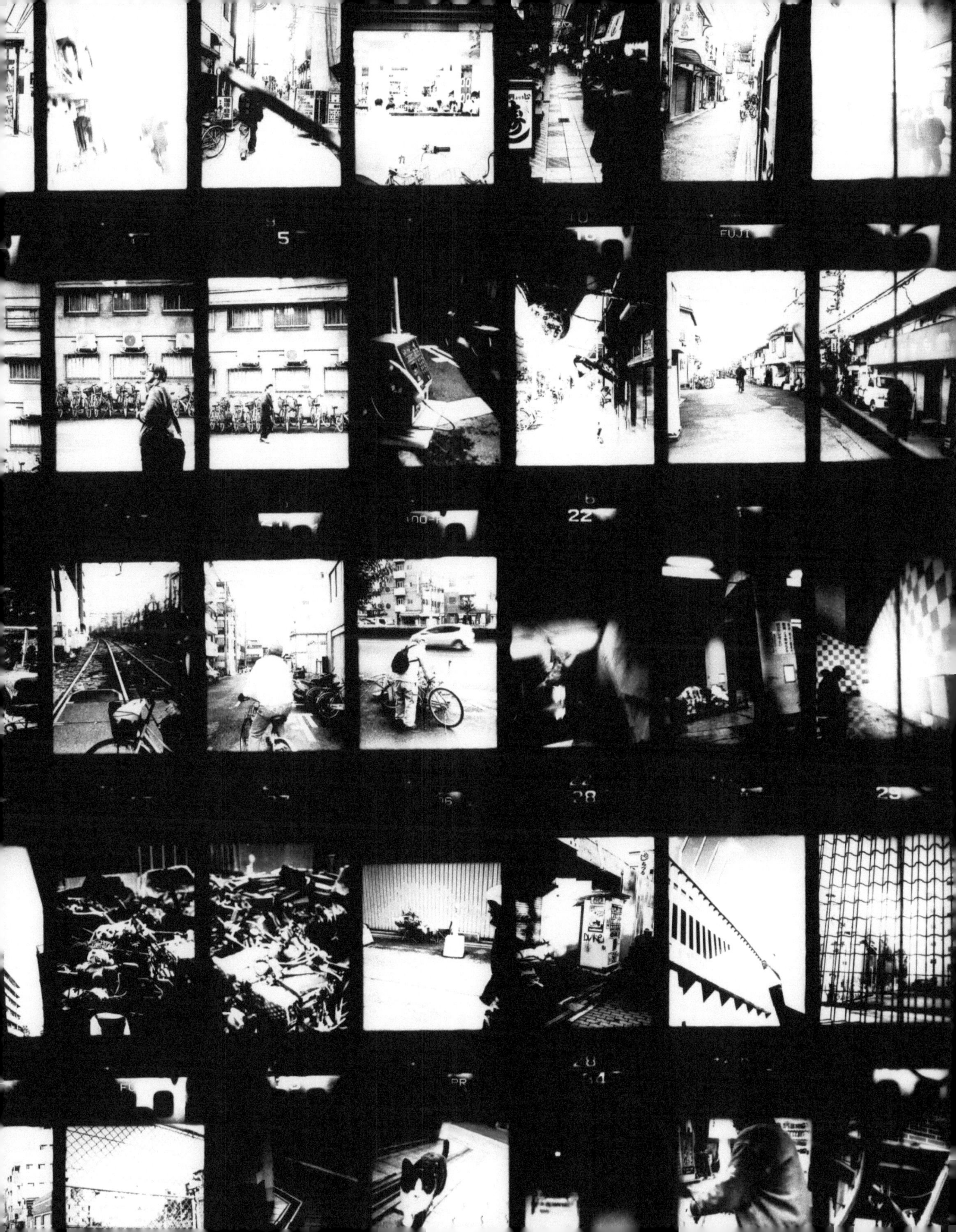

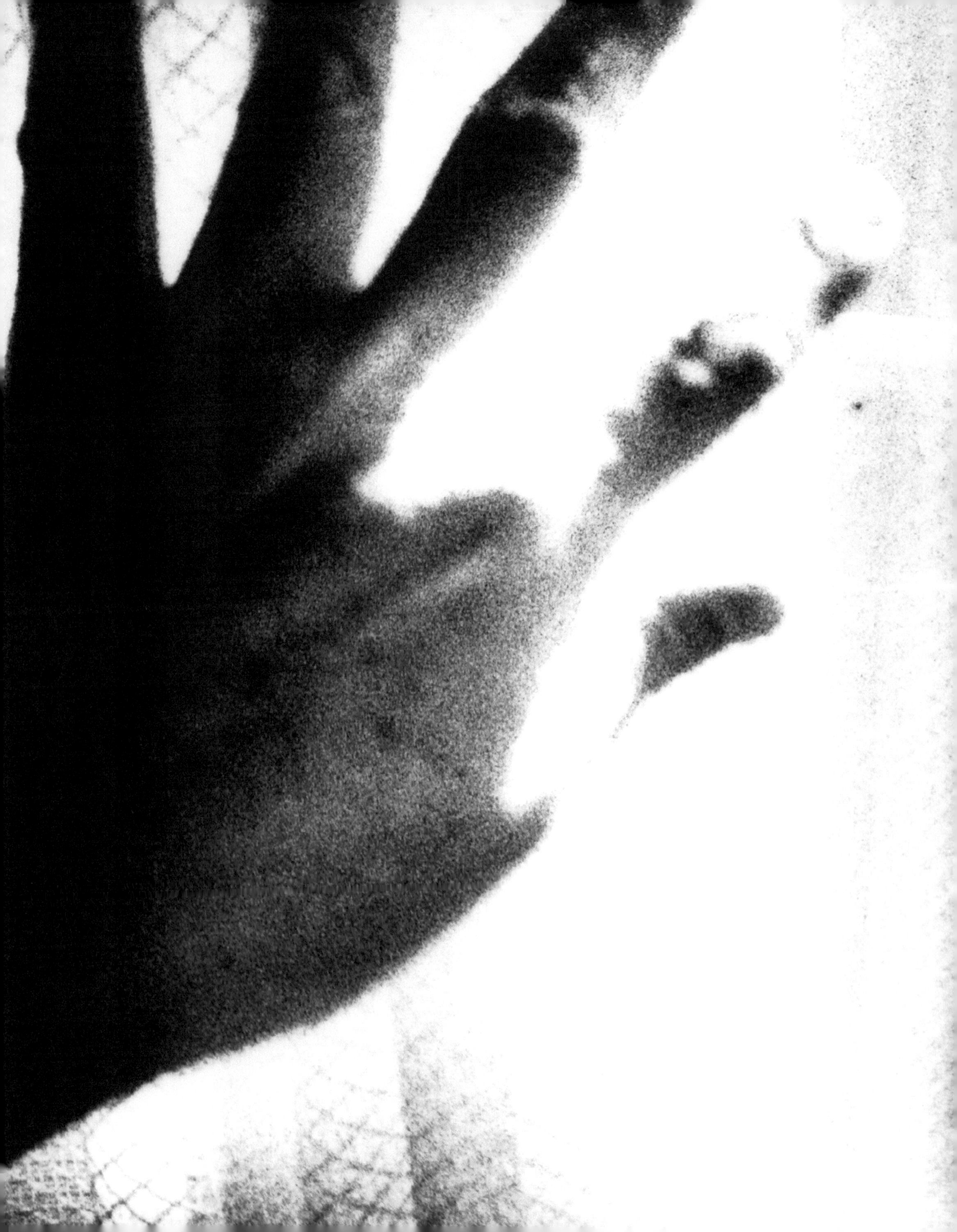

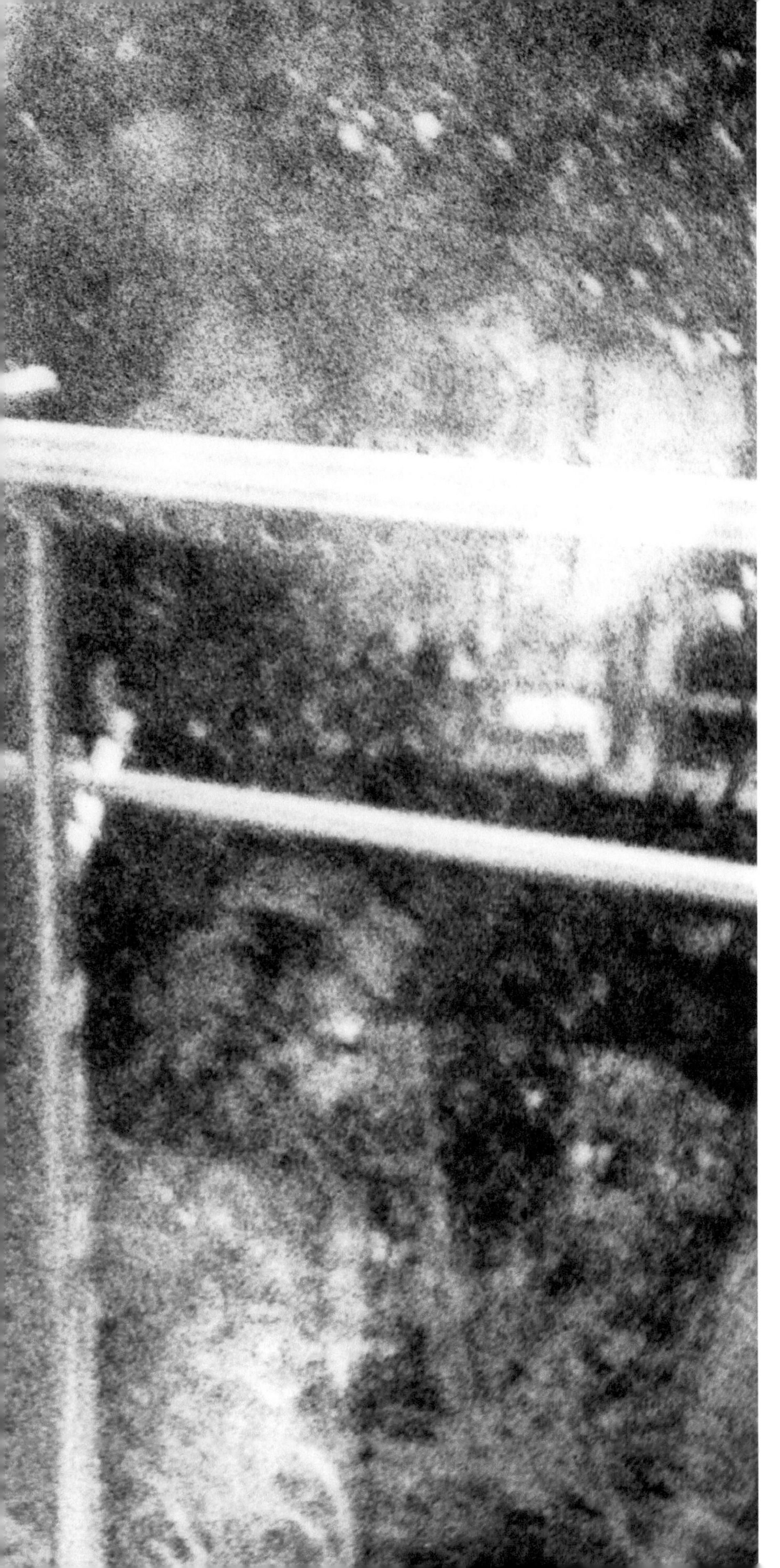

61

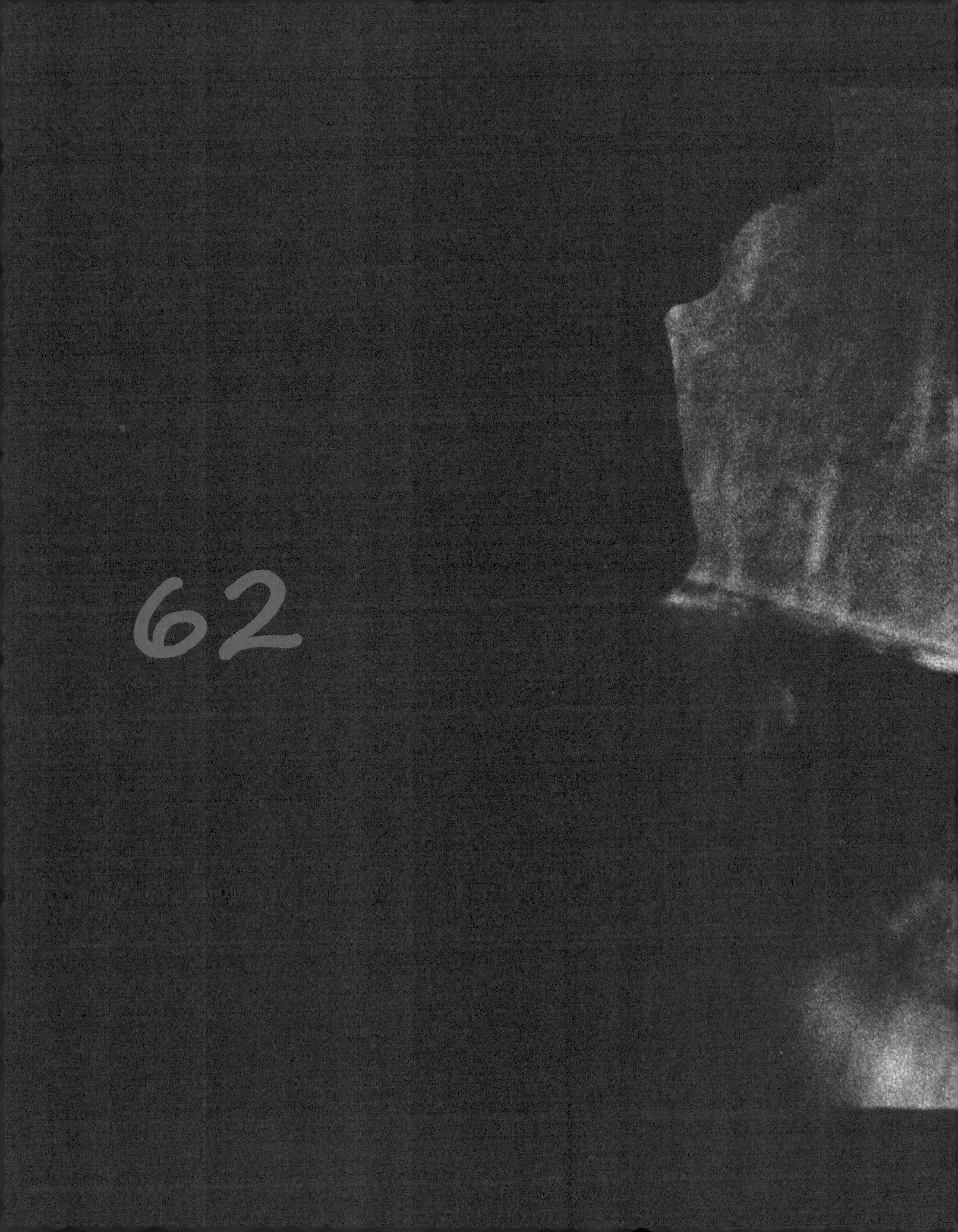

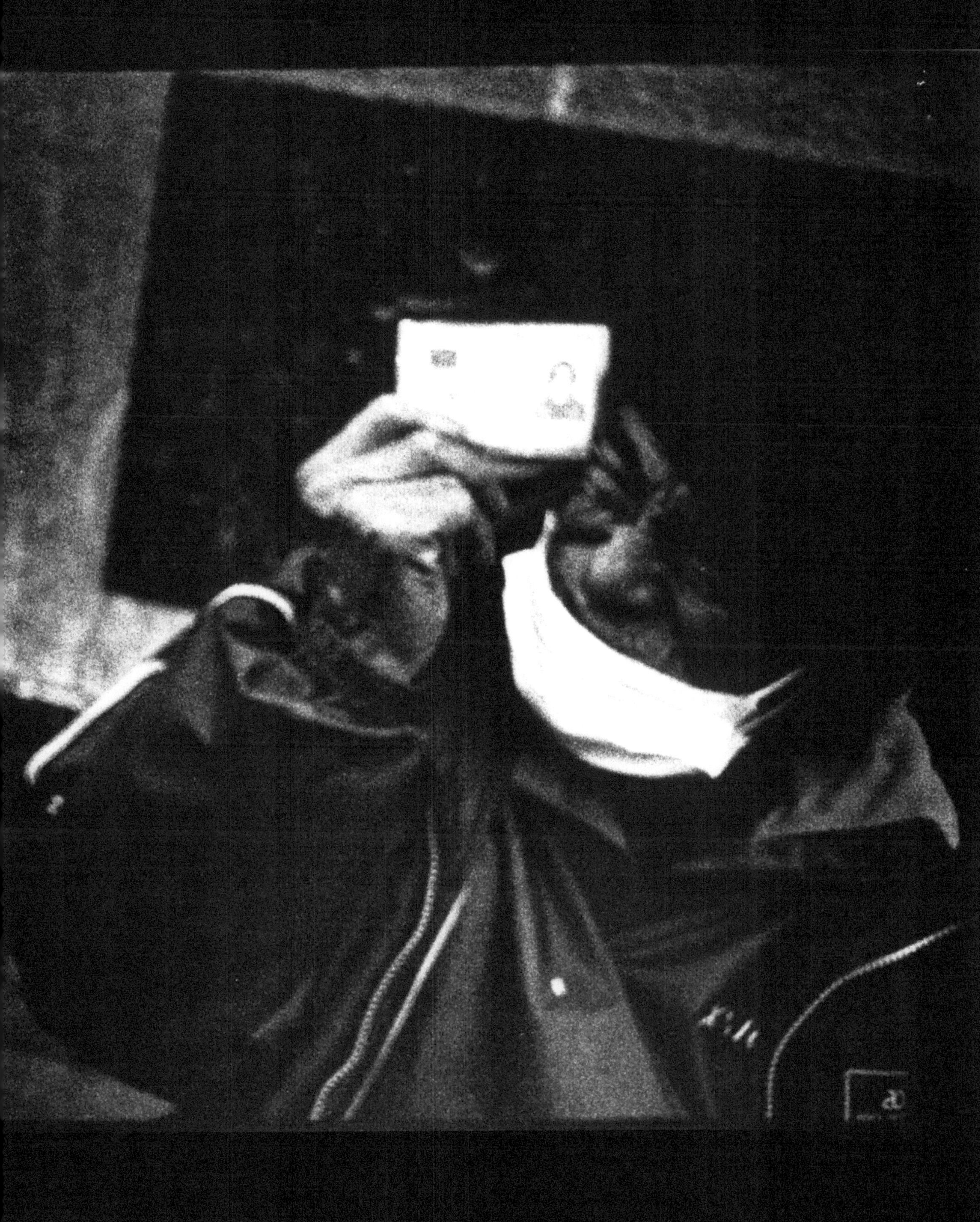

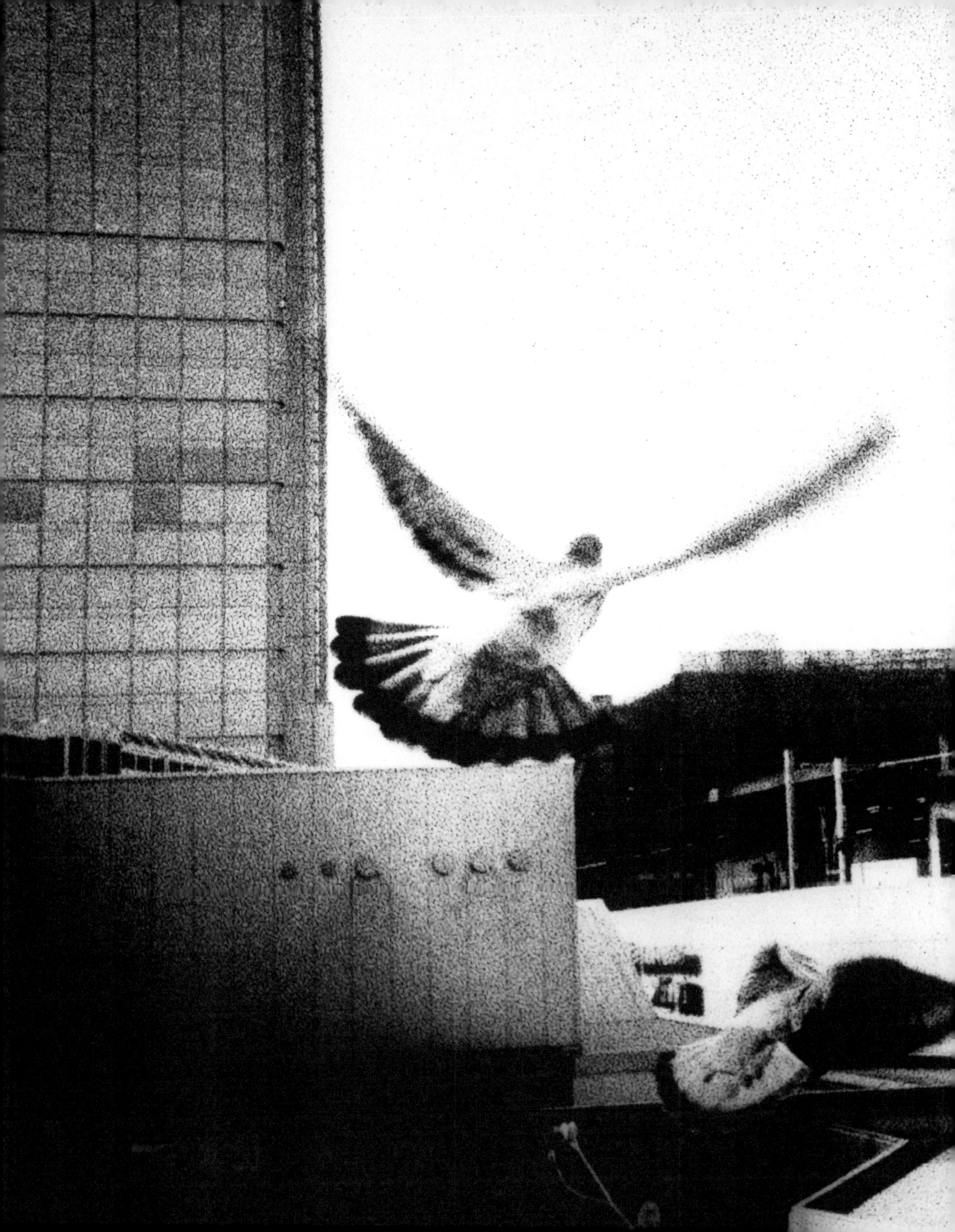

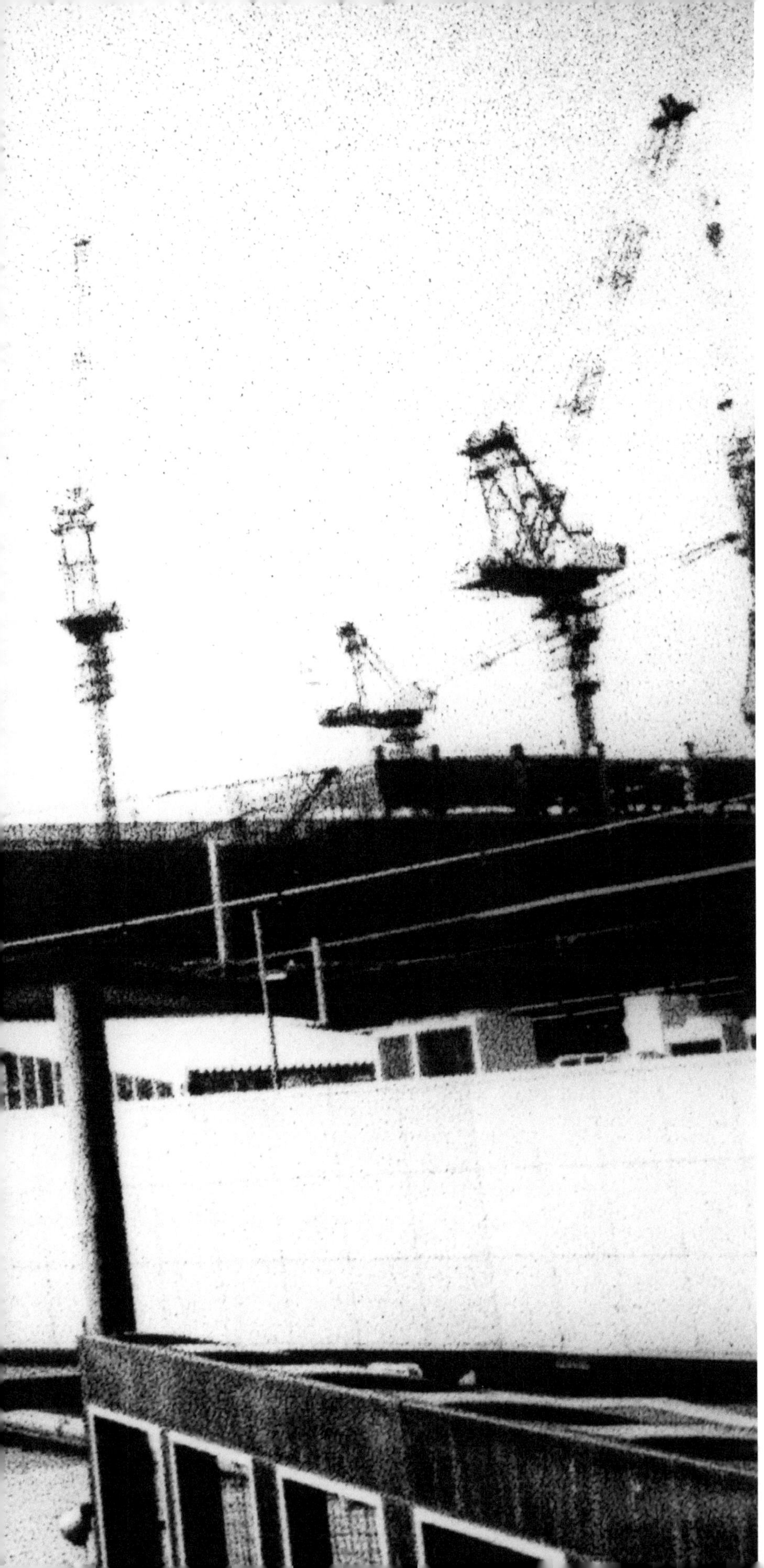

63

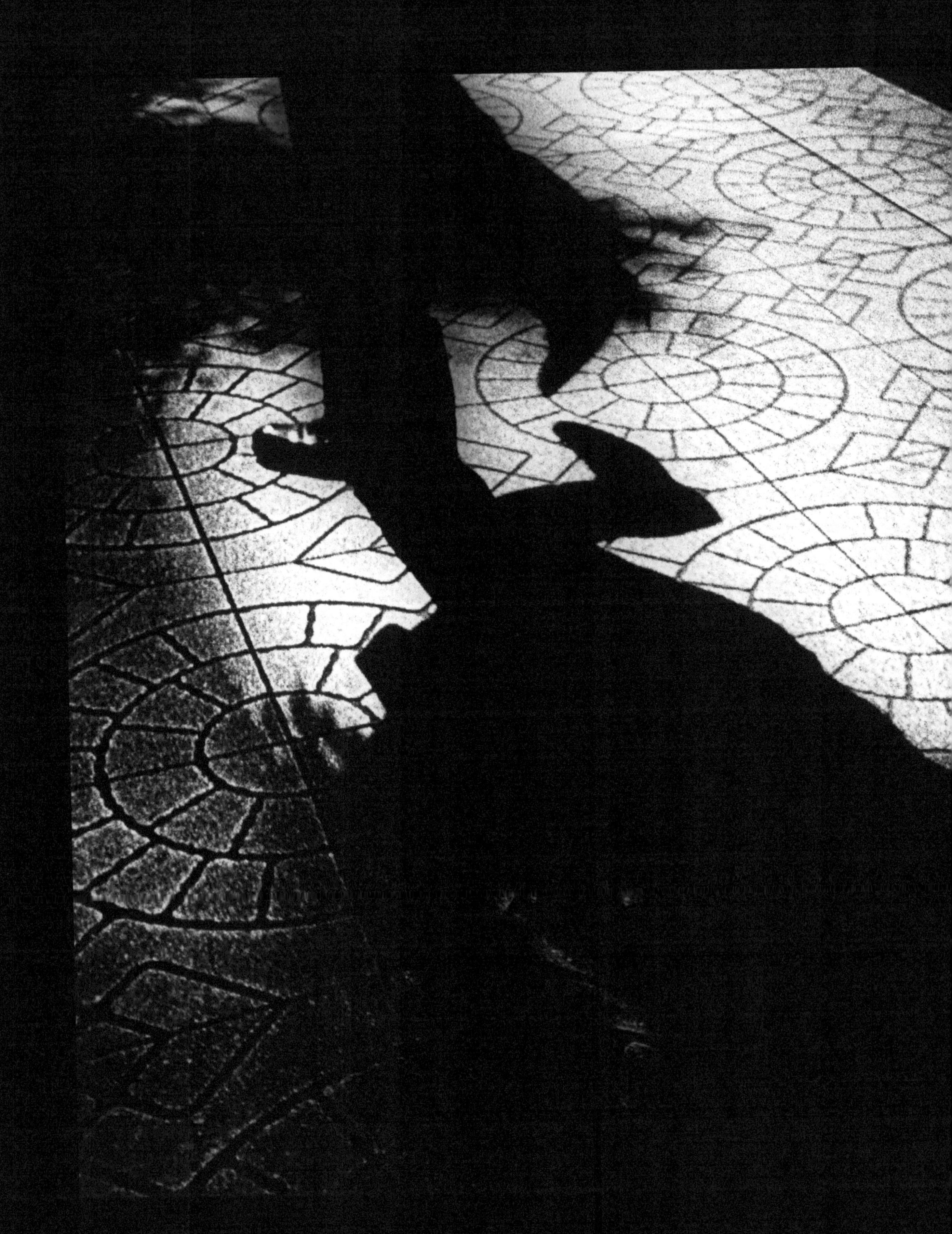

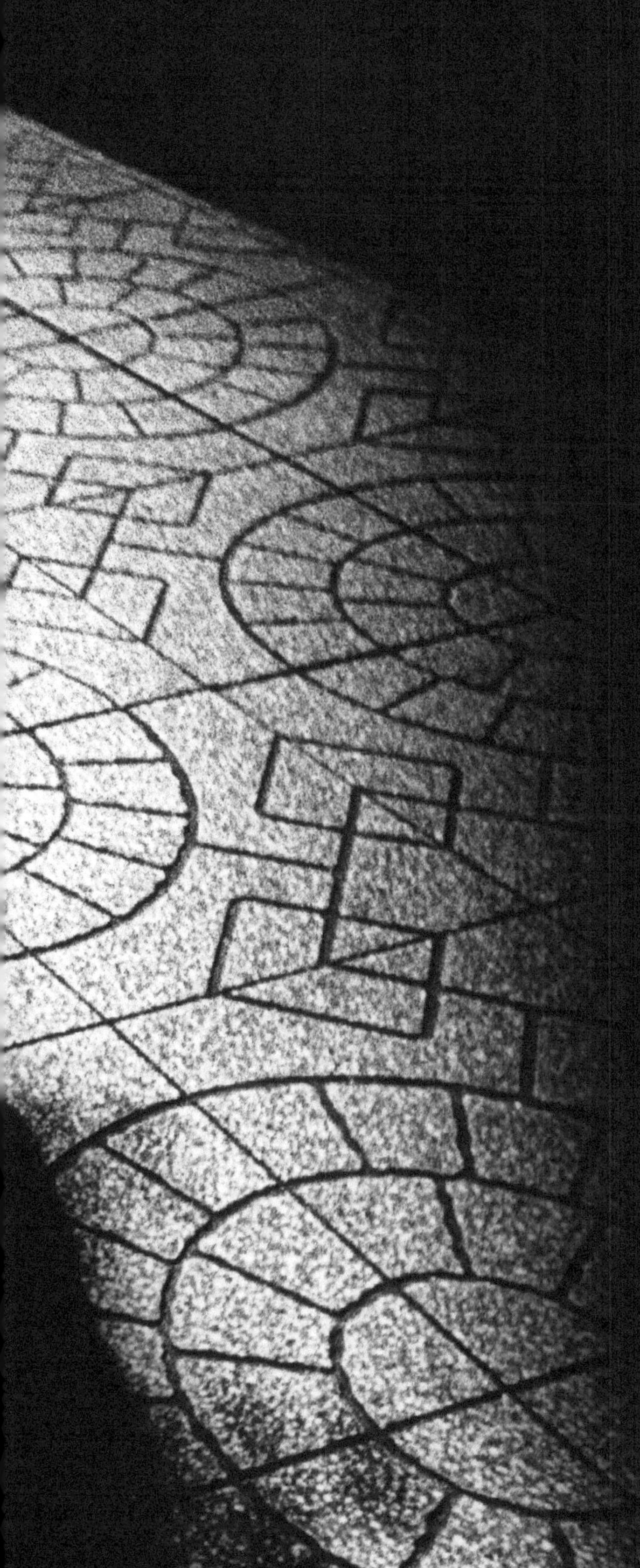

64

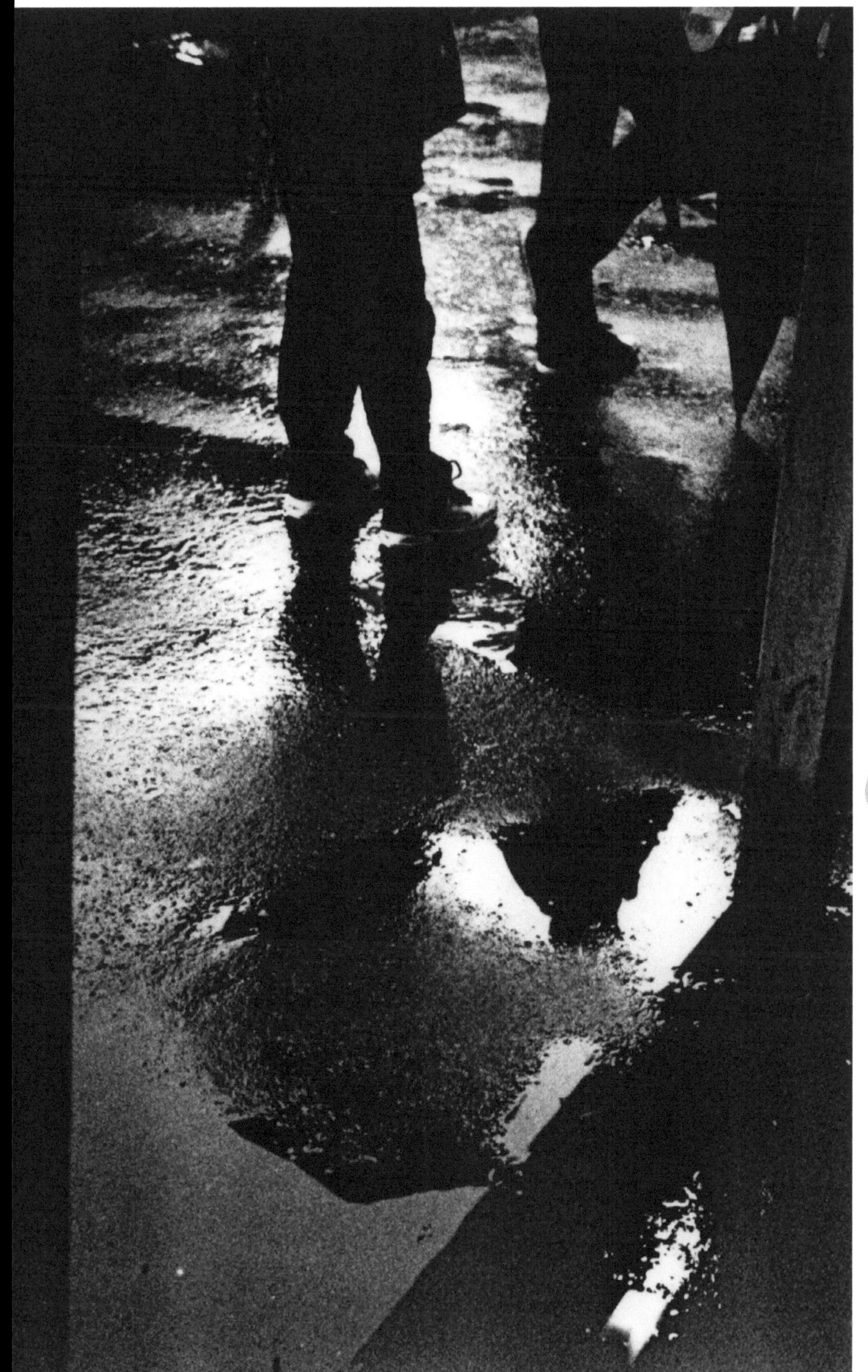

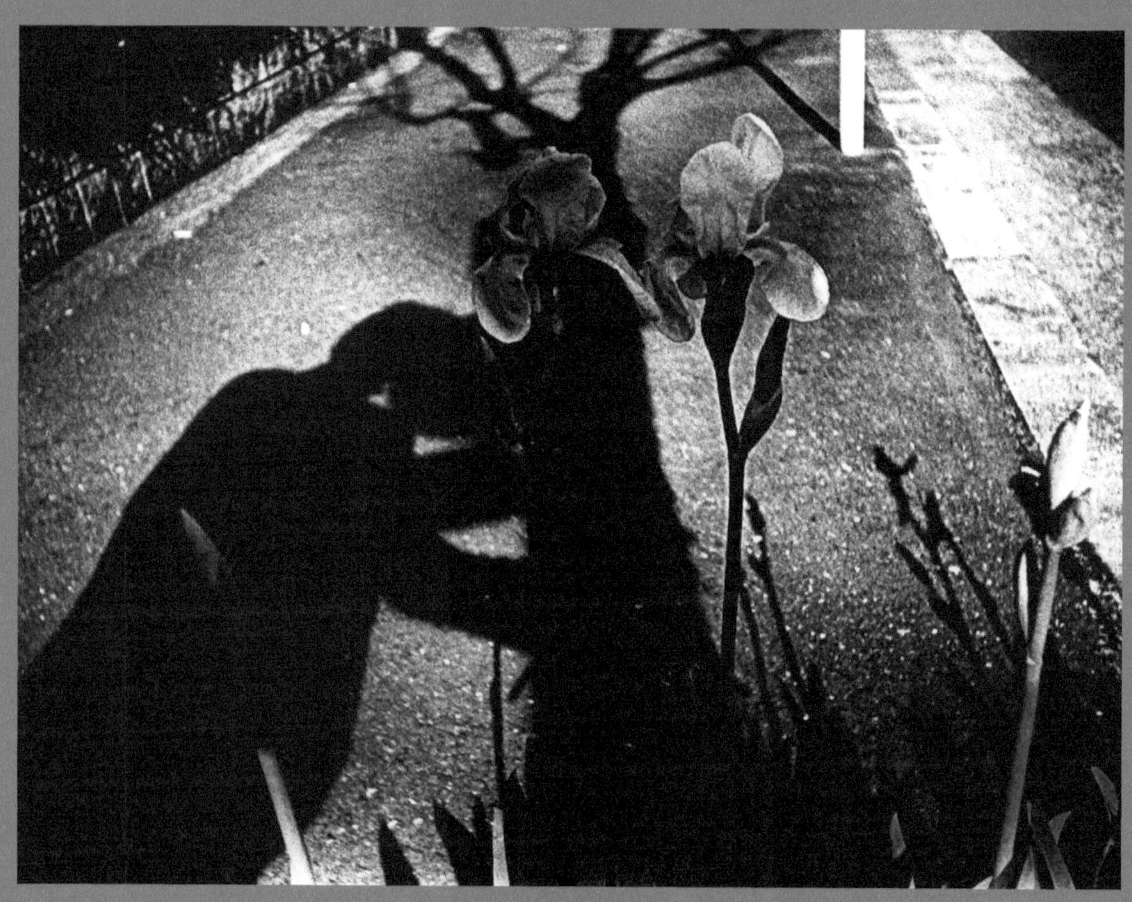

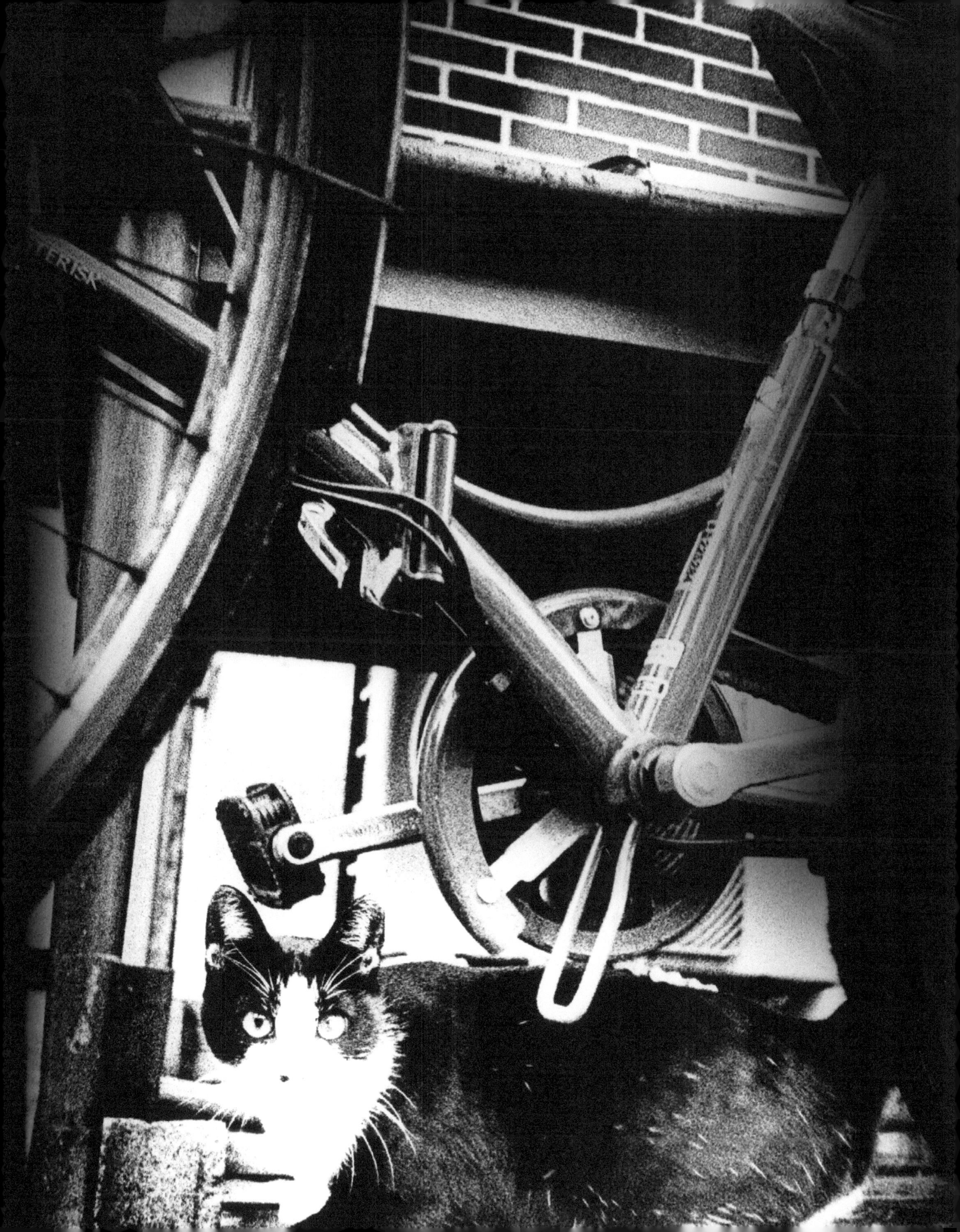

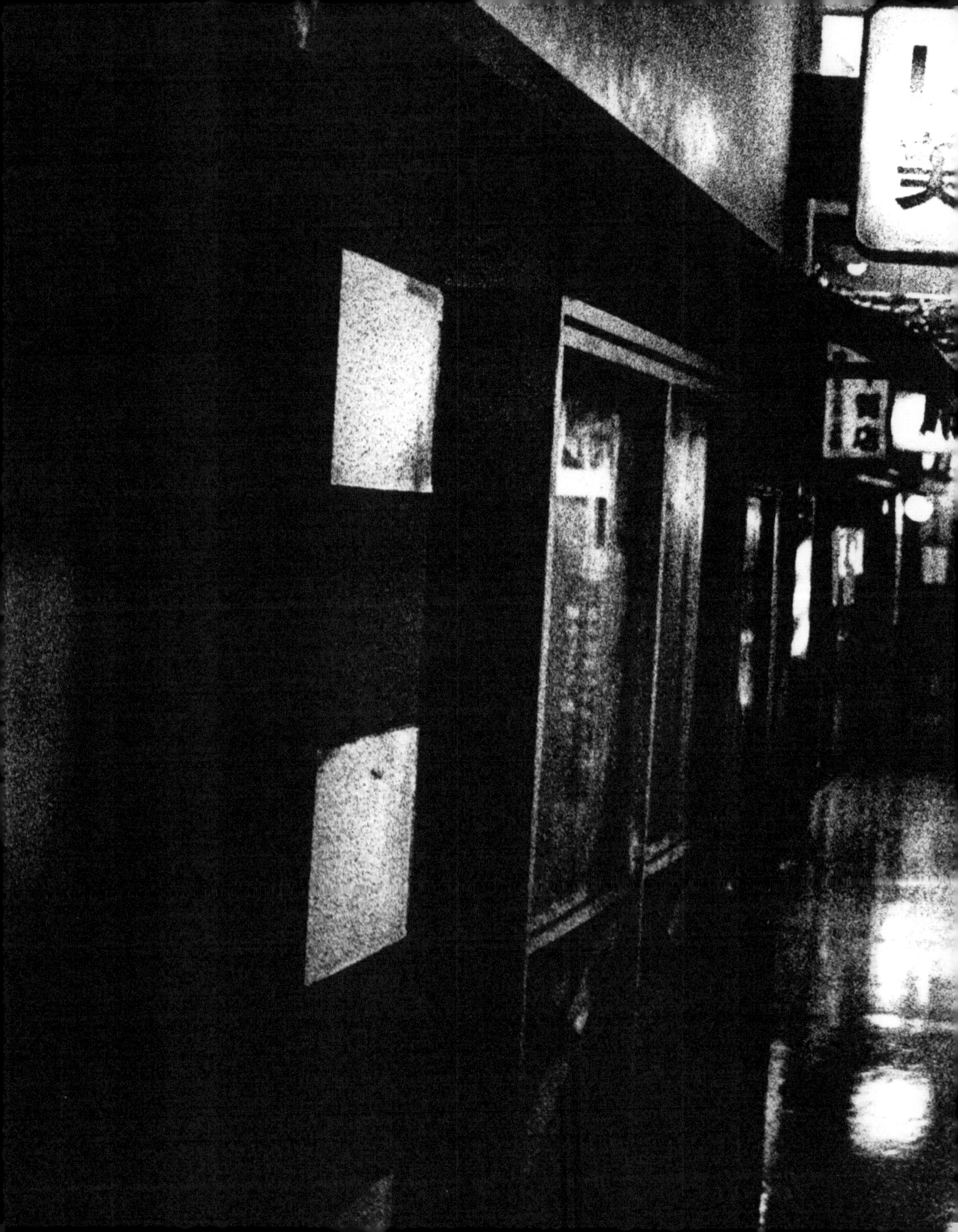

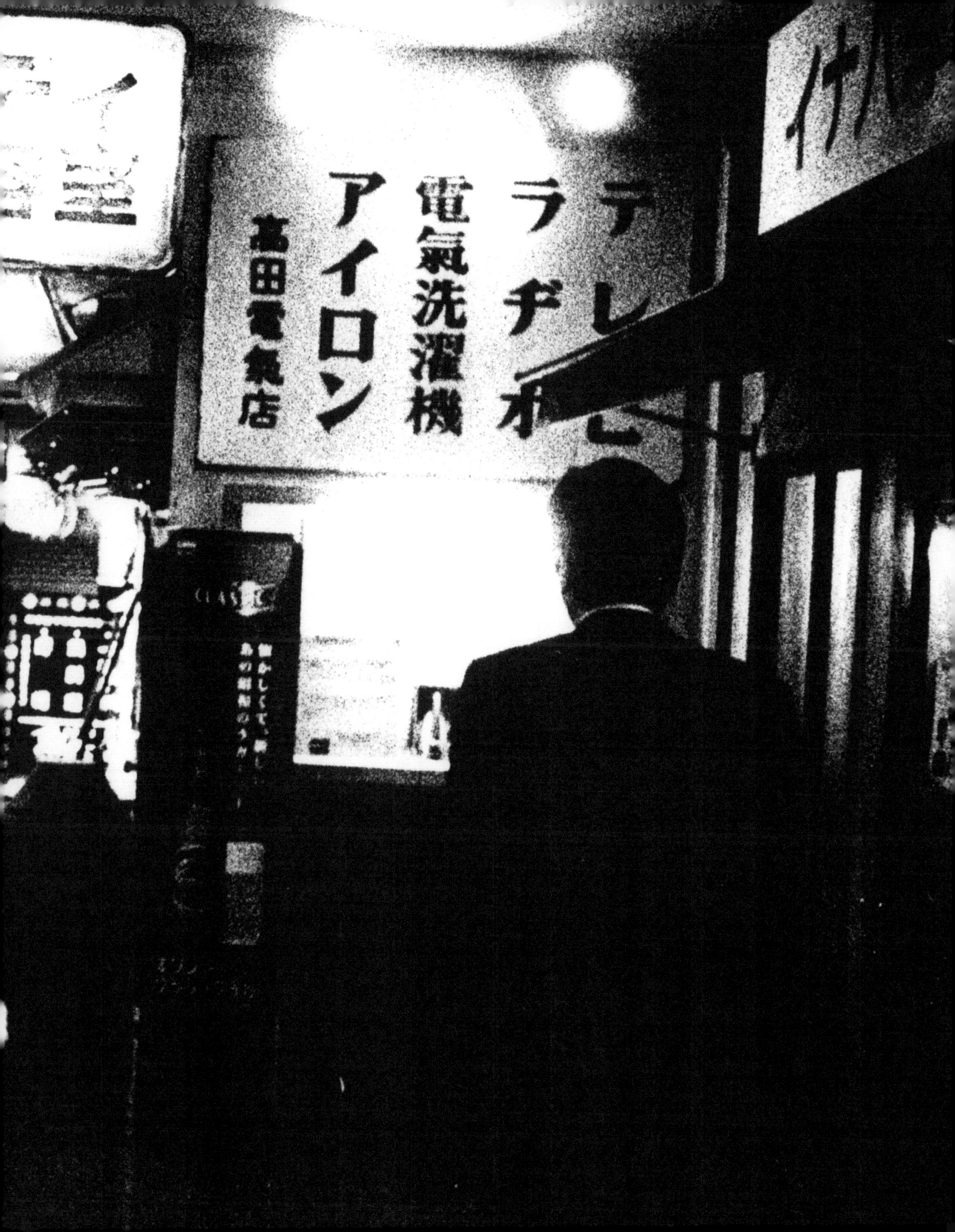

テレビ
ラヂオ
電氣洗濯機
アイロン
高田電氣店
イケハ
CLASSIC

70

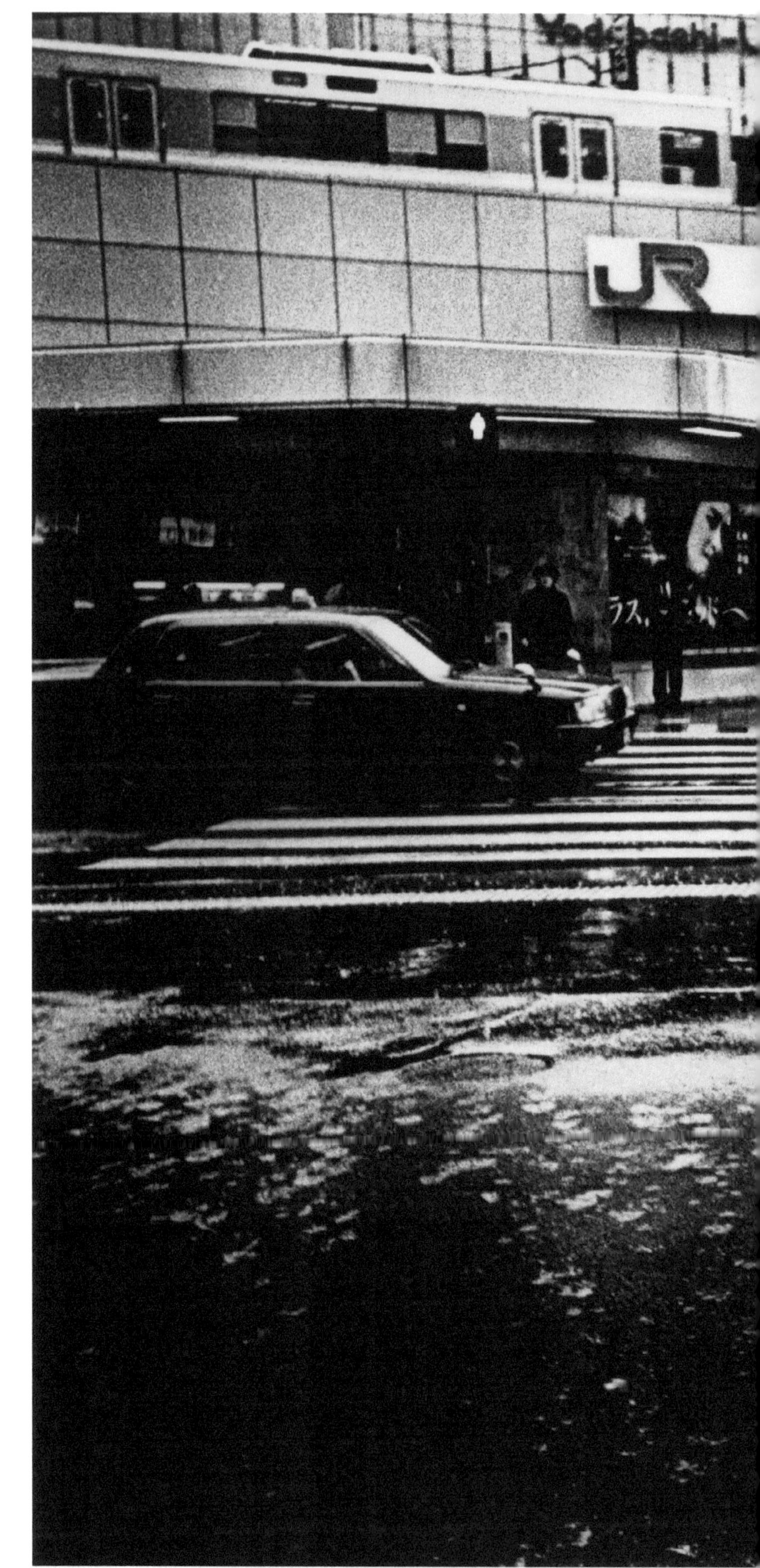

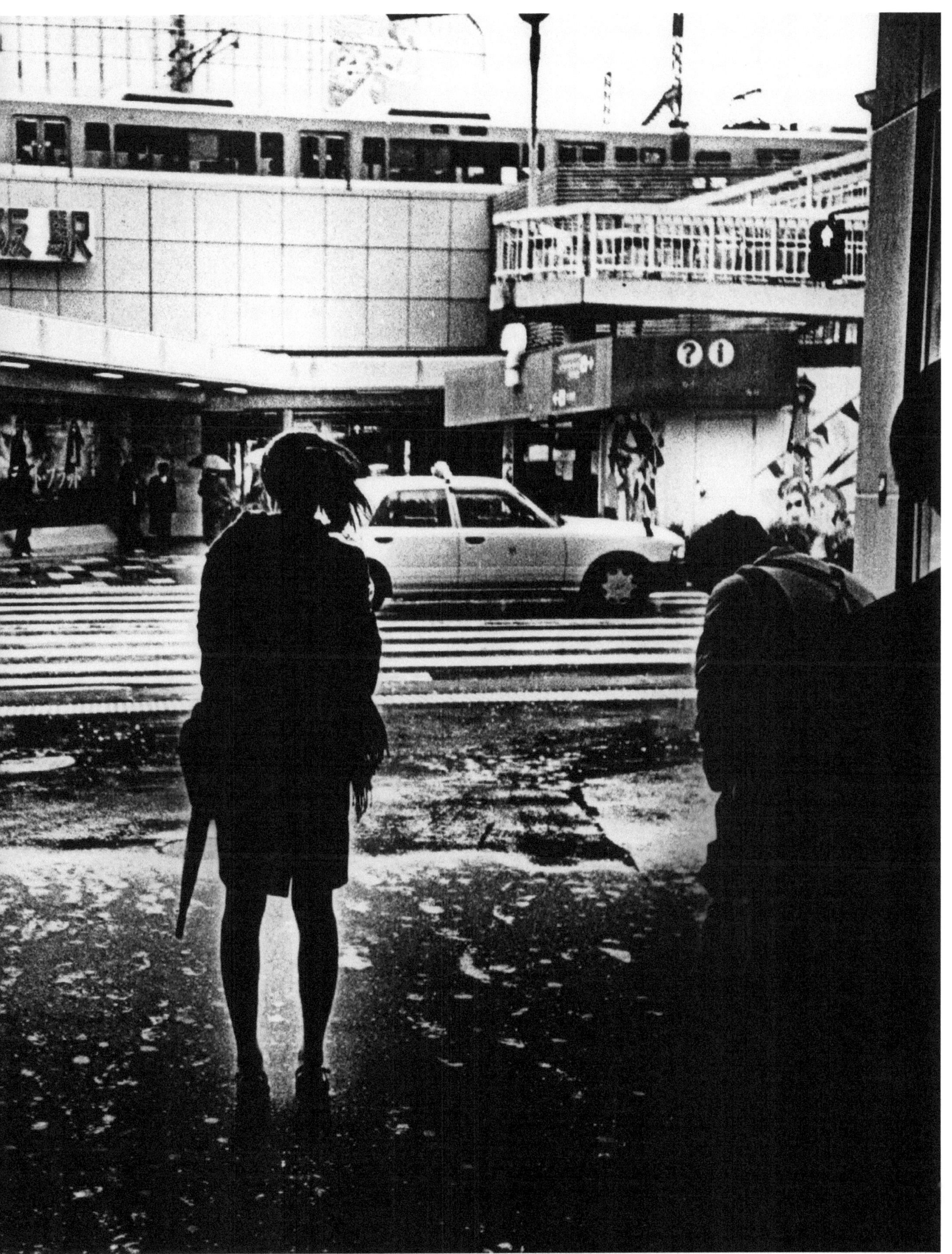

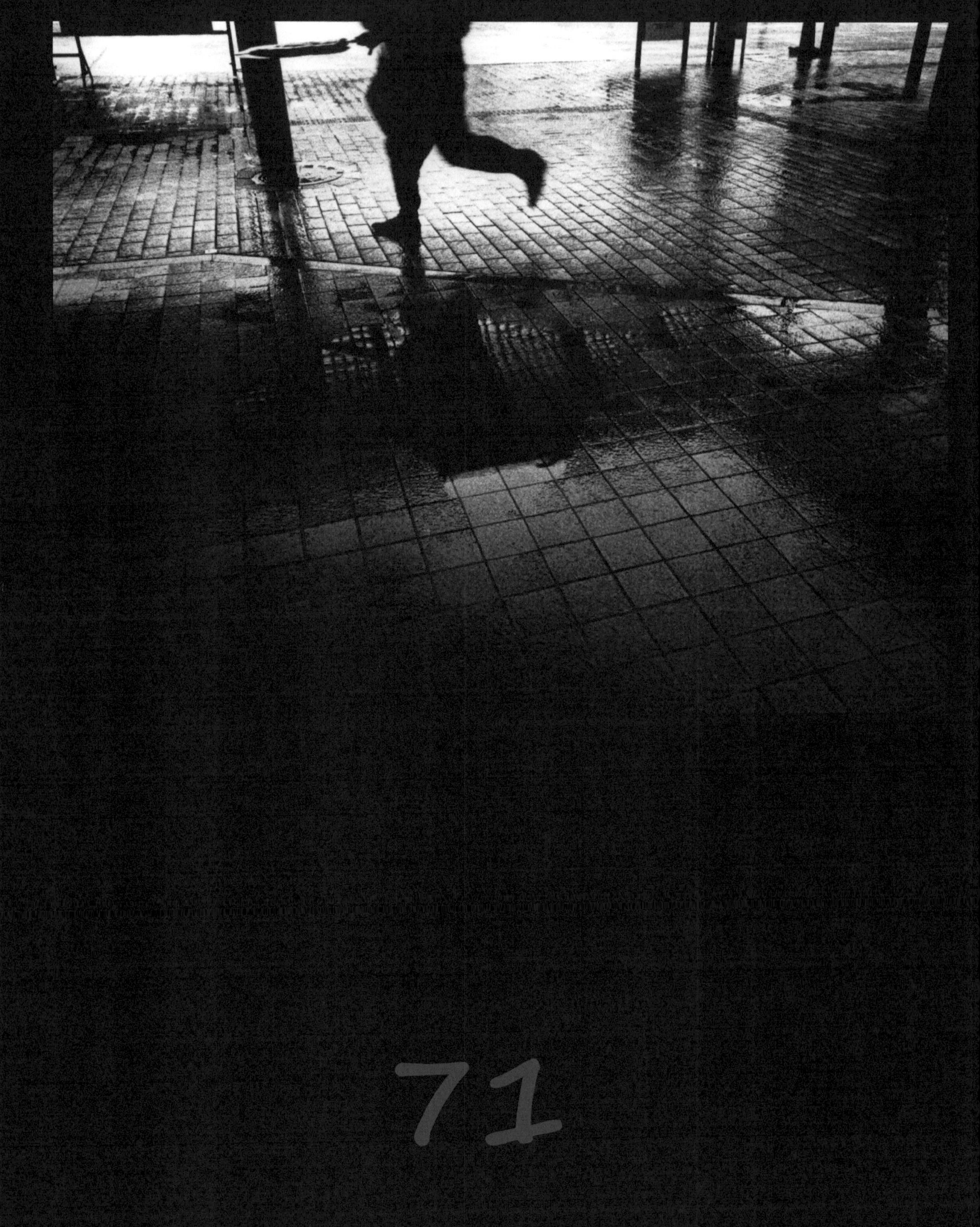

71

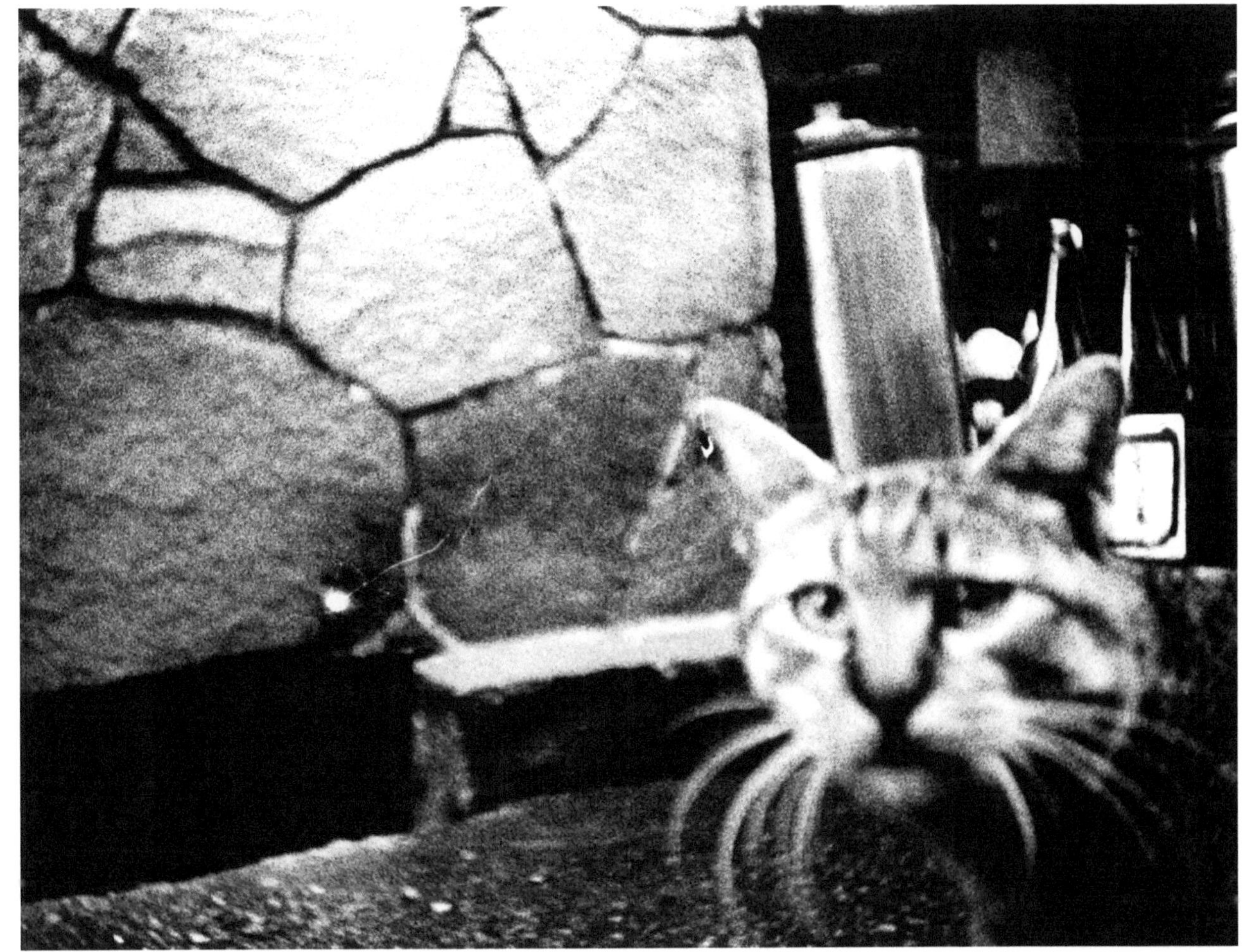

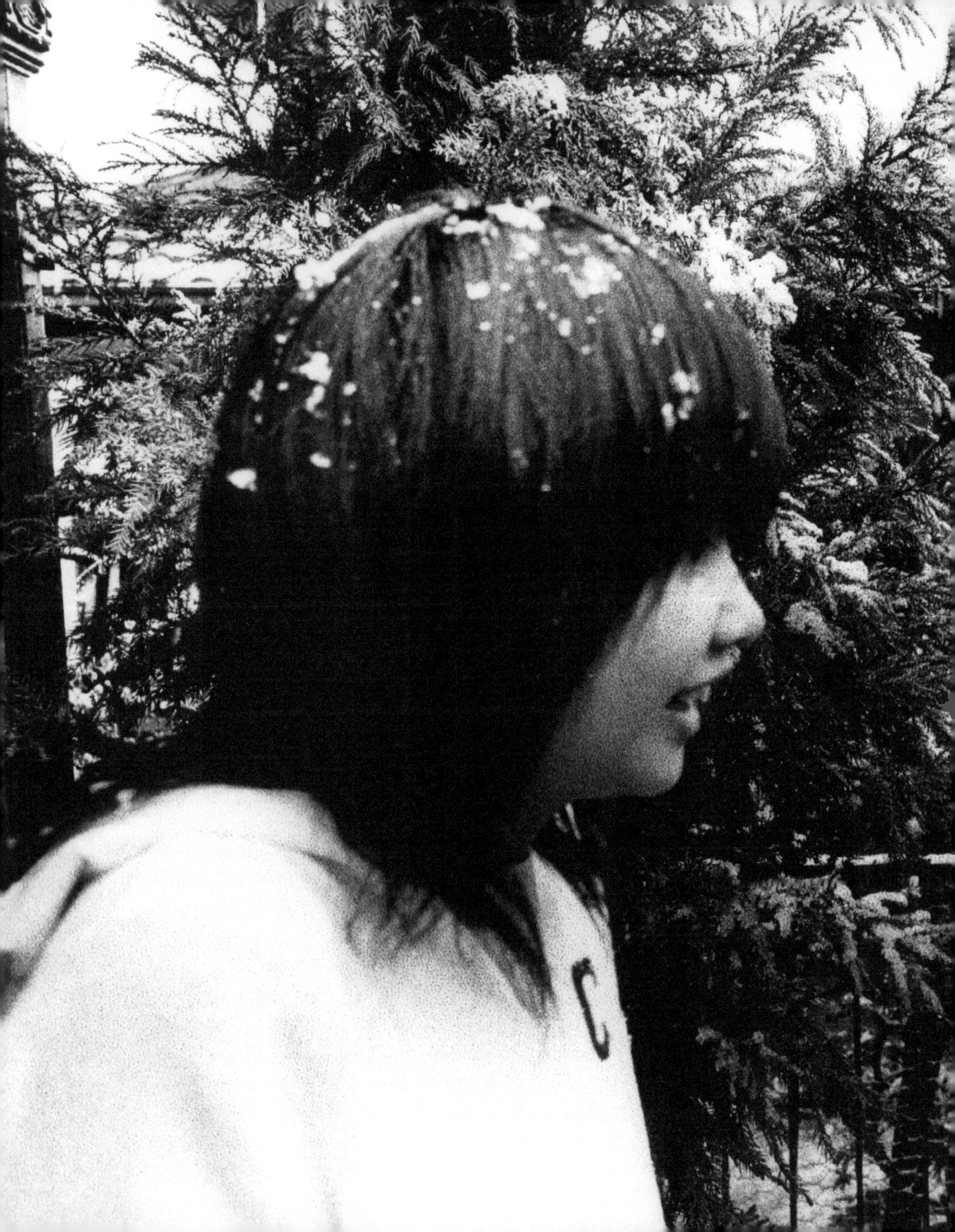

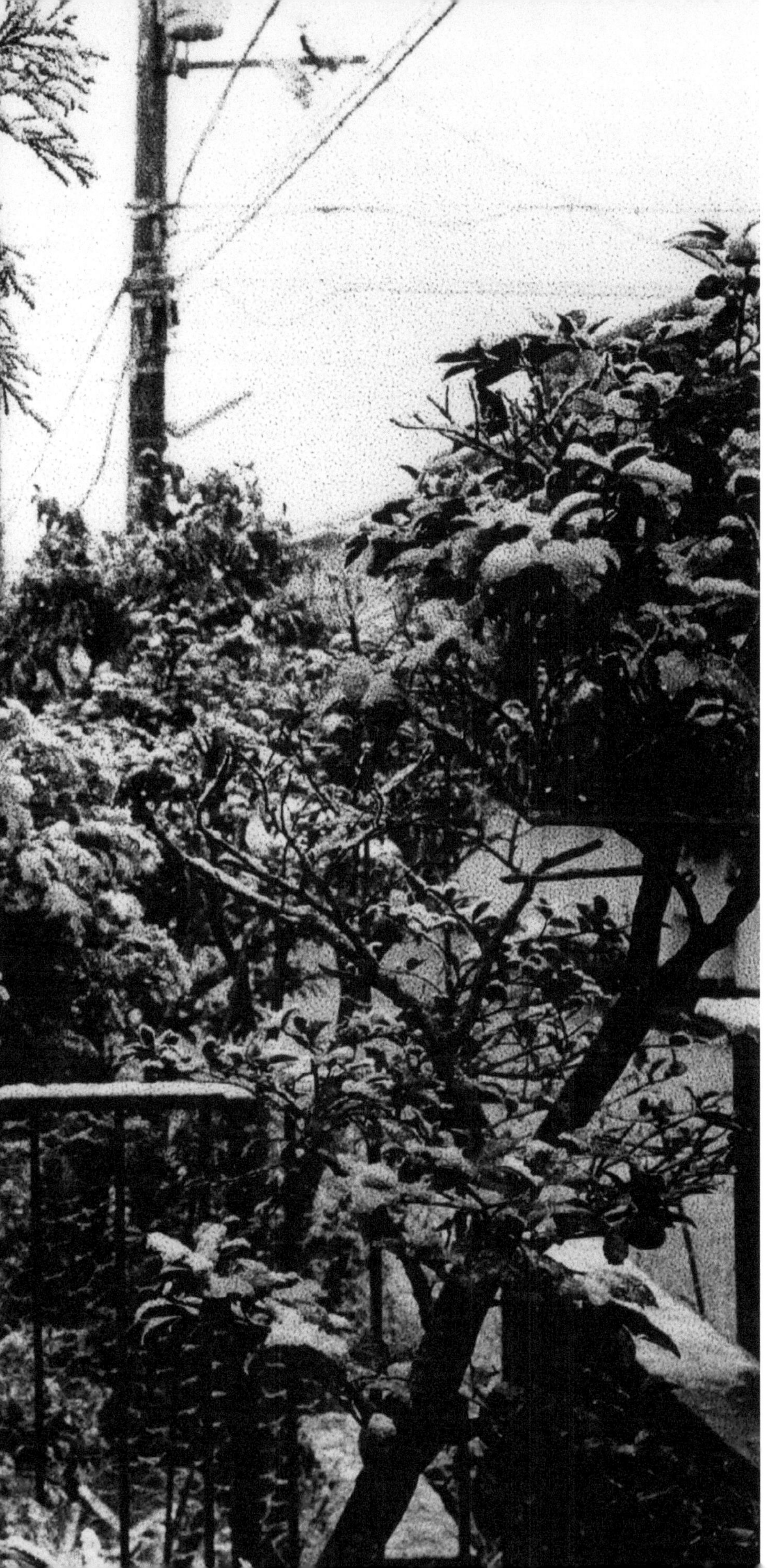

73

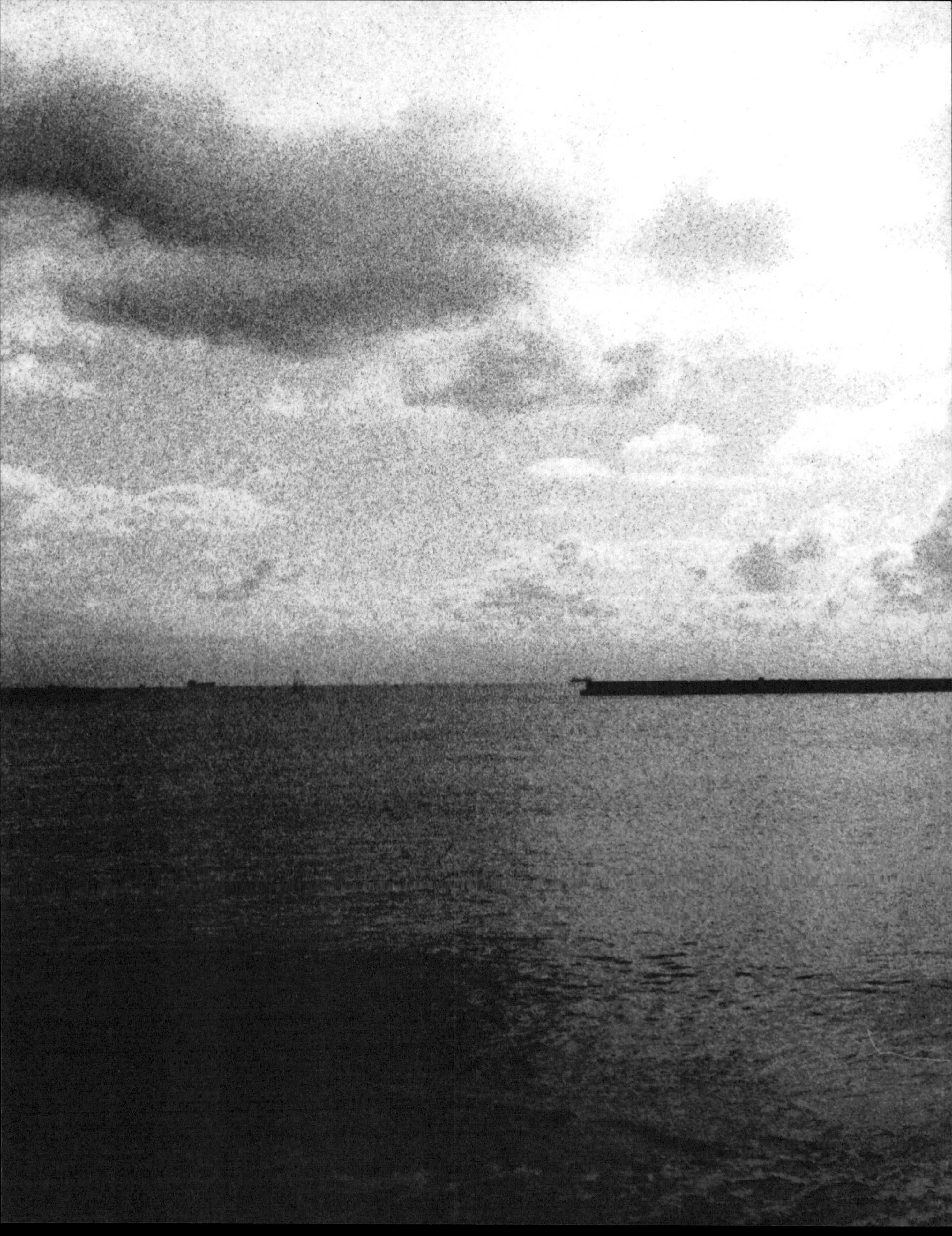

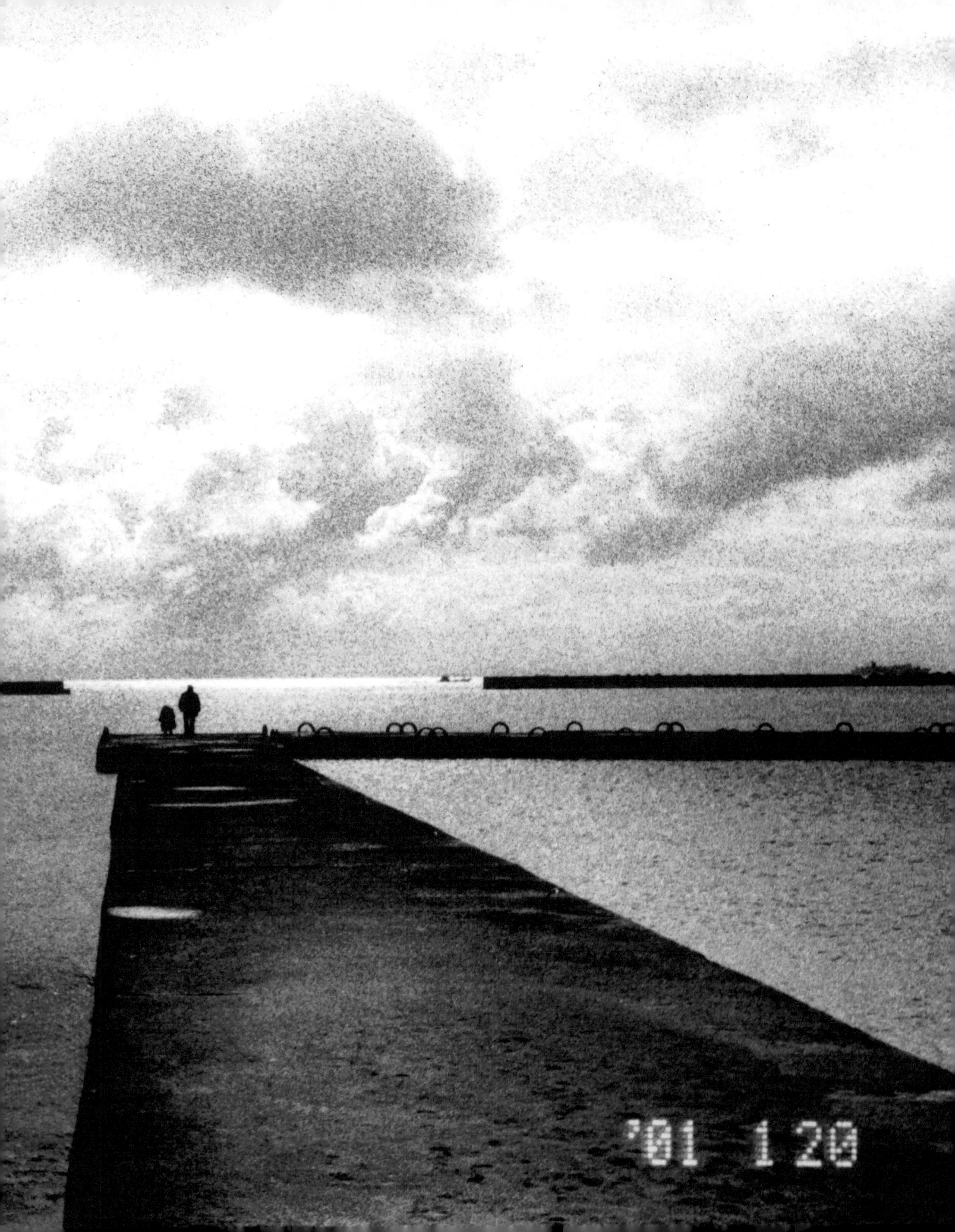
'01 1 20

75

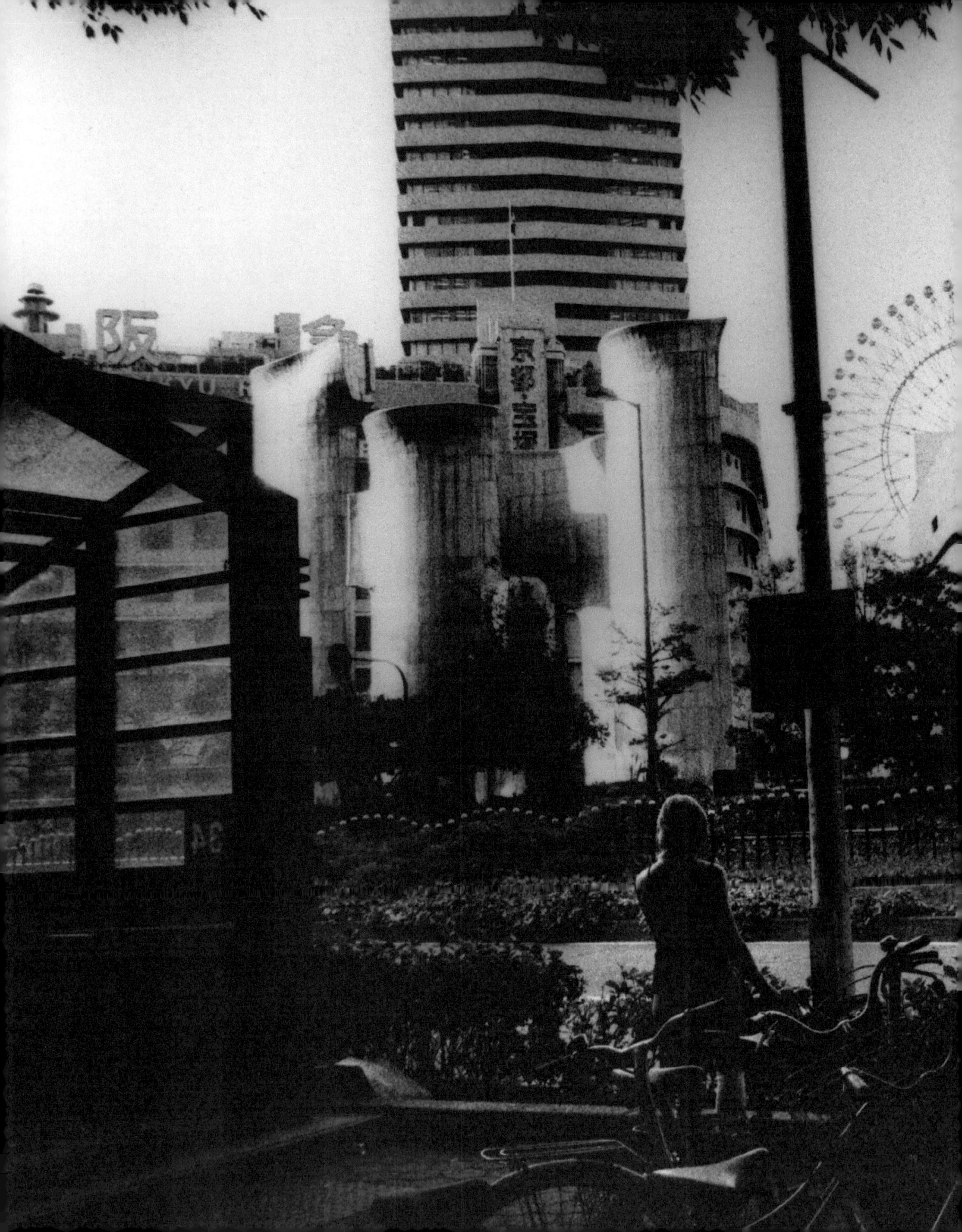

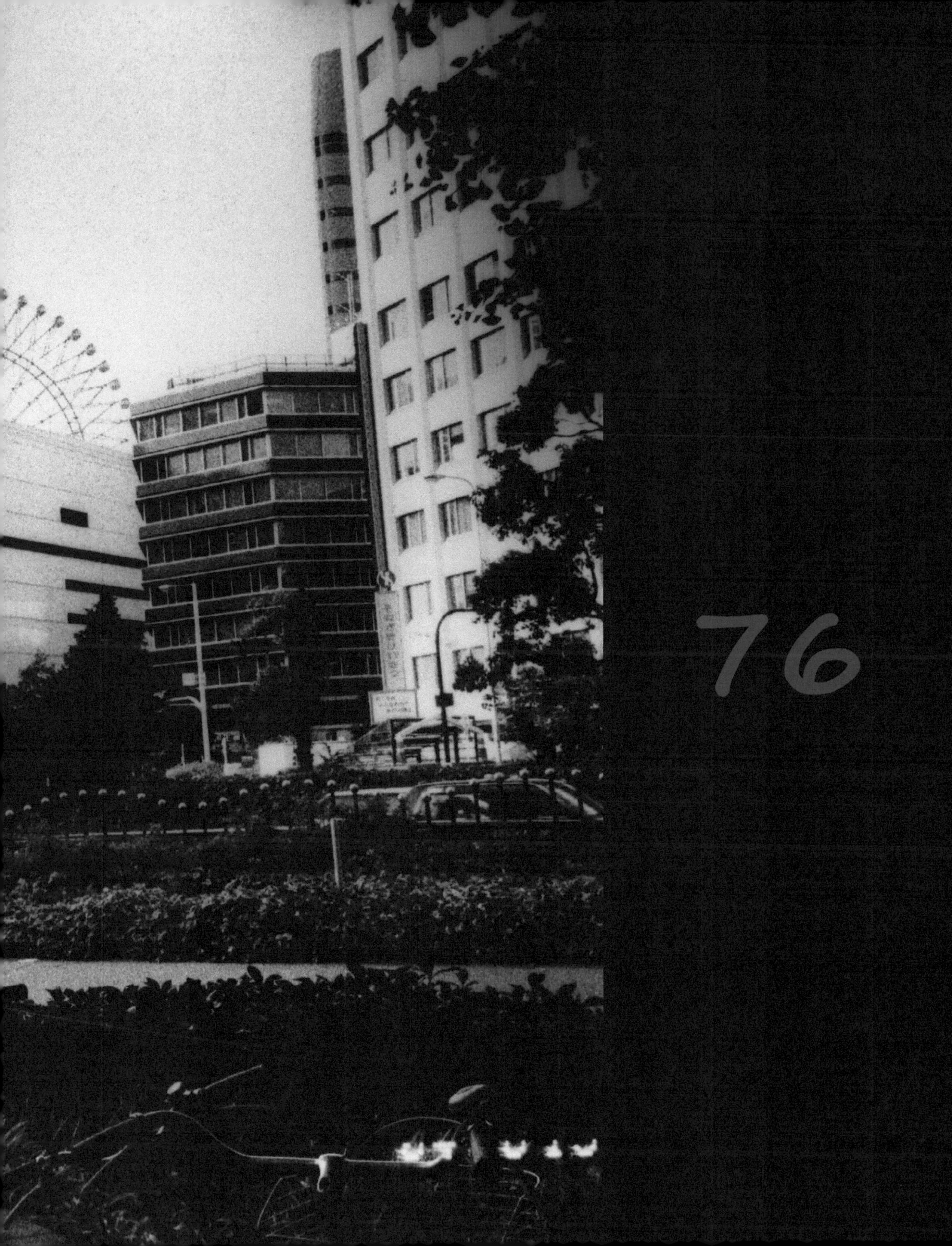

76

77

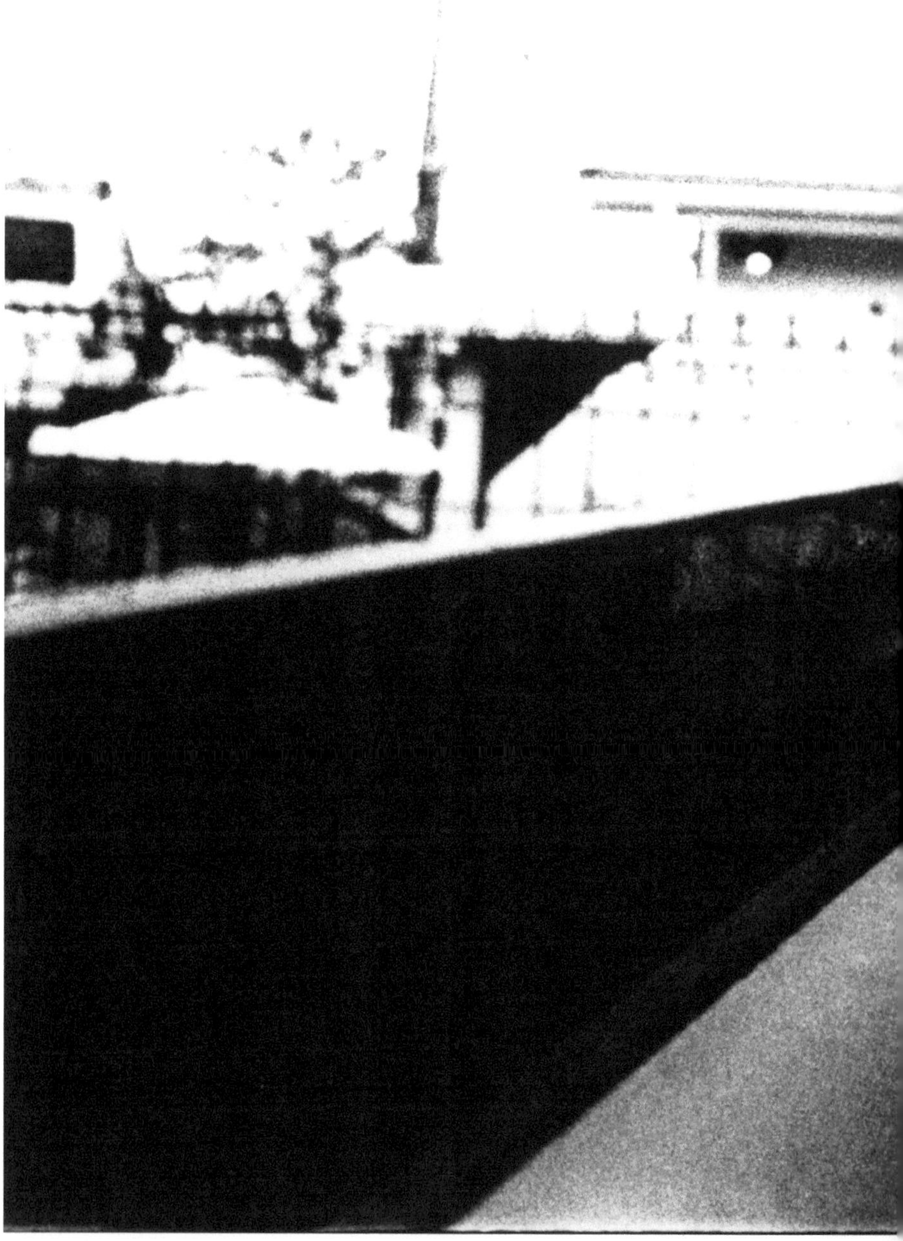

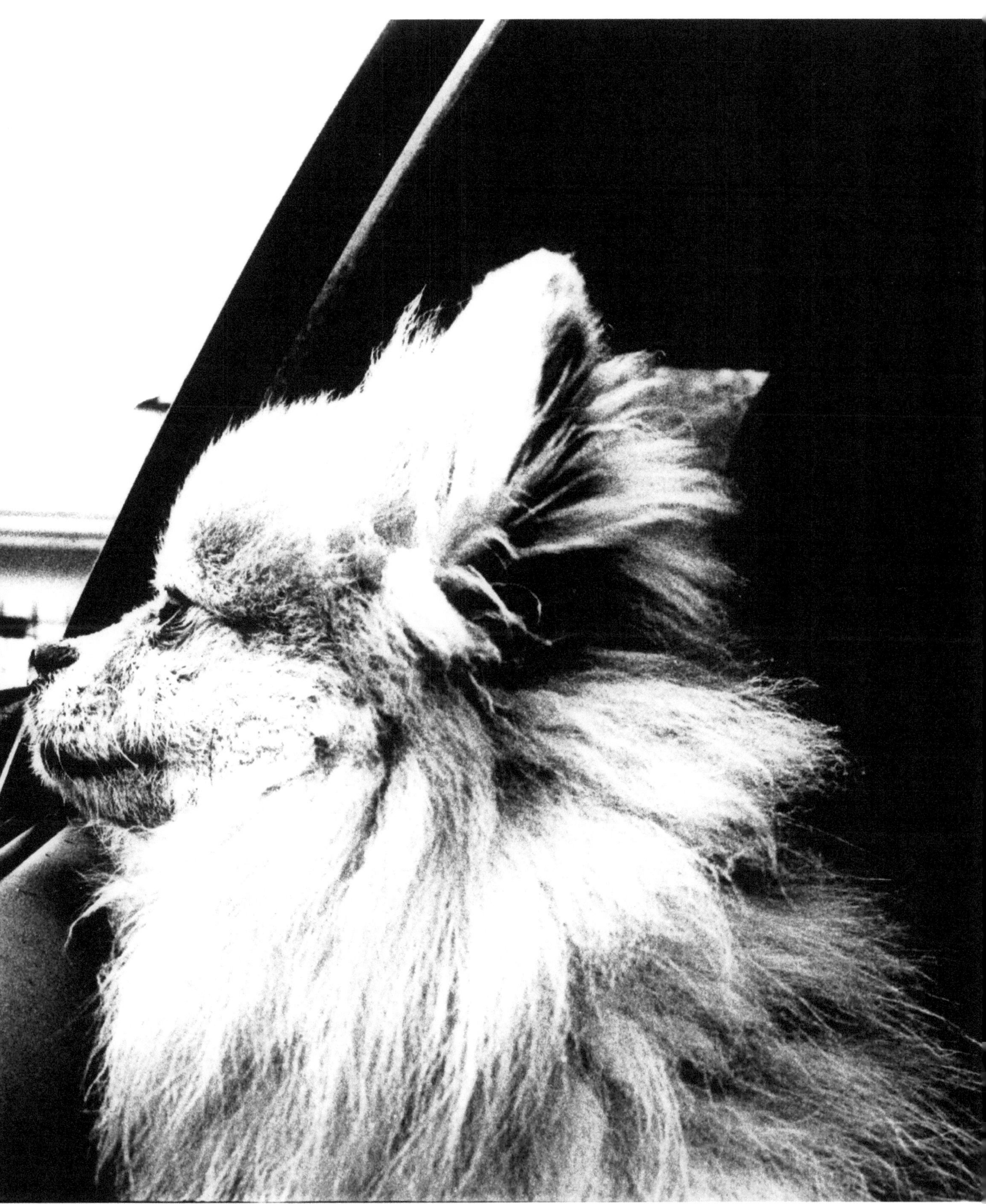

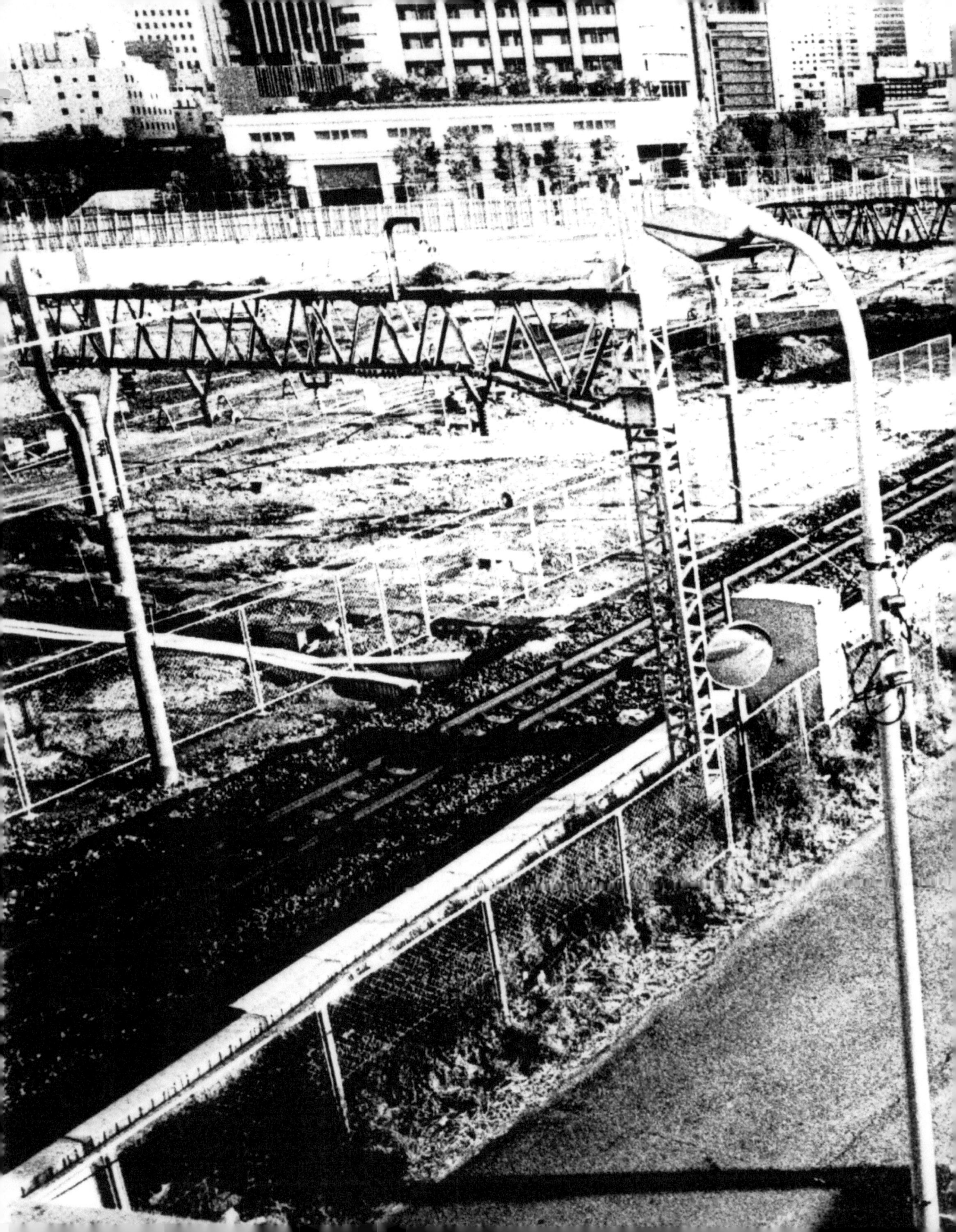

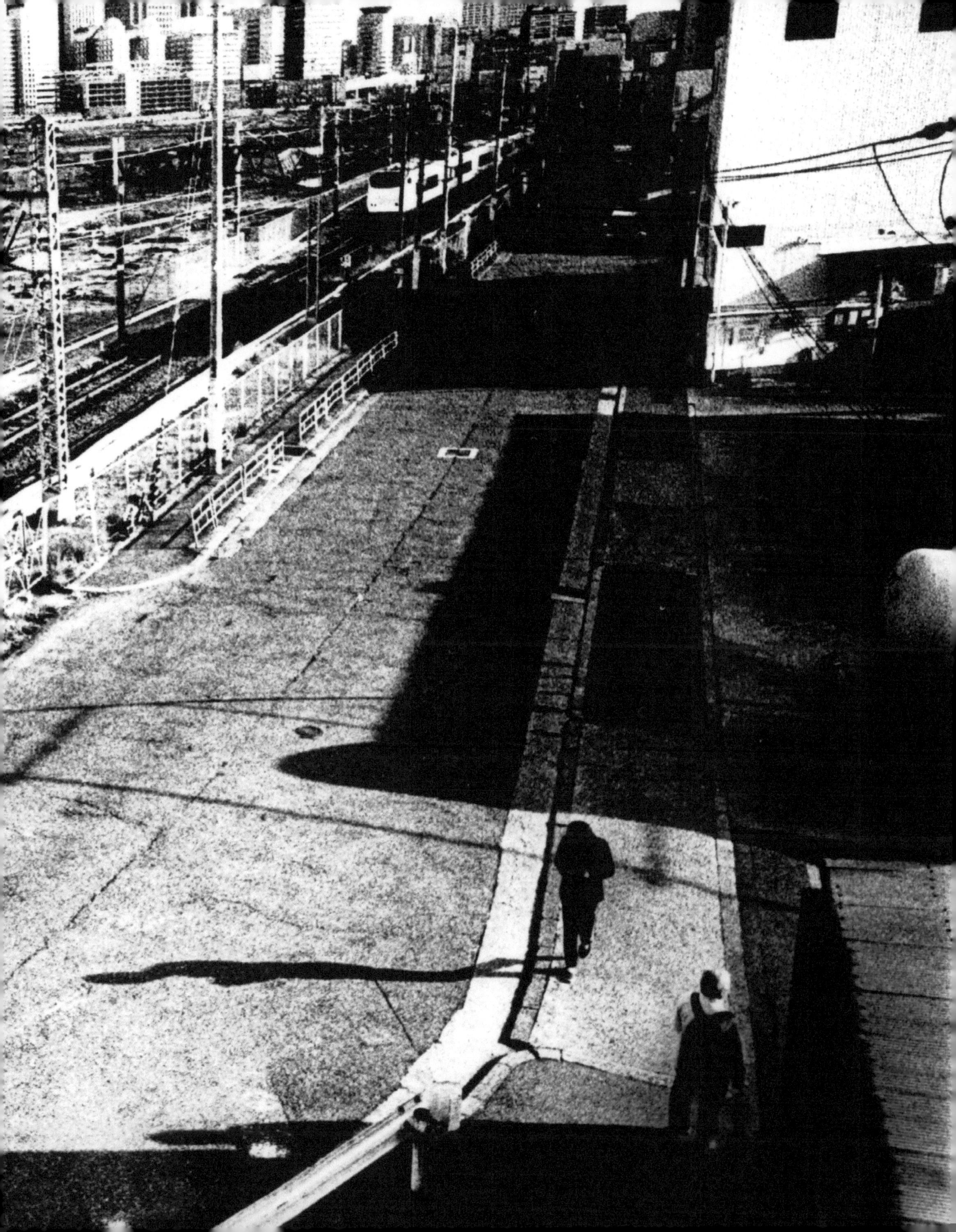

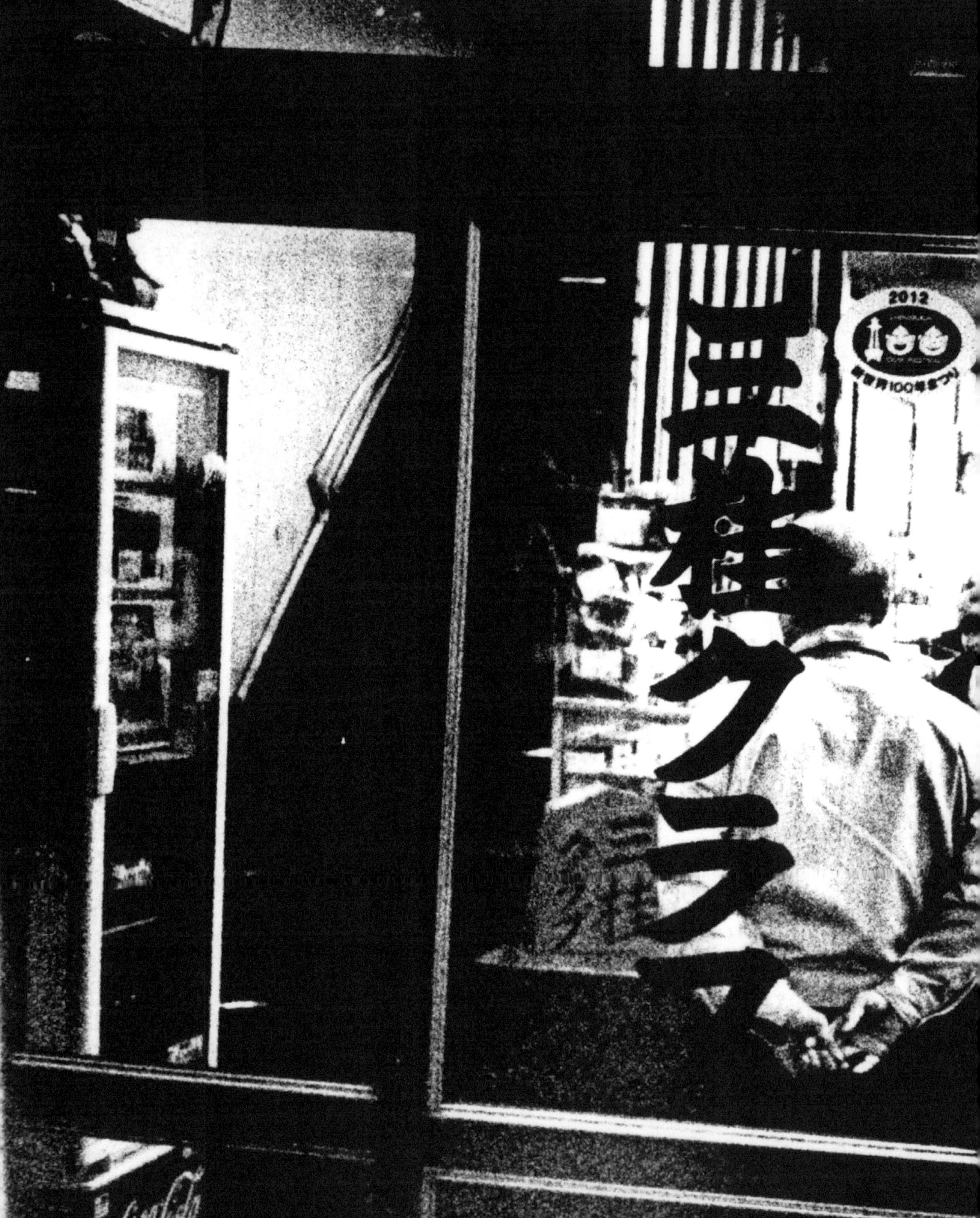

2012

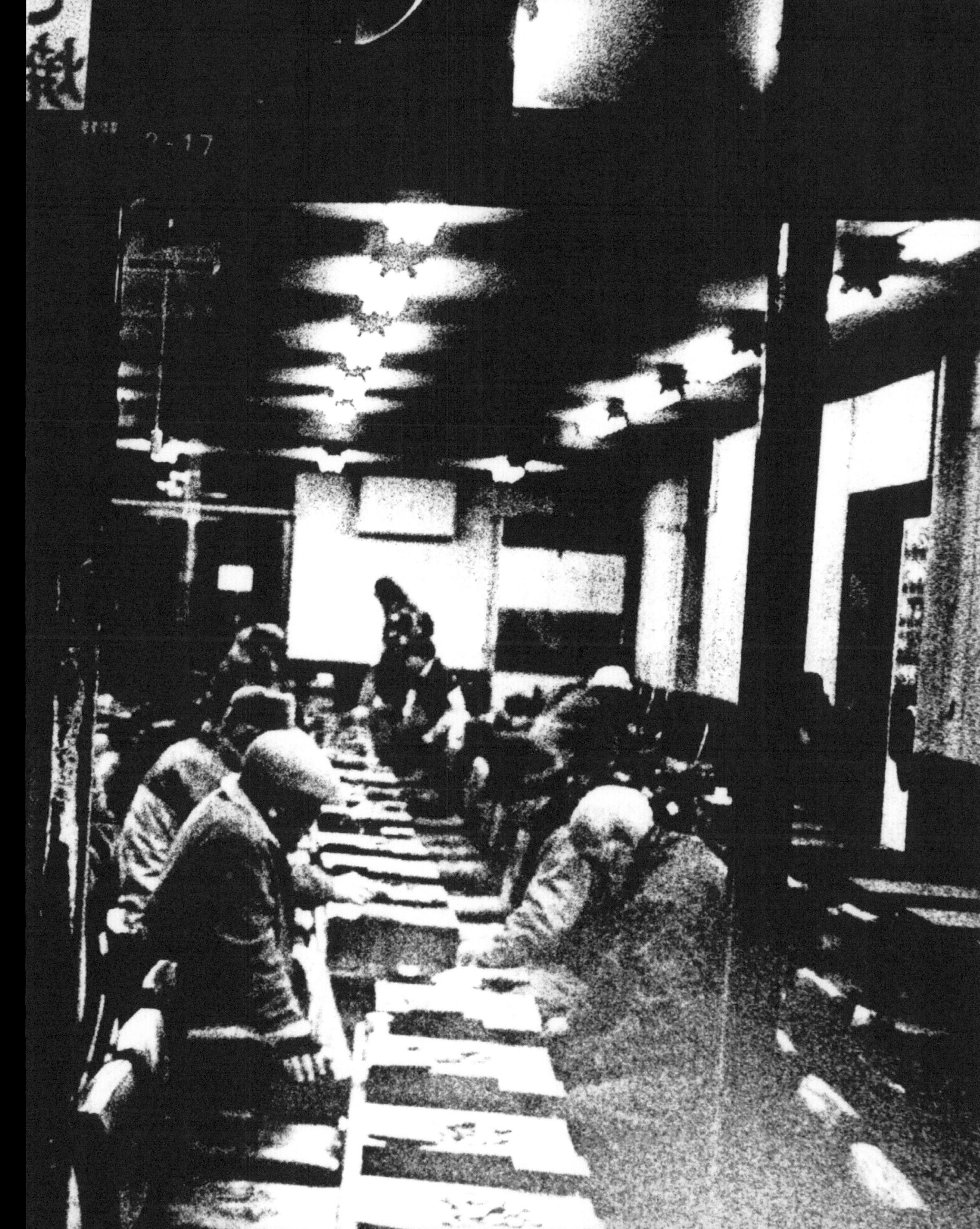

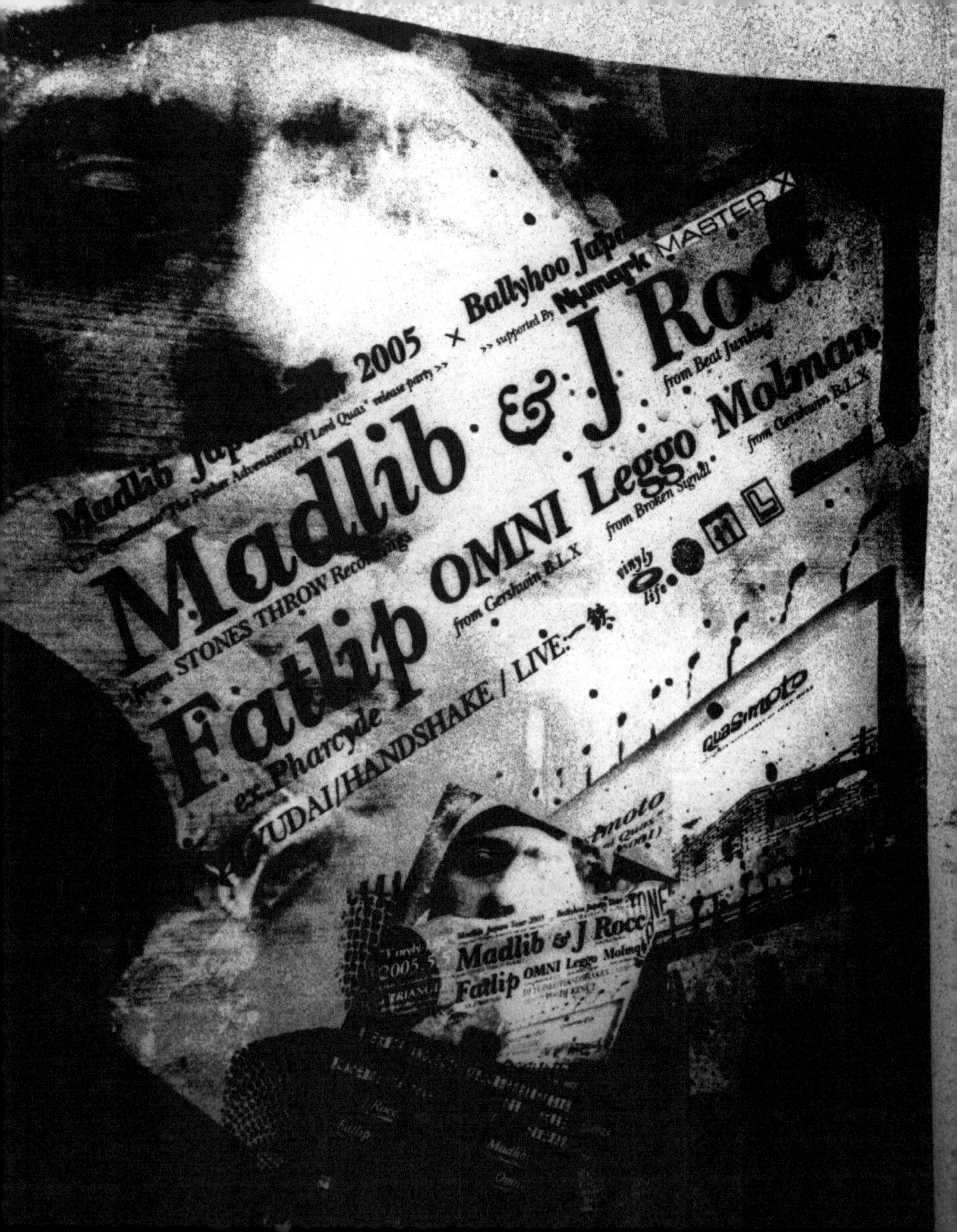

Madlib Japan Tour 2005 × Ballyhoo Japan

>> supported By Numark MASTER X

>> "The Further Adventures Of Lord Quas" release party >>

Madlib & J Rocc

from STONES THROW Recordings

from Beat Junkies

Fatlip OMNI Leggo · Molman

ex. Pharcyde

from Gershwin B.L.X

from Broken Signal

from Gershwin B.L.X

vinyl life

FUDAI/HANDSHAKE / LIVE:一鉄

Quasimoto

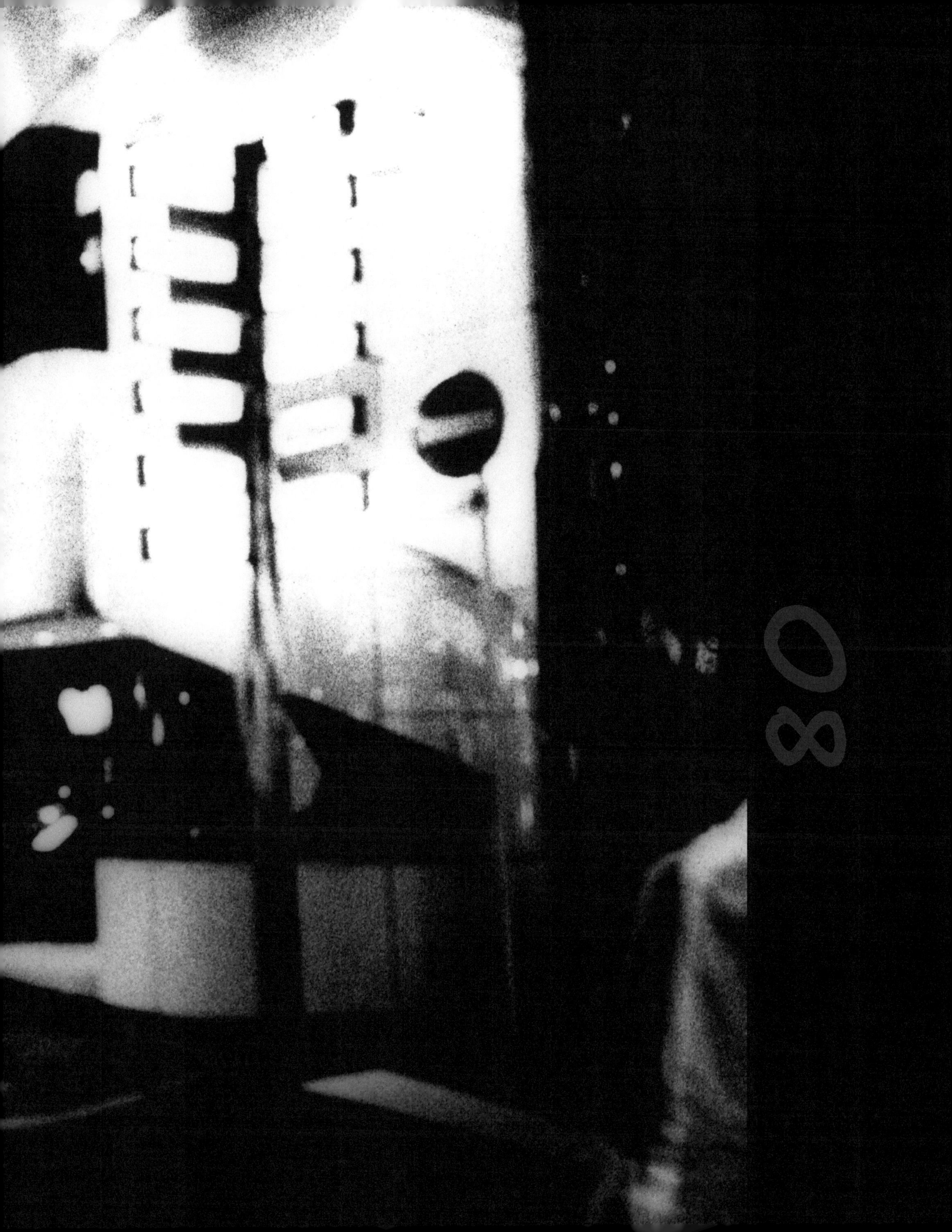
80

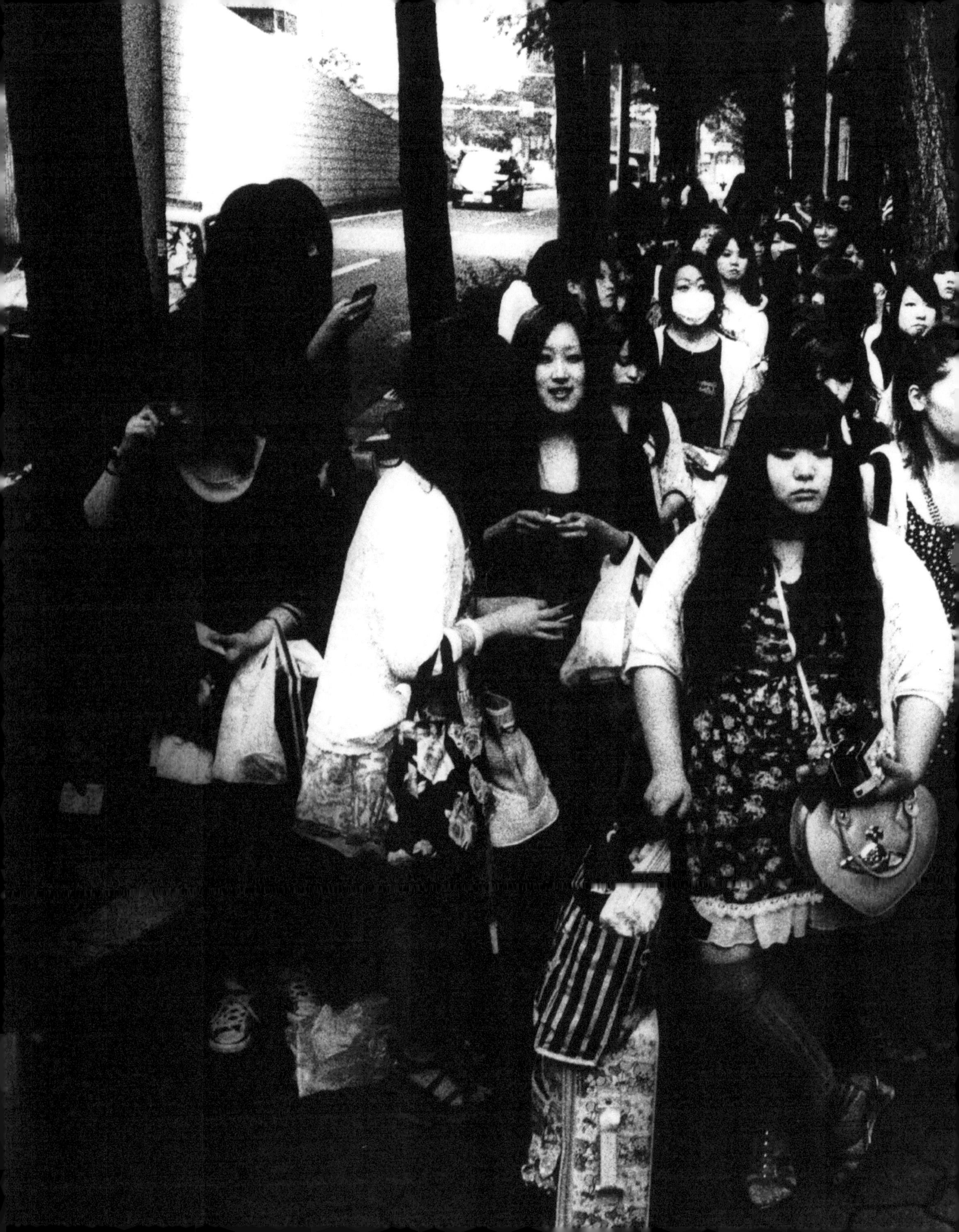

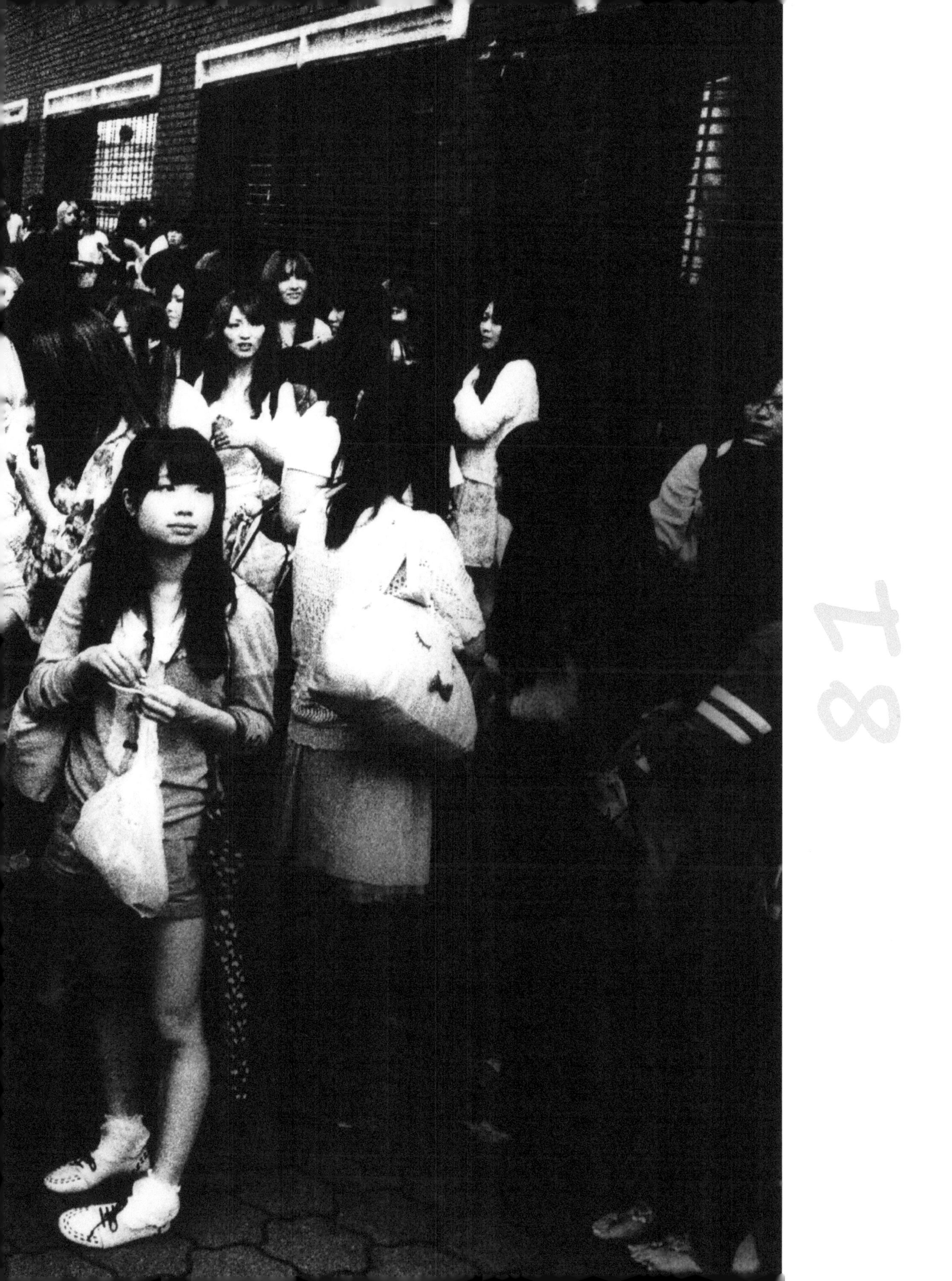

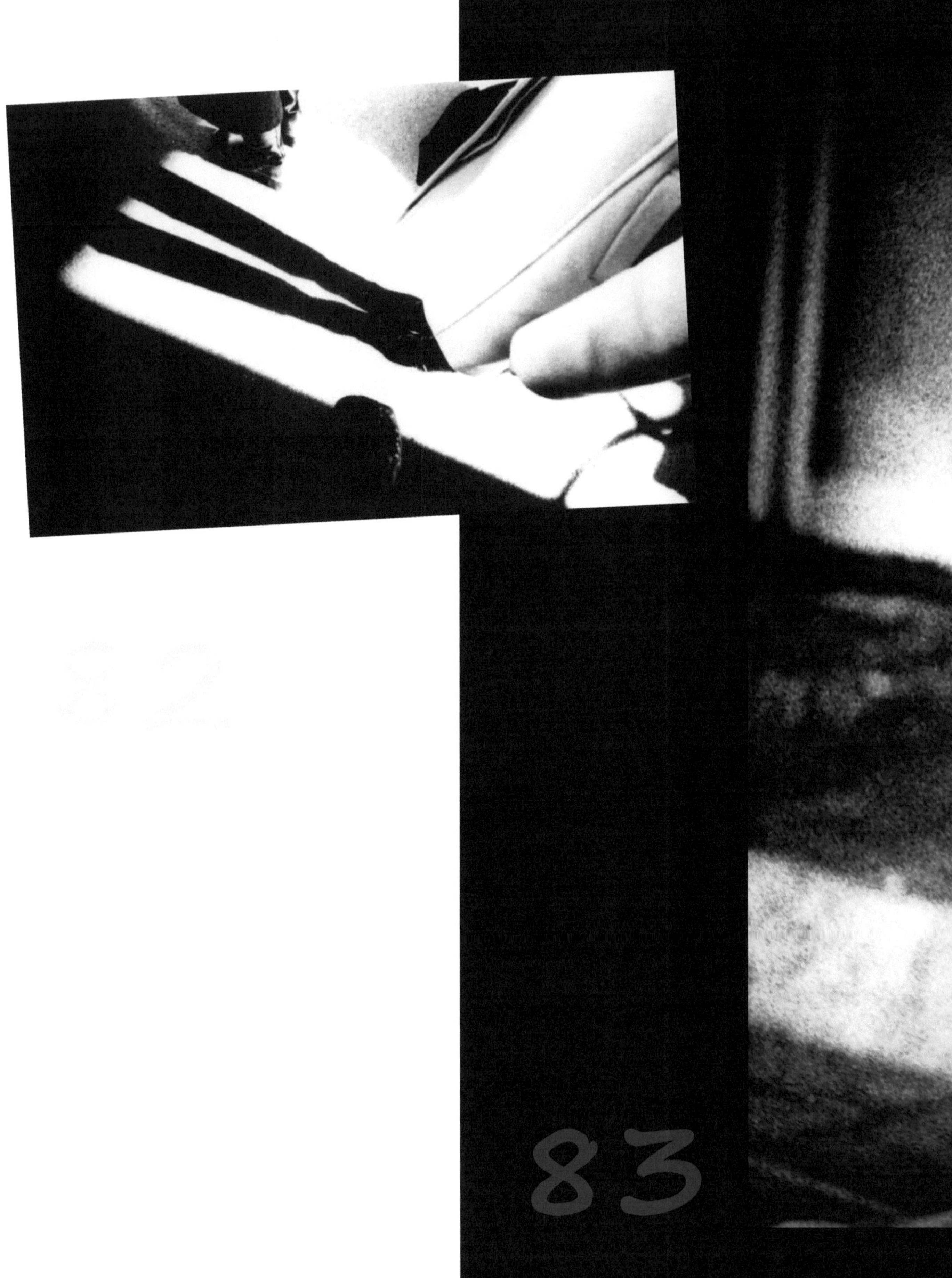

83

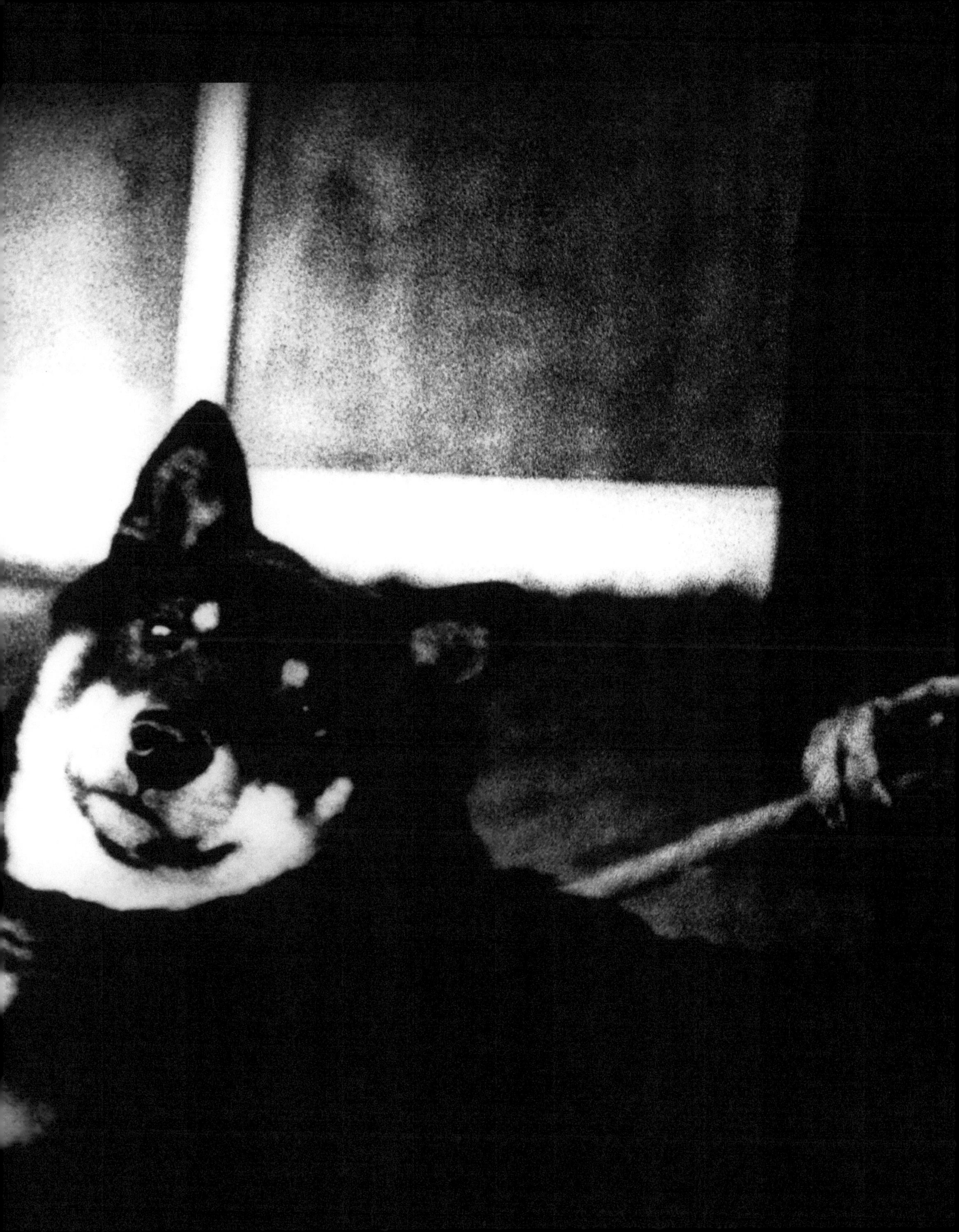

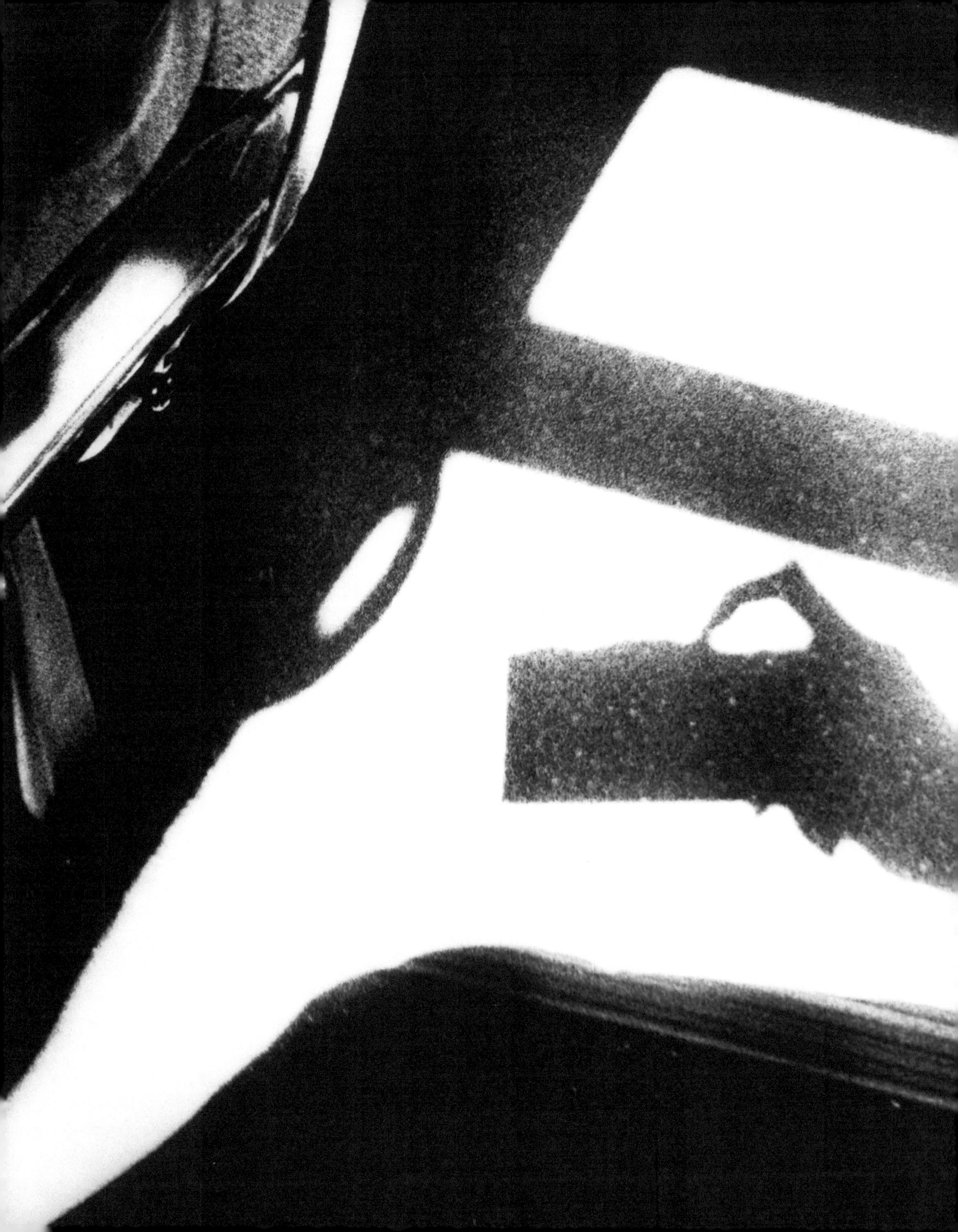

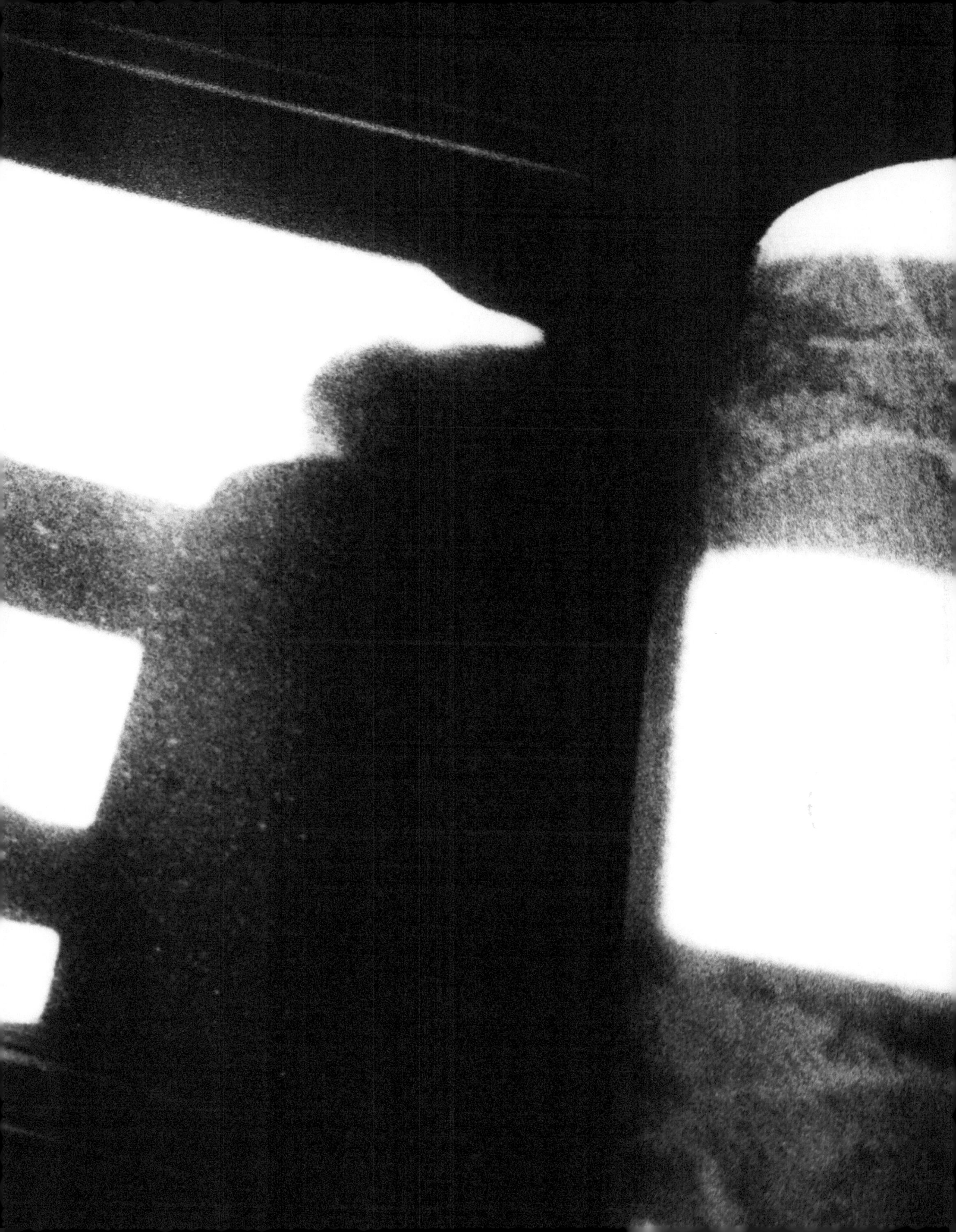

85-86

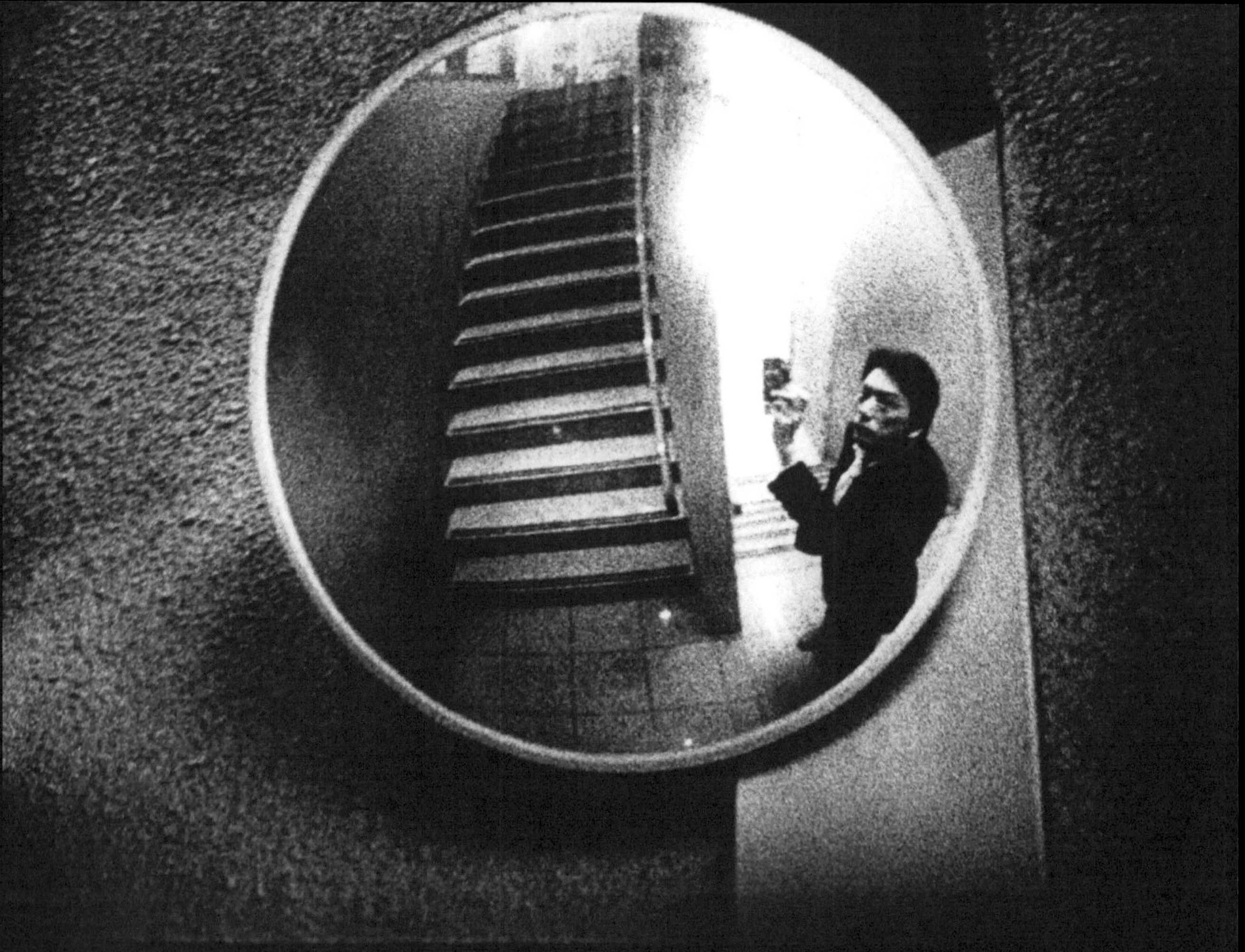

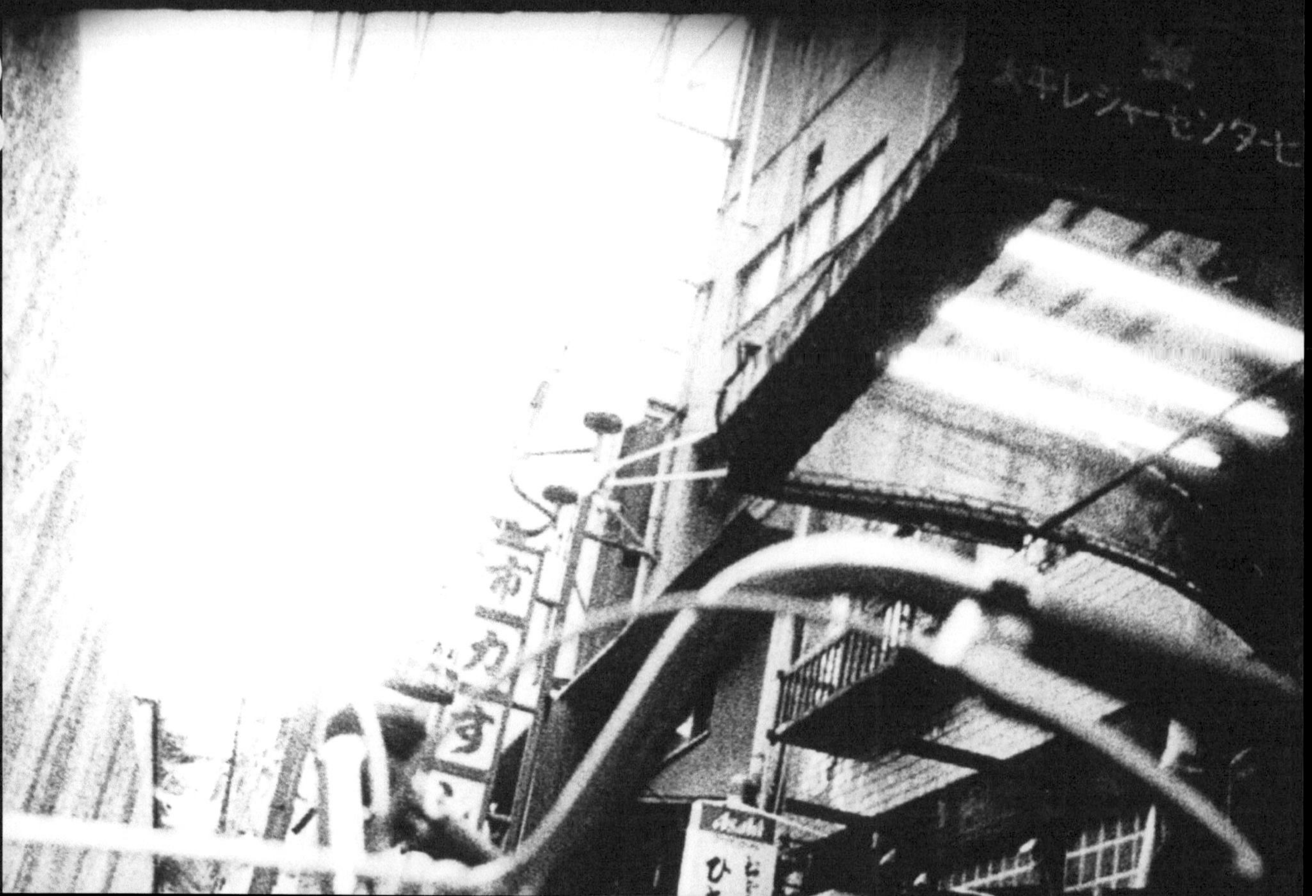

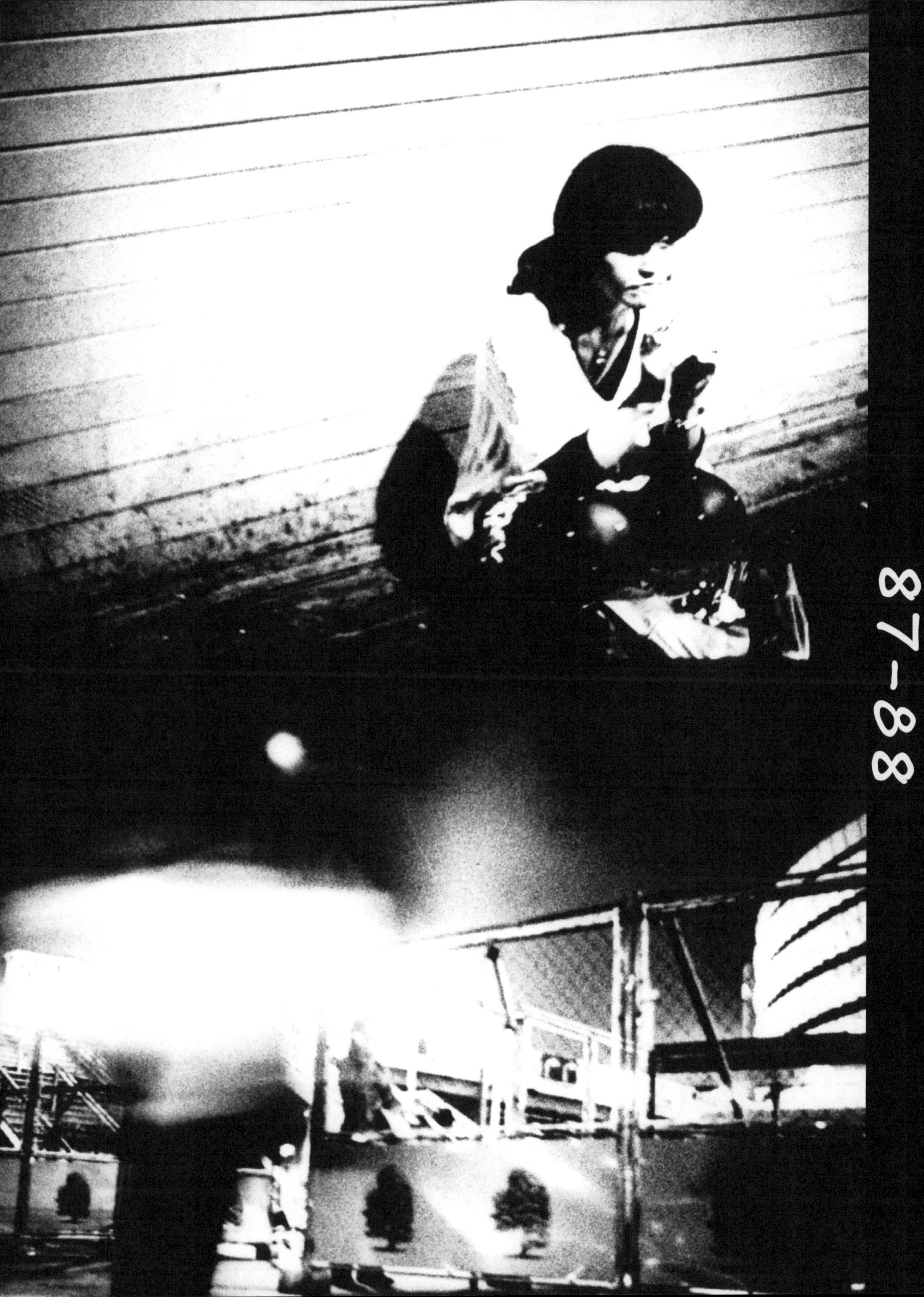

87-88

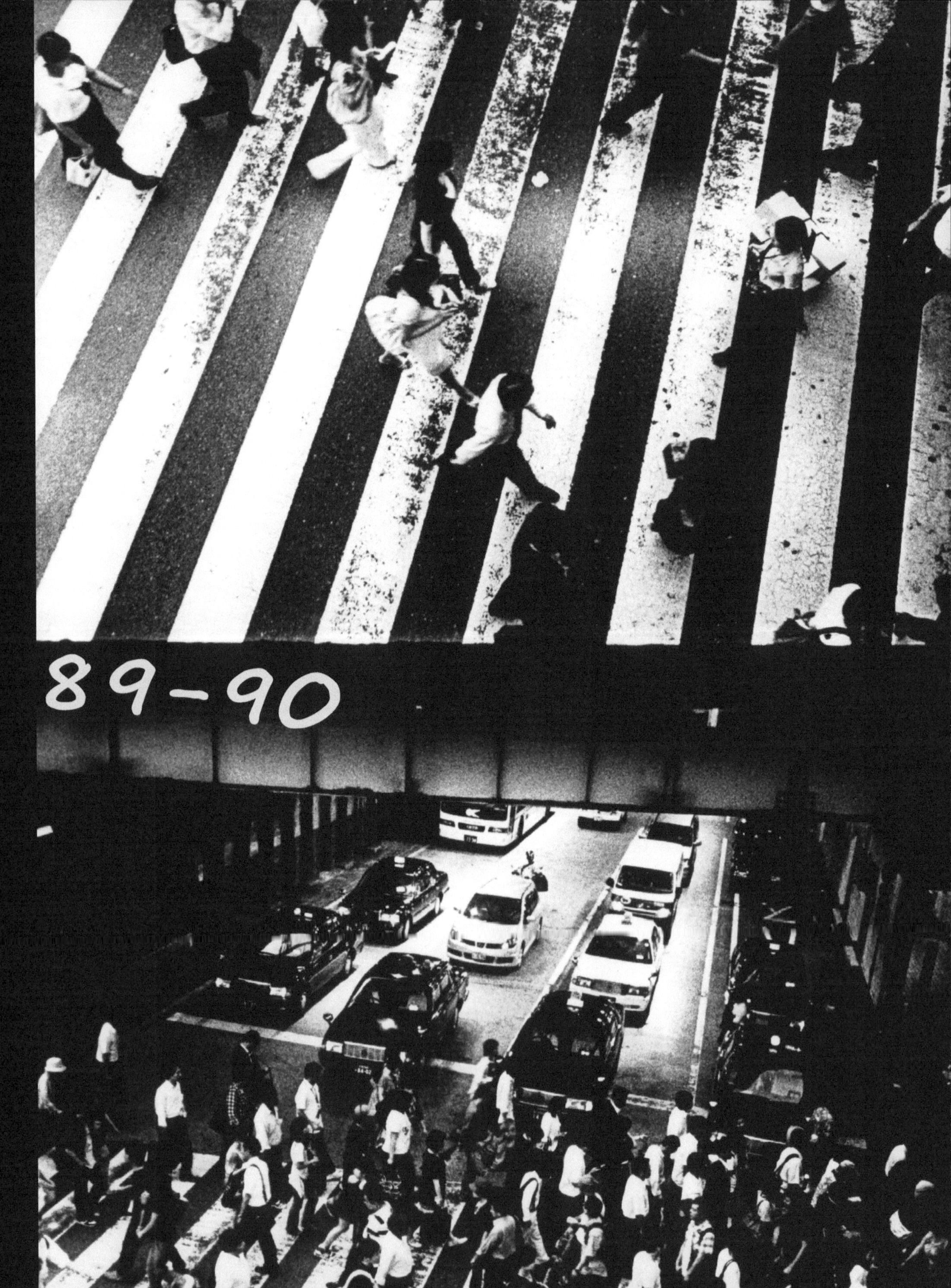

89-90

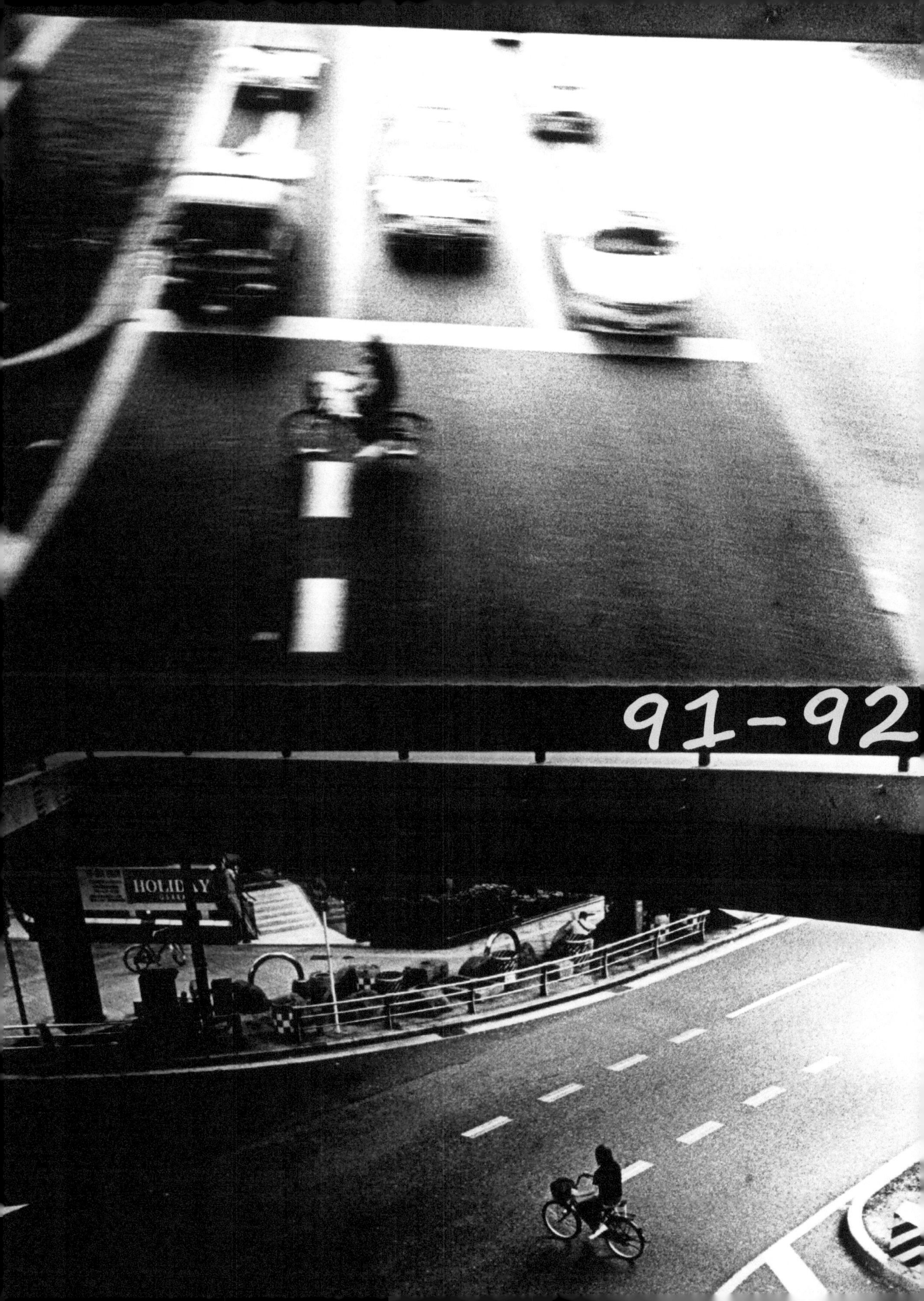

91-92
HOLIDAY

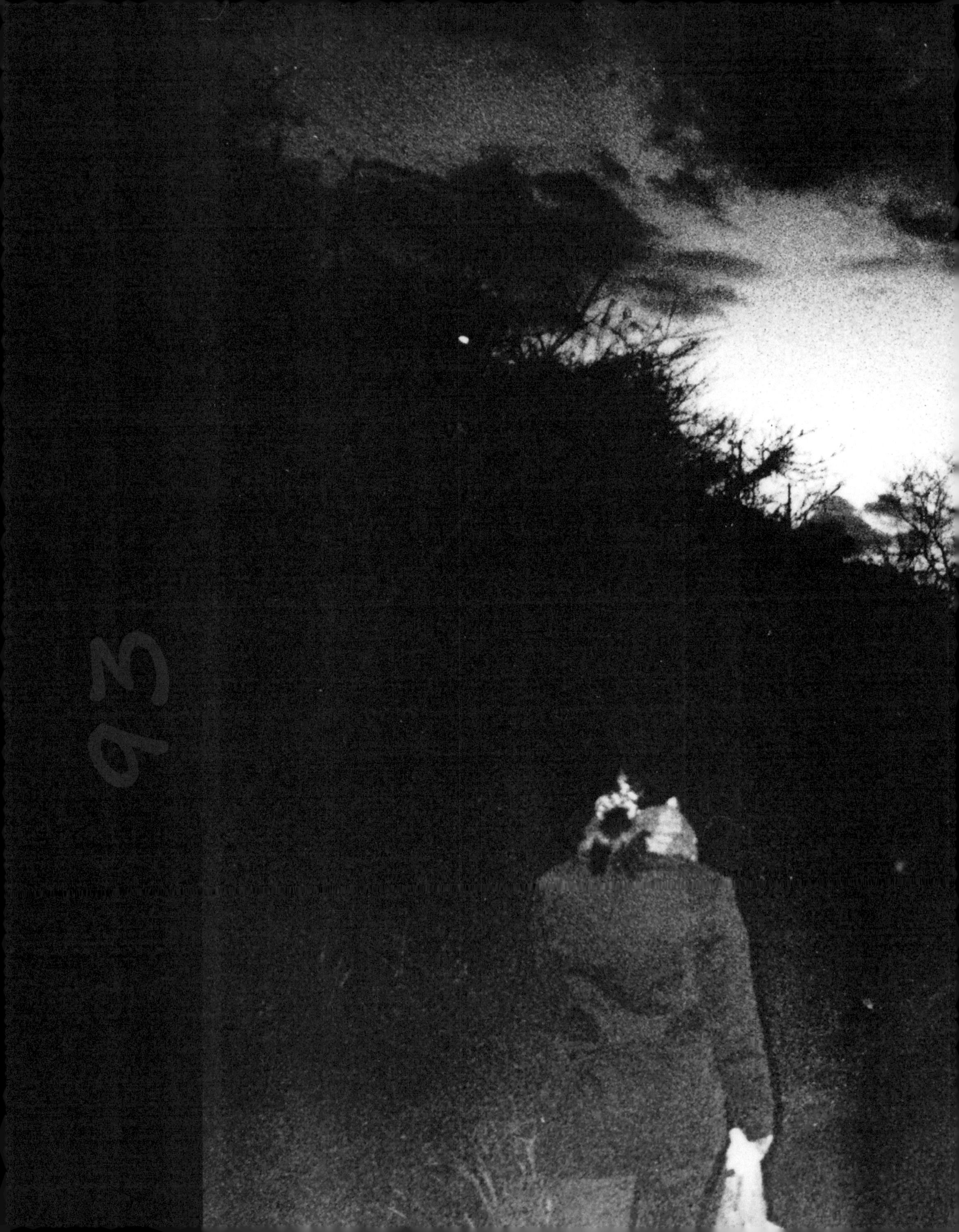

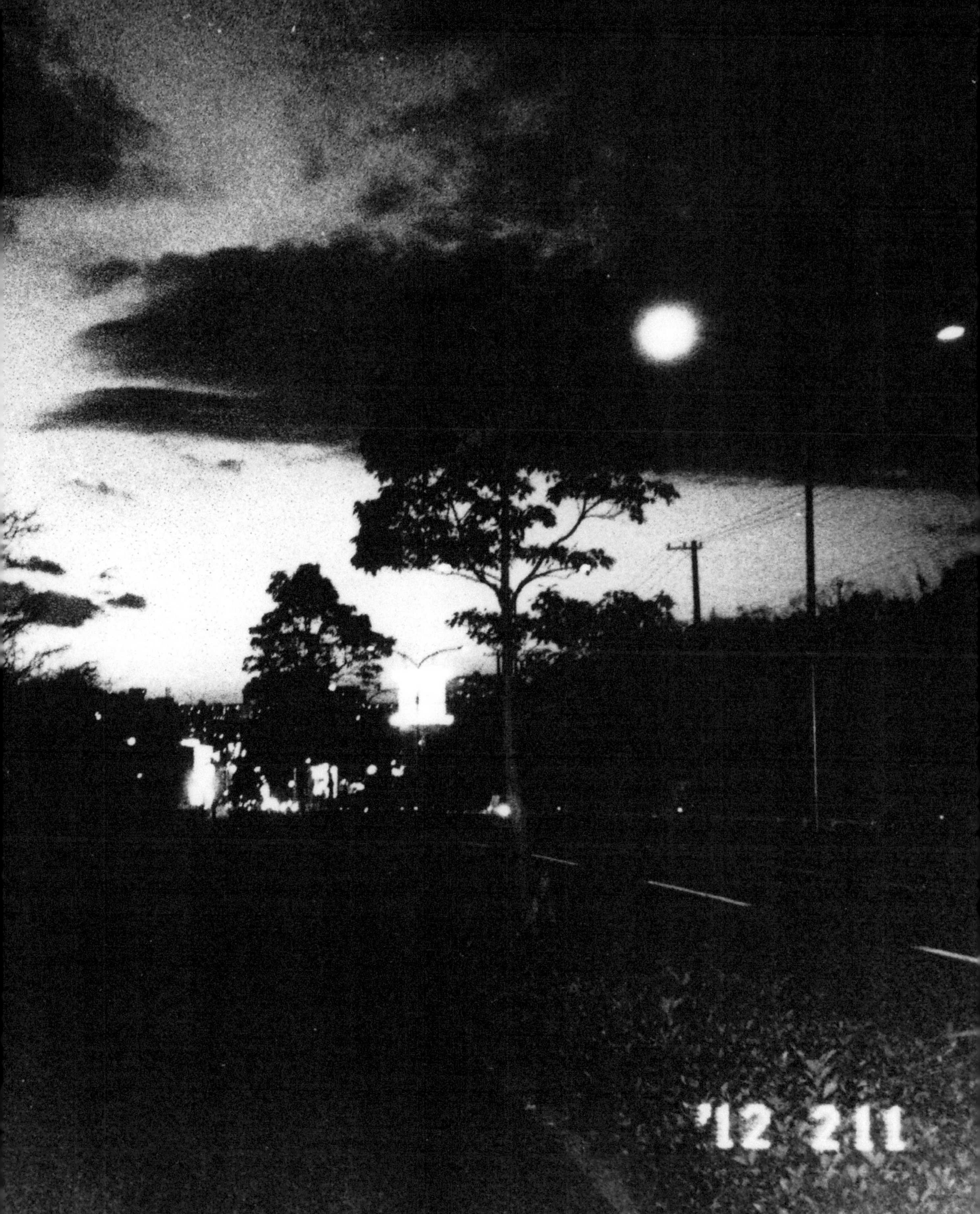
'12 211

94

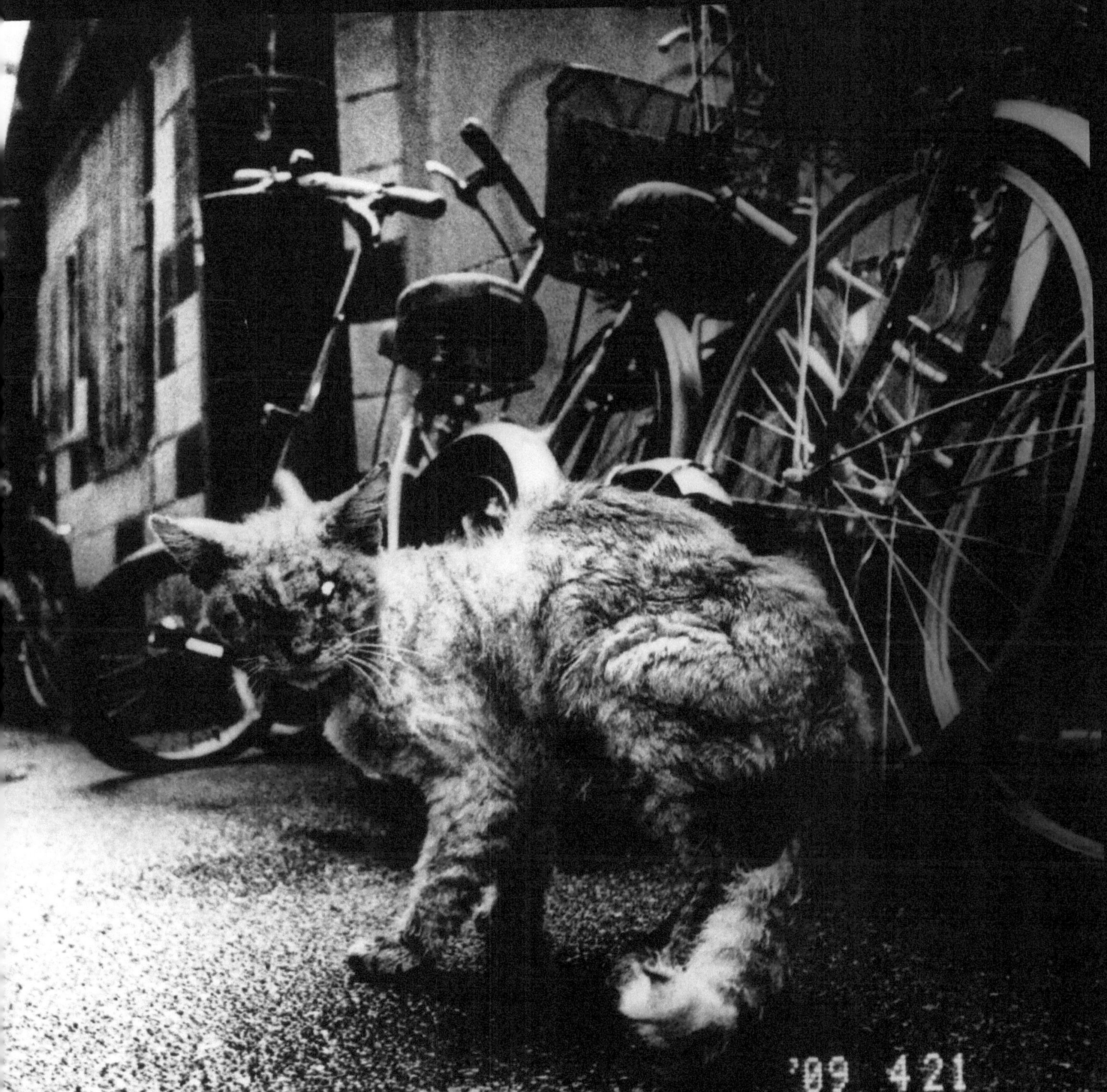
'09 4 21

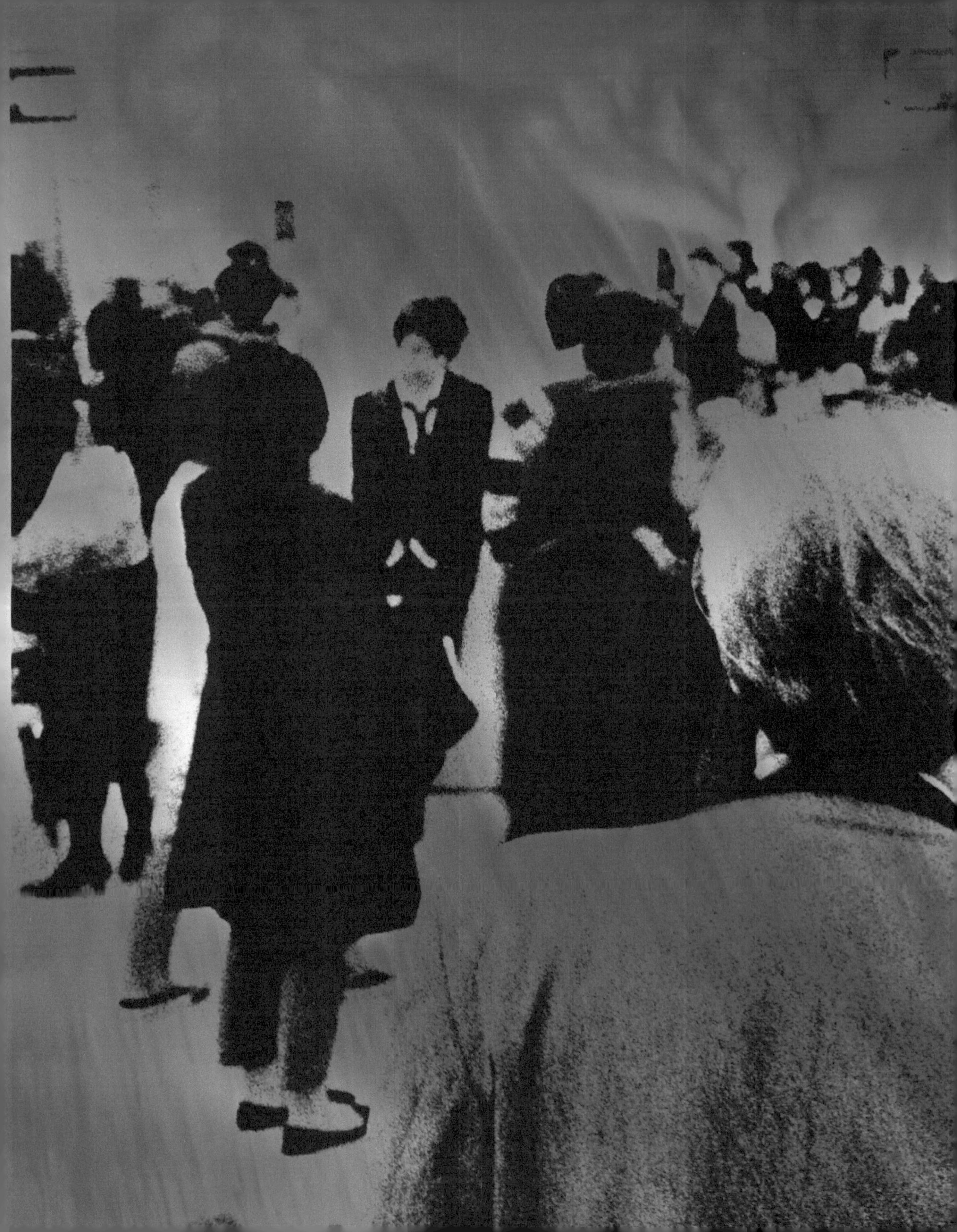

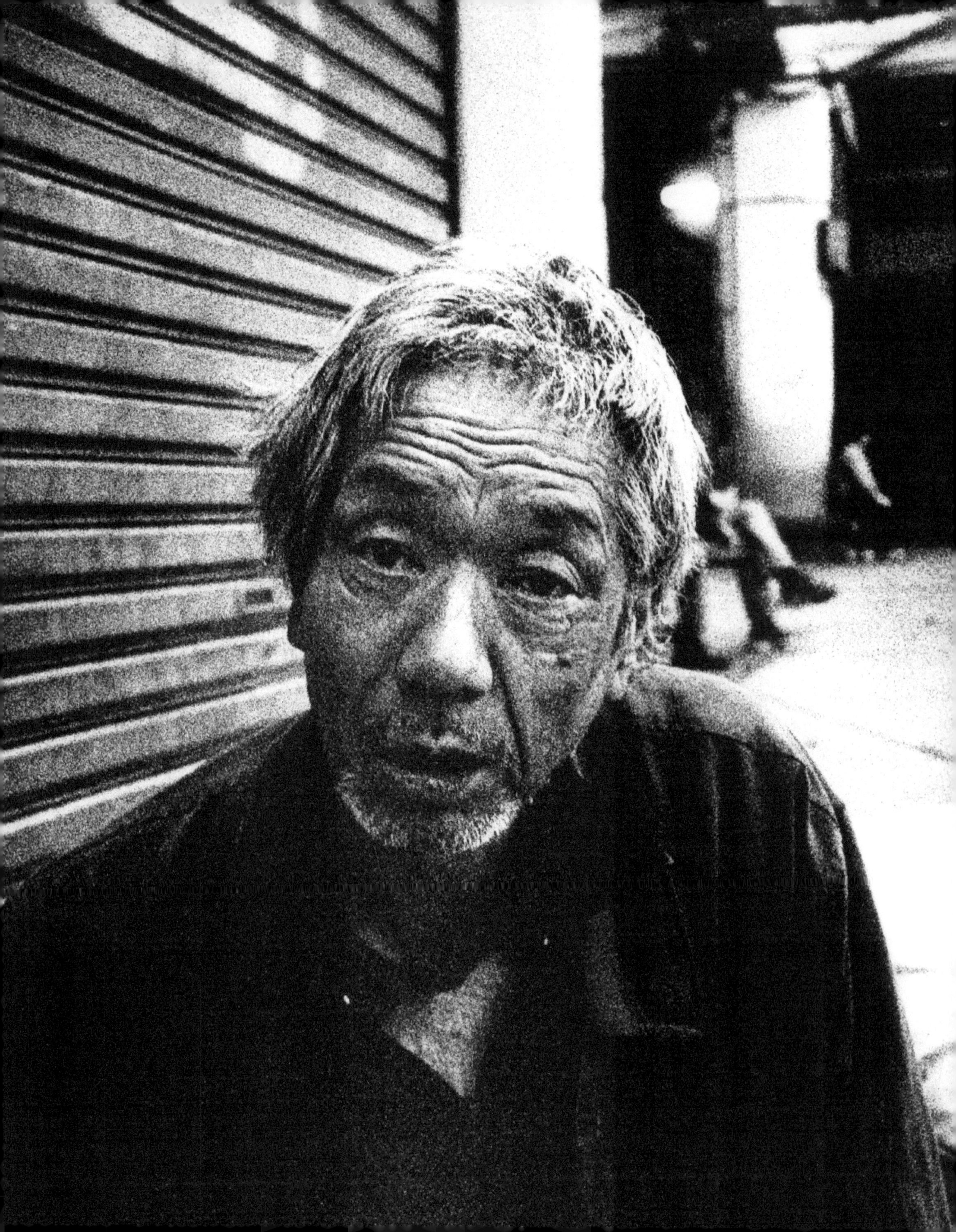

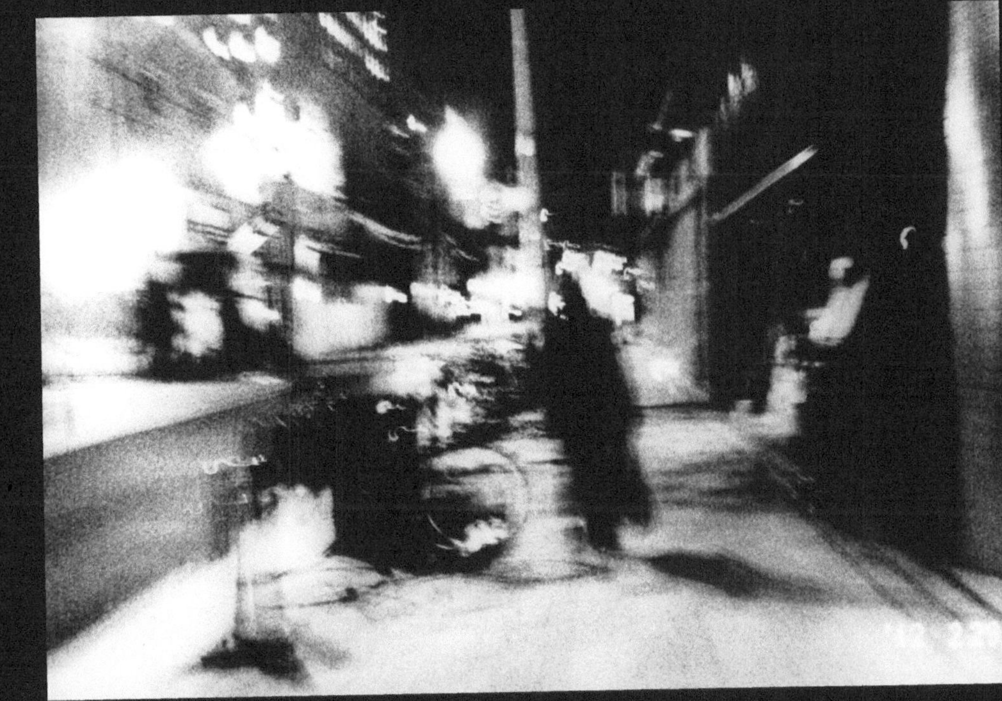

96

97

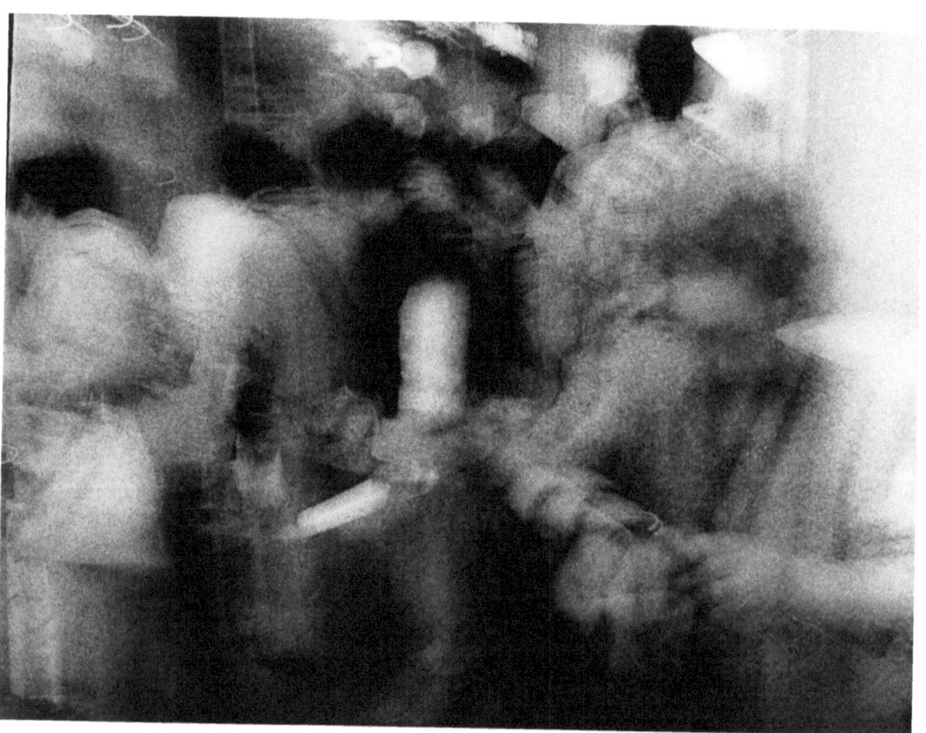

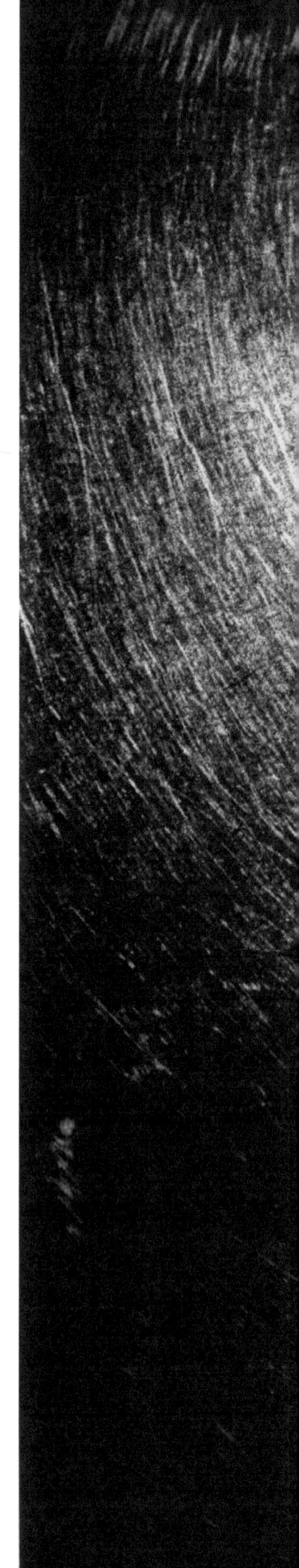

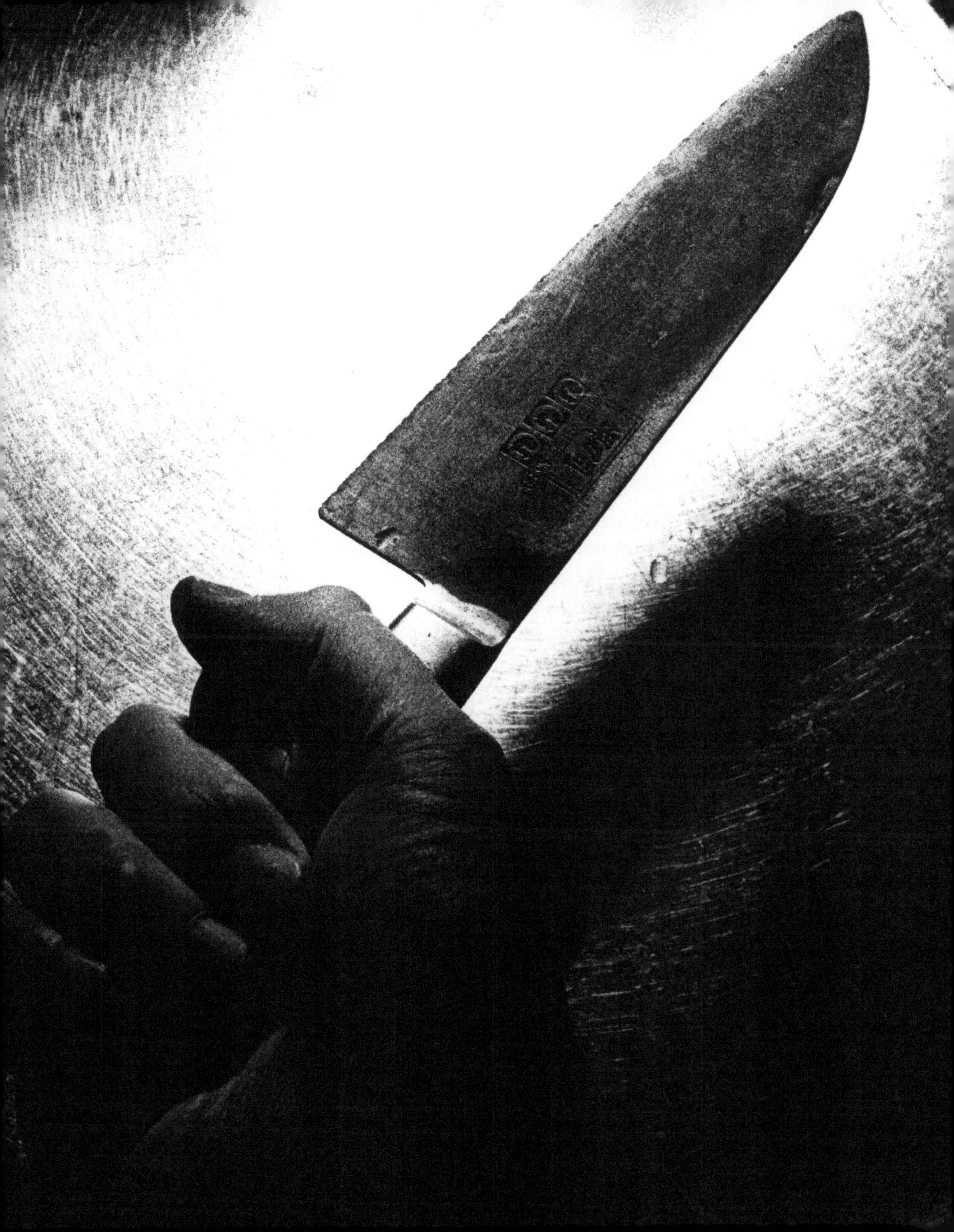

100

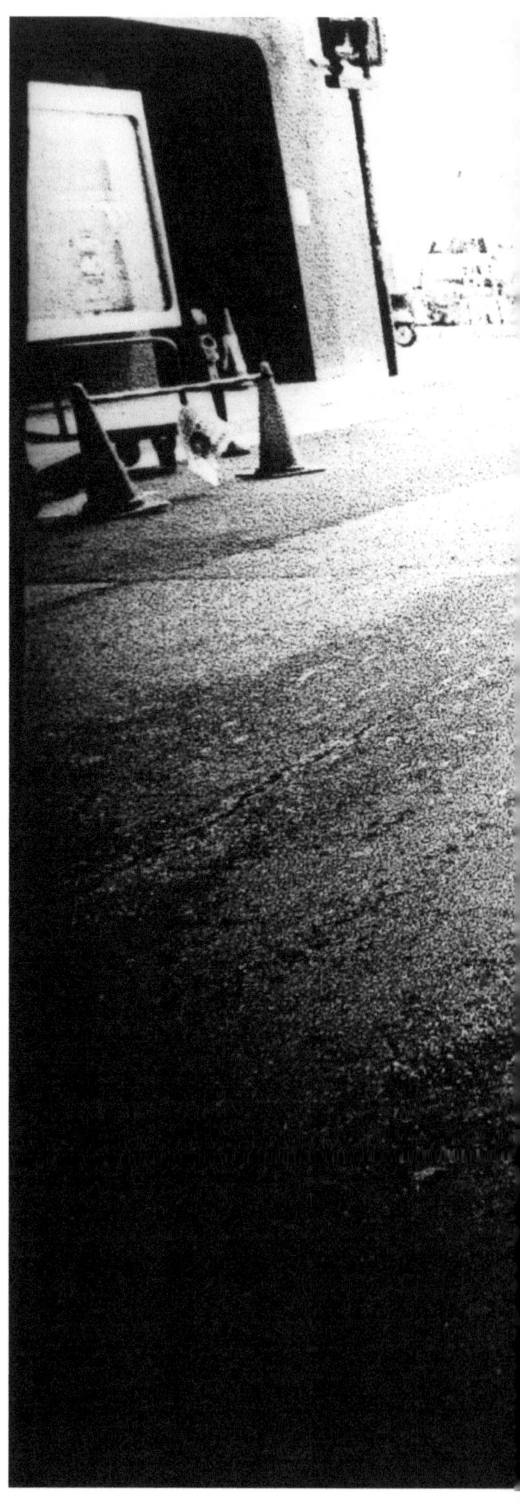

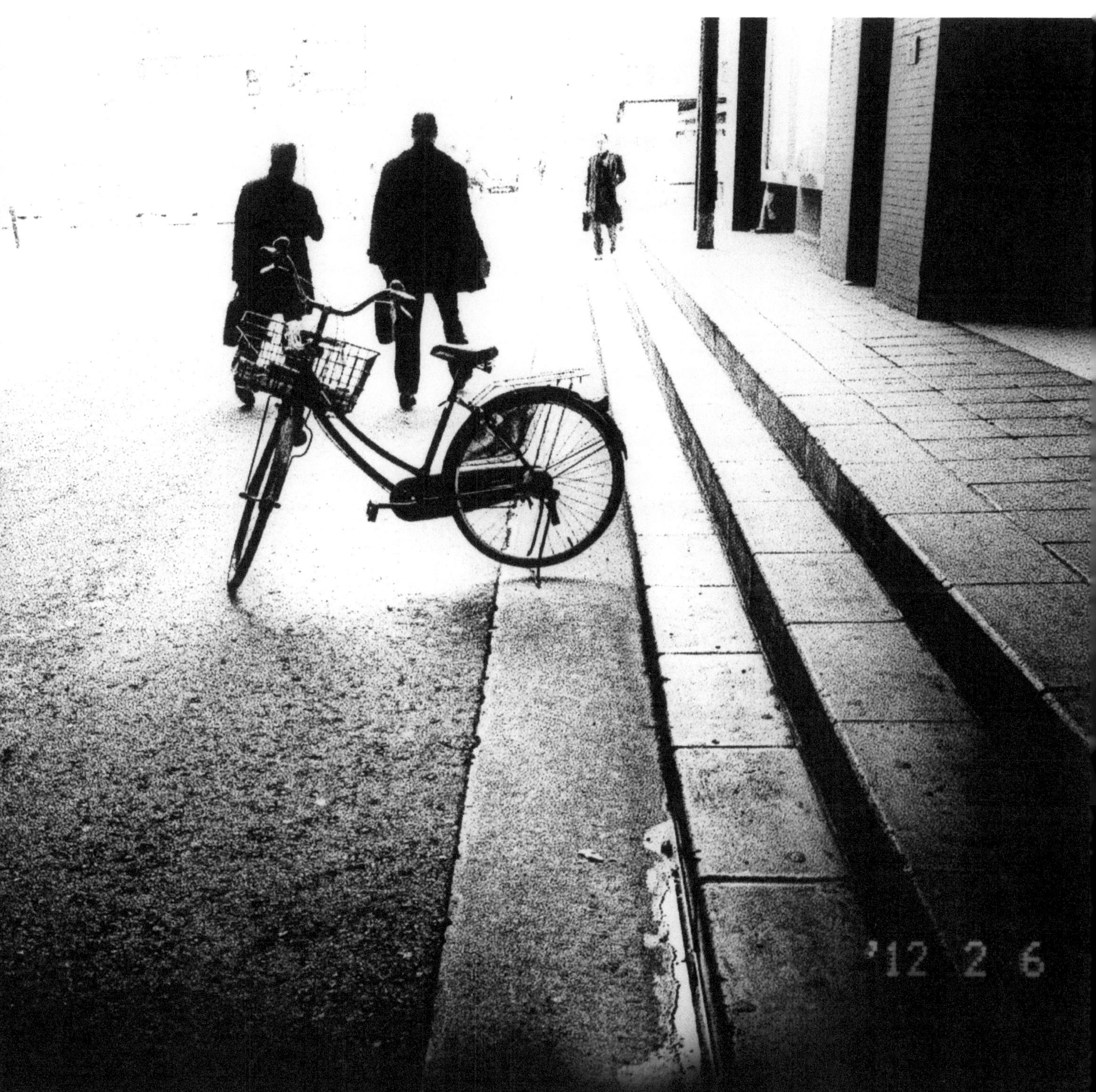
'12 2 6

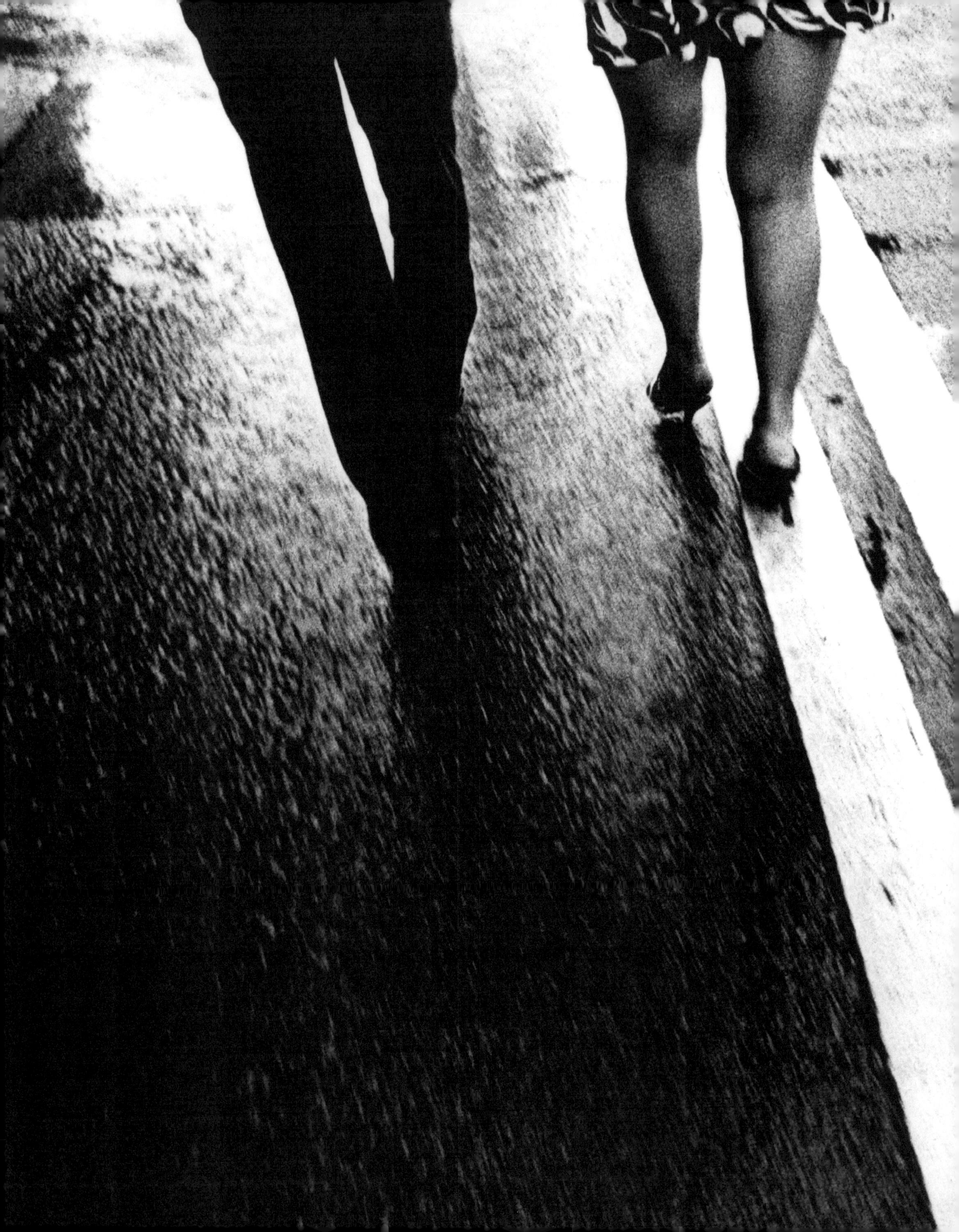

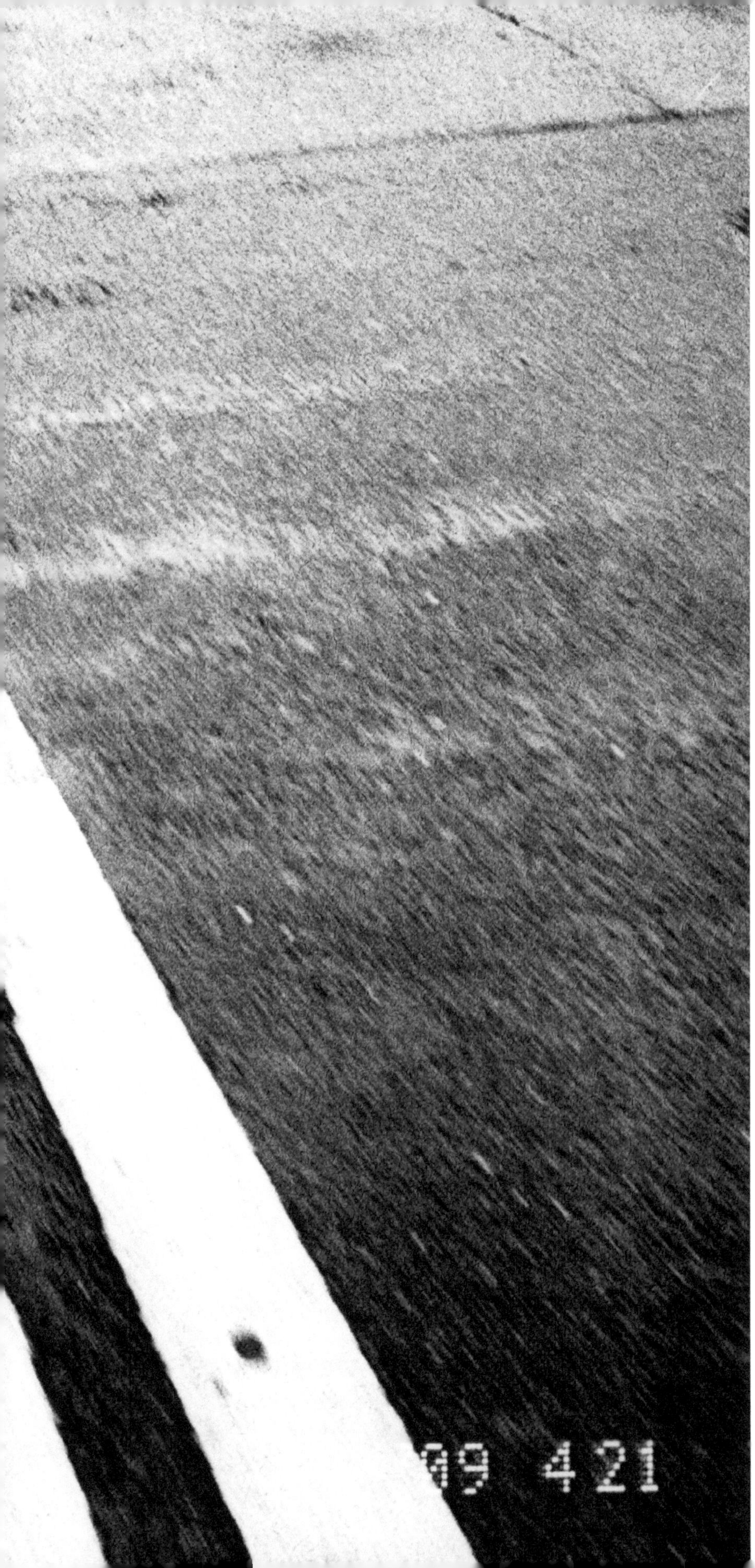

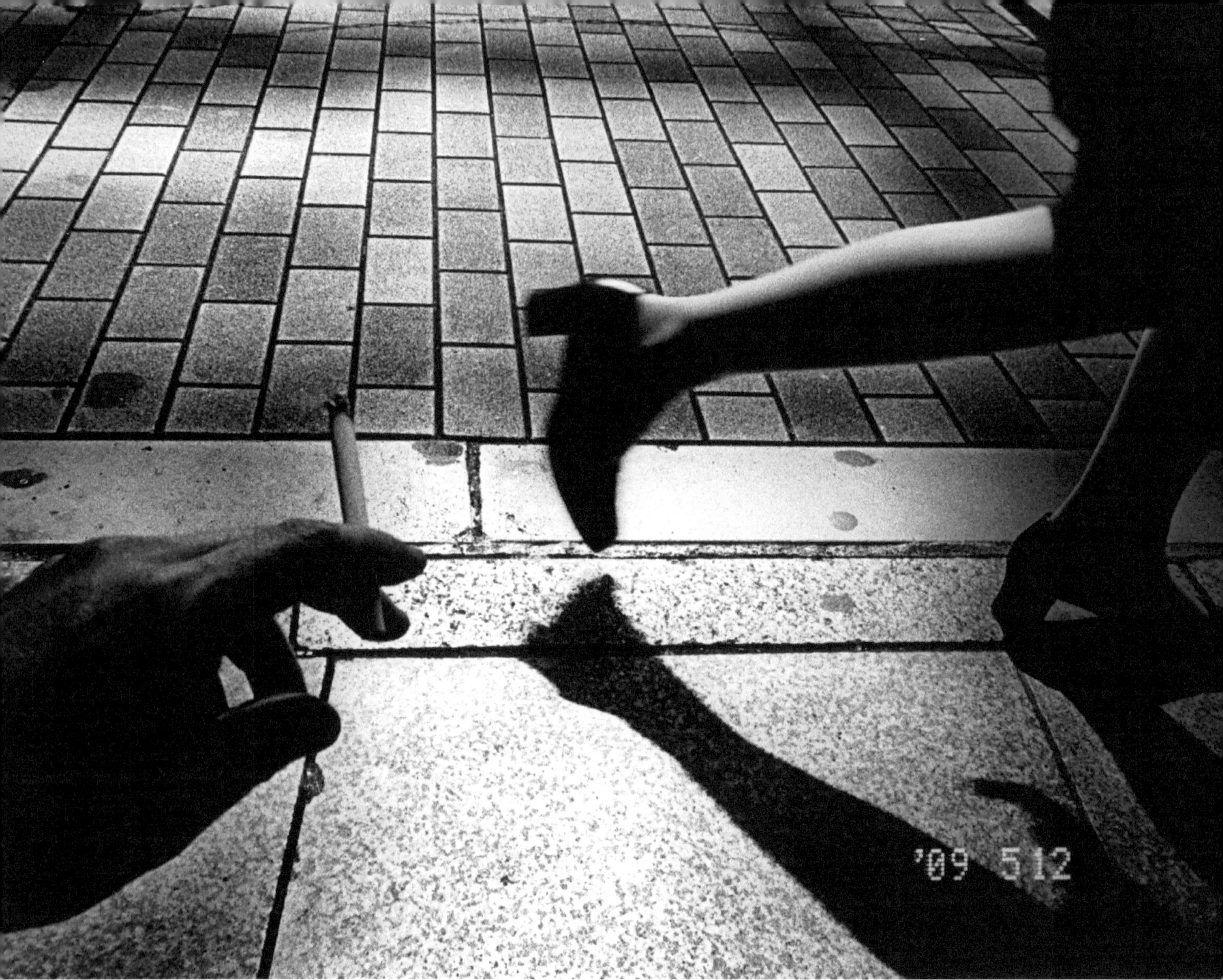

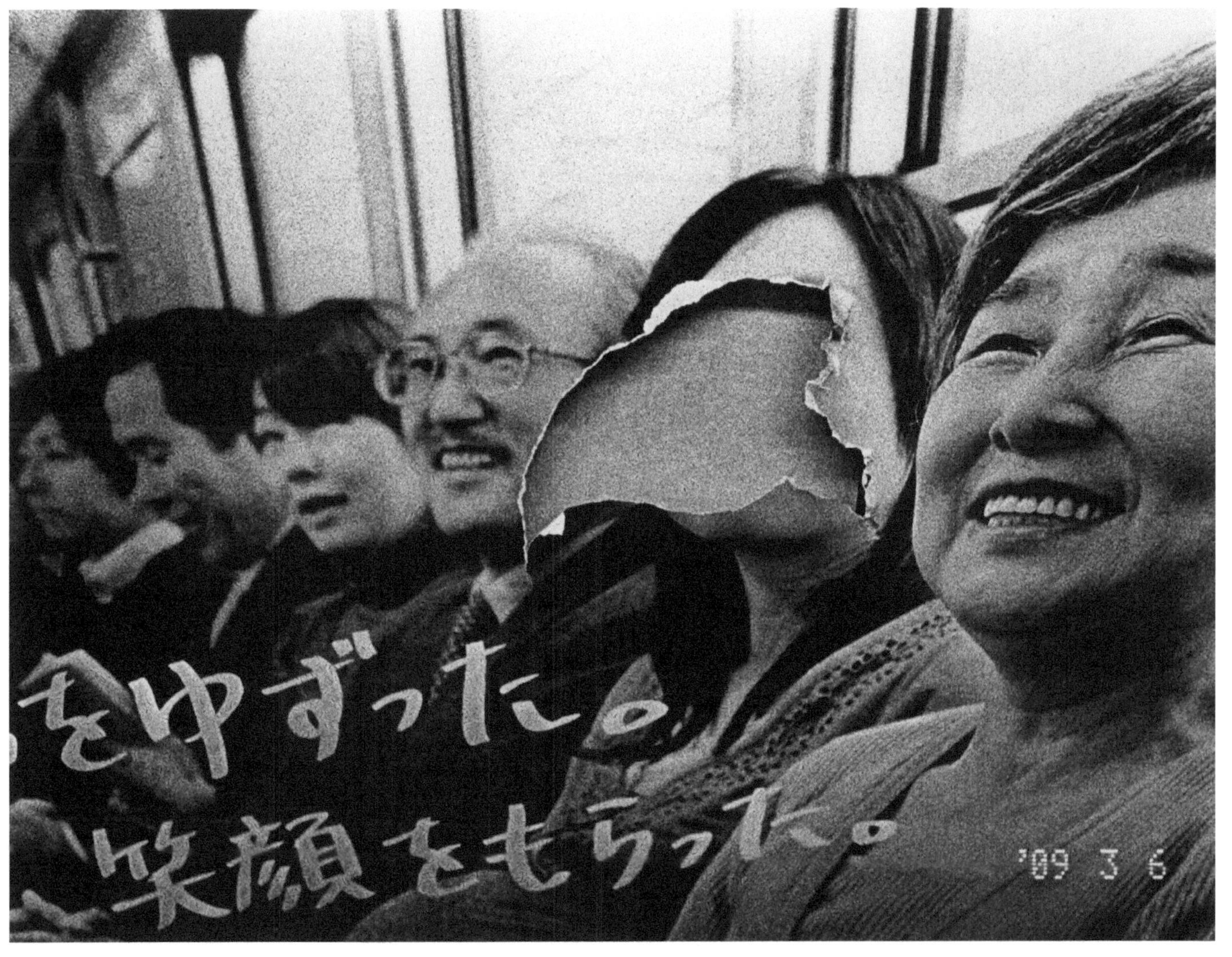
をゆずった。
笑顔をもらった。
'09 3 6

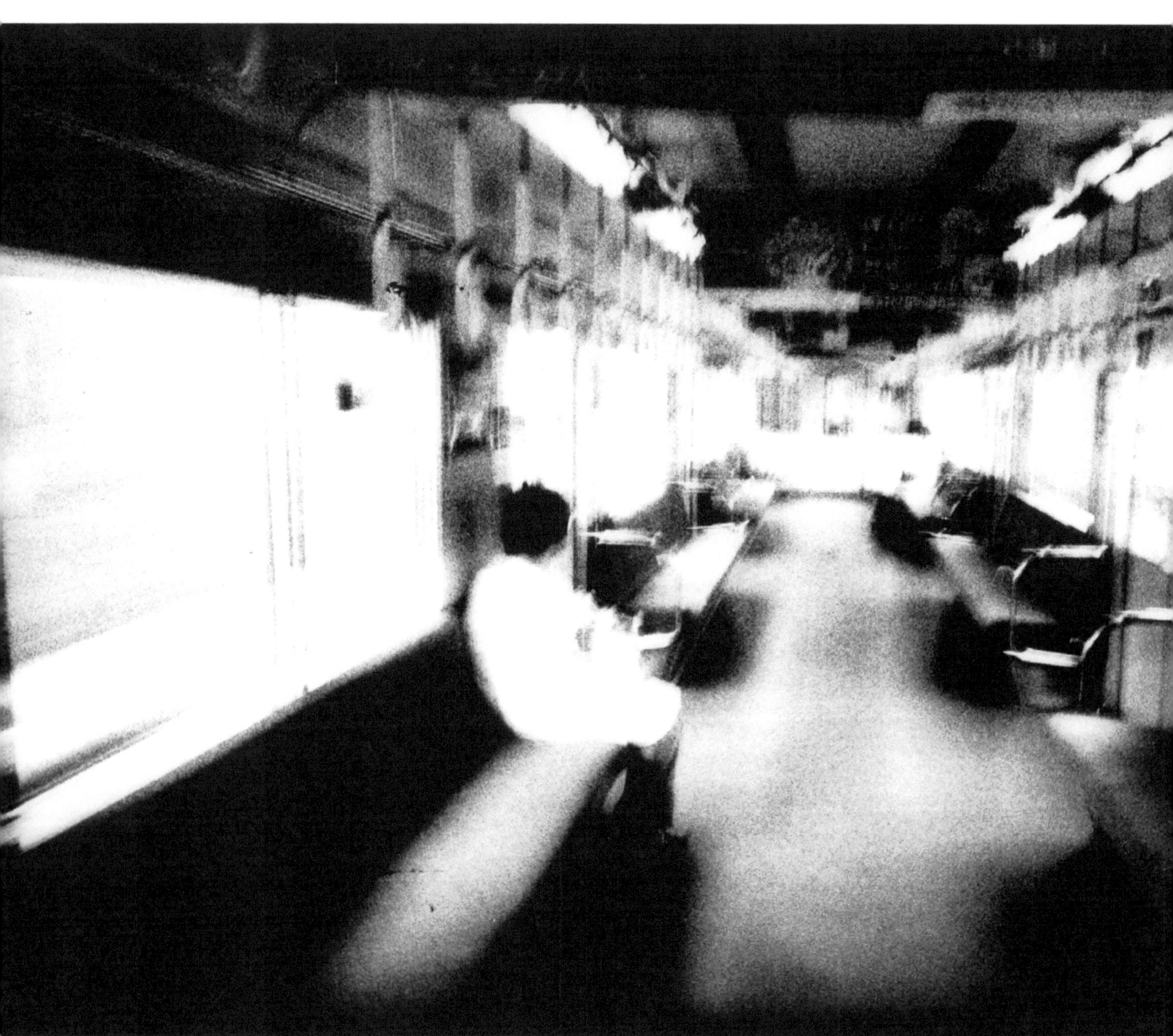

104

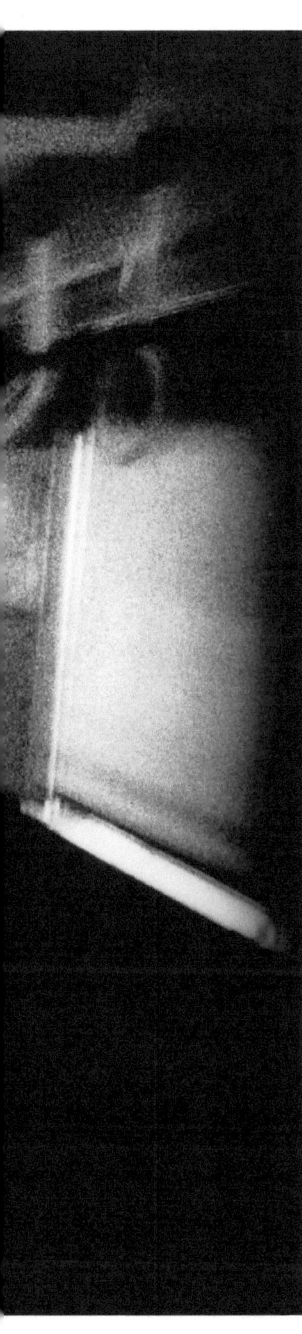

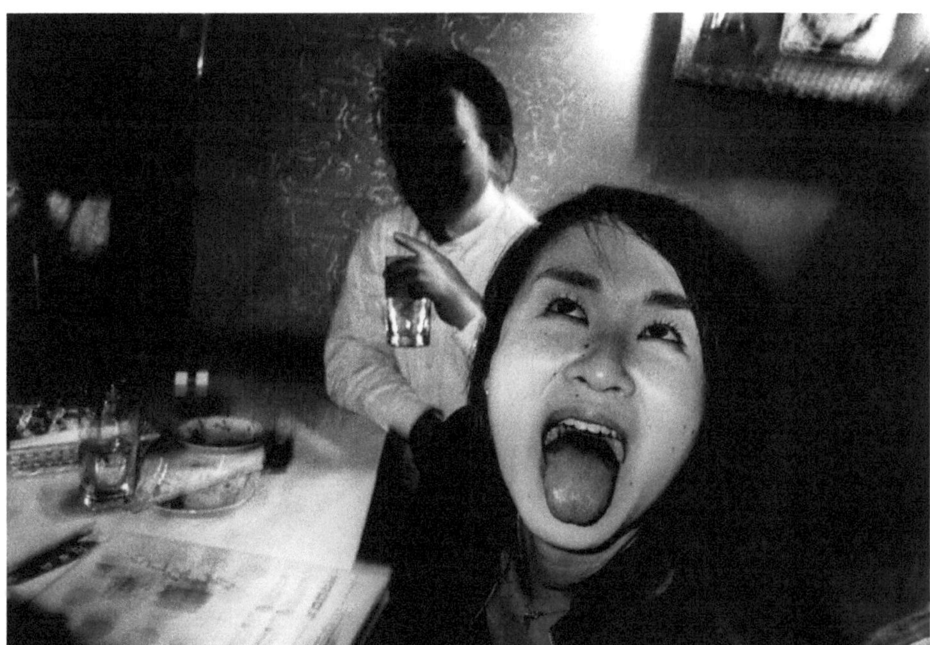

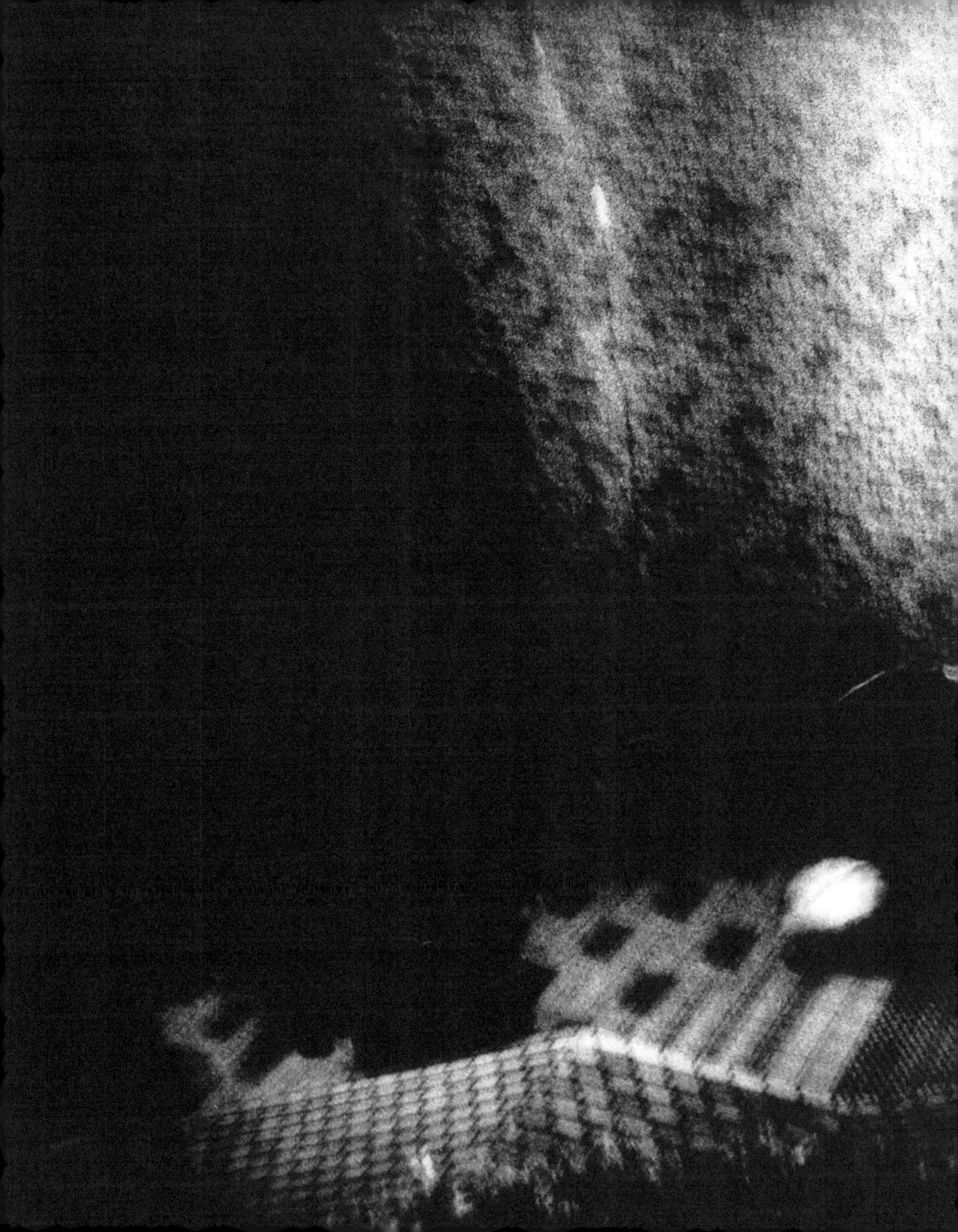

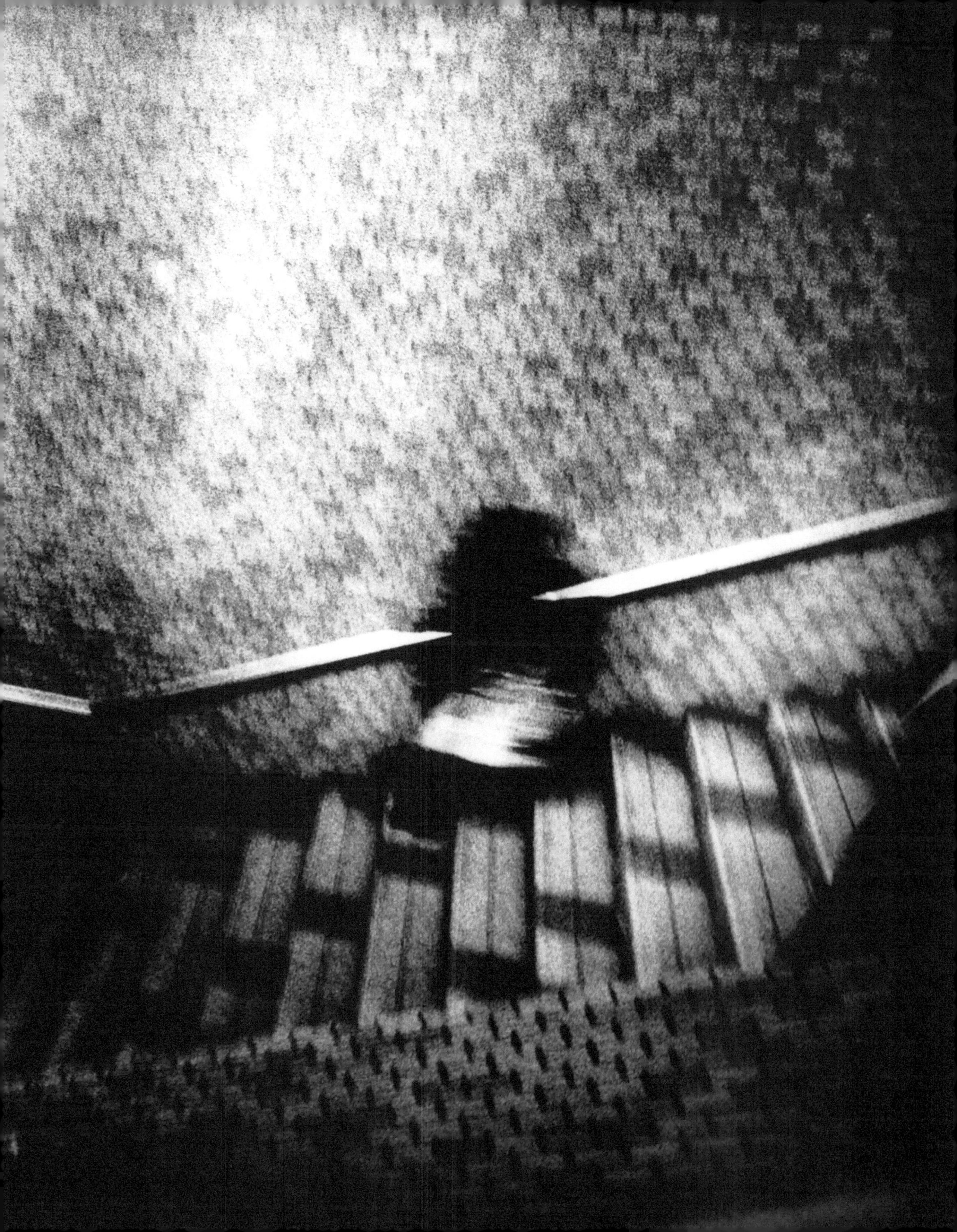

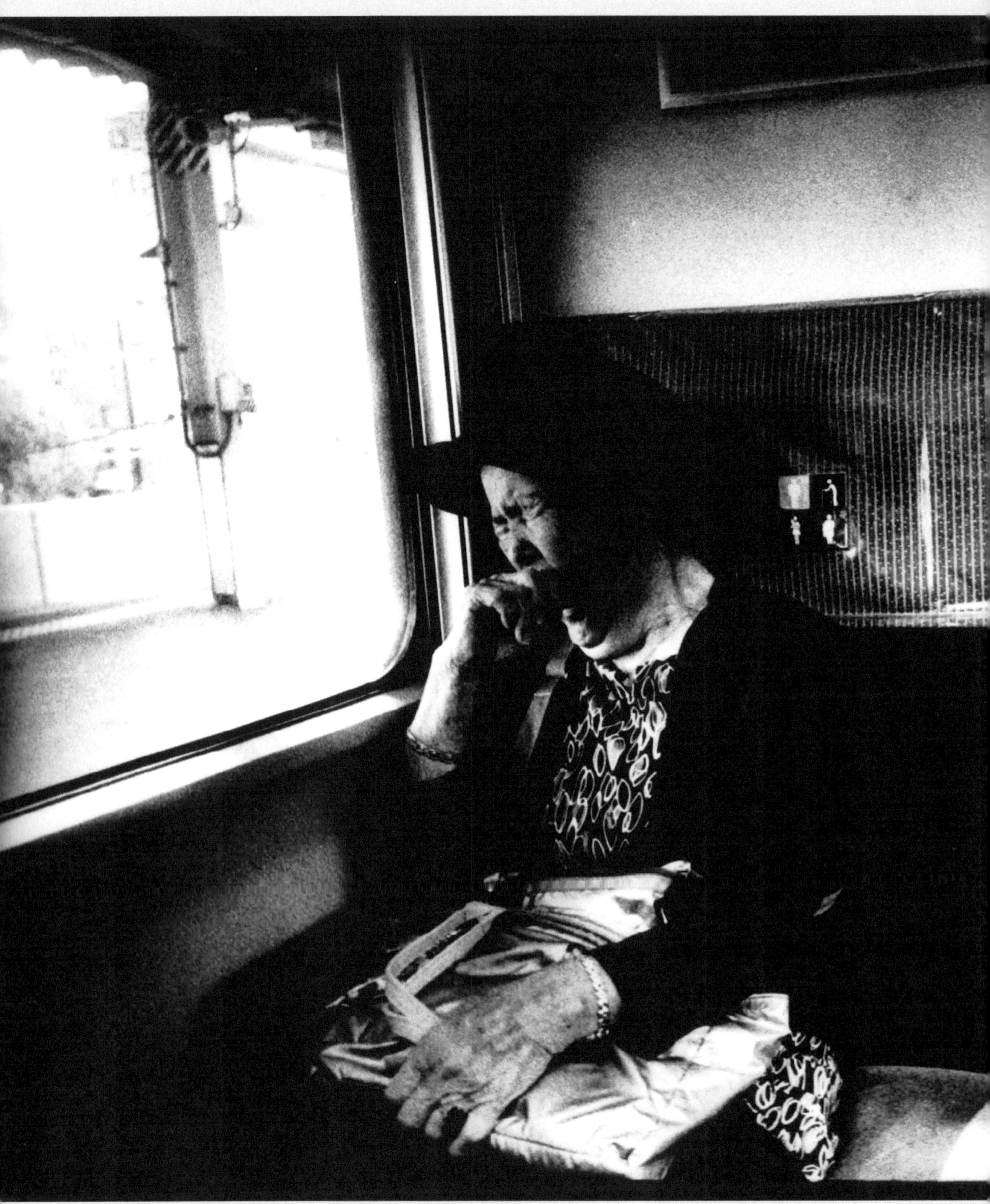

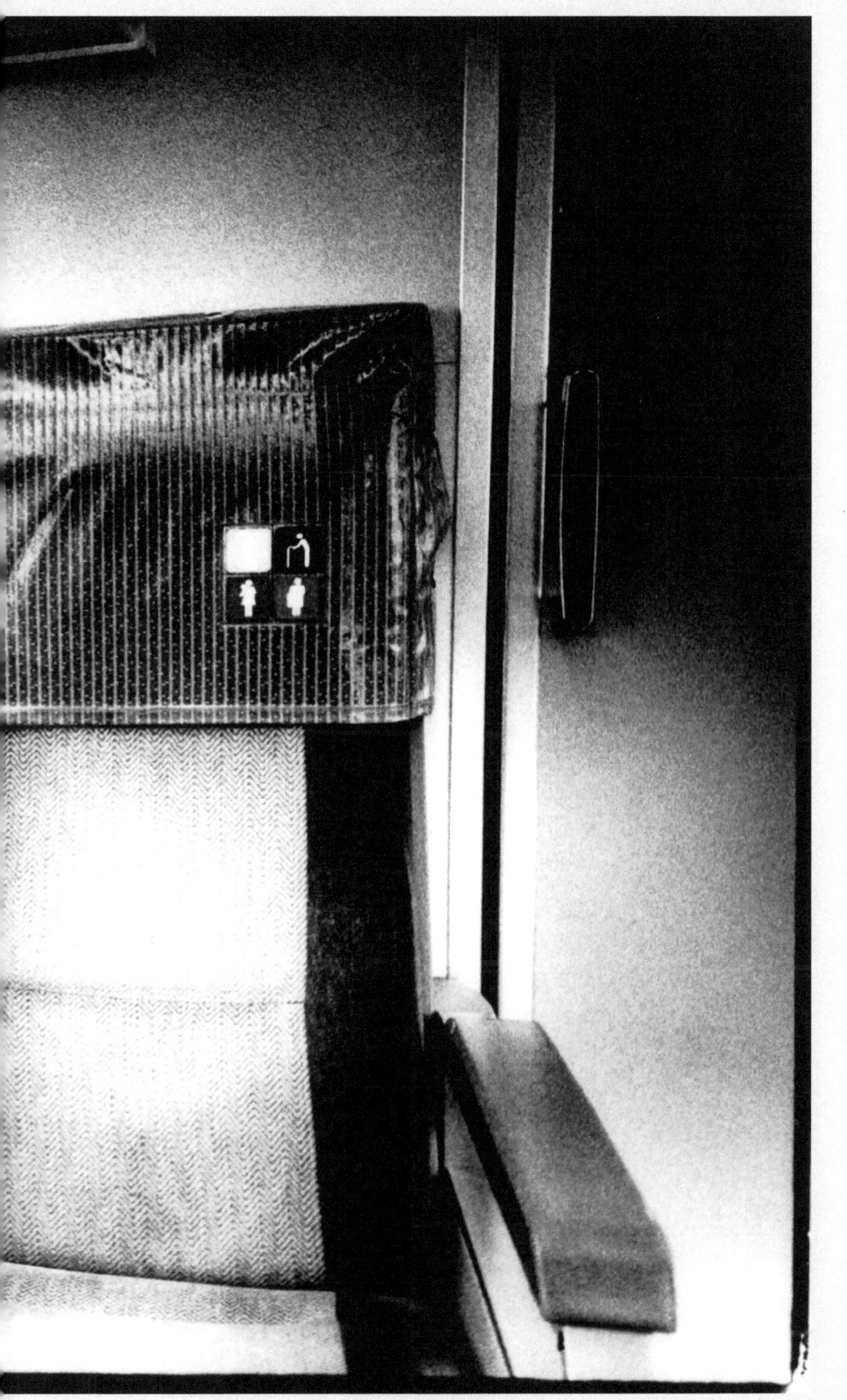

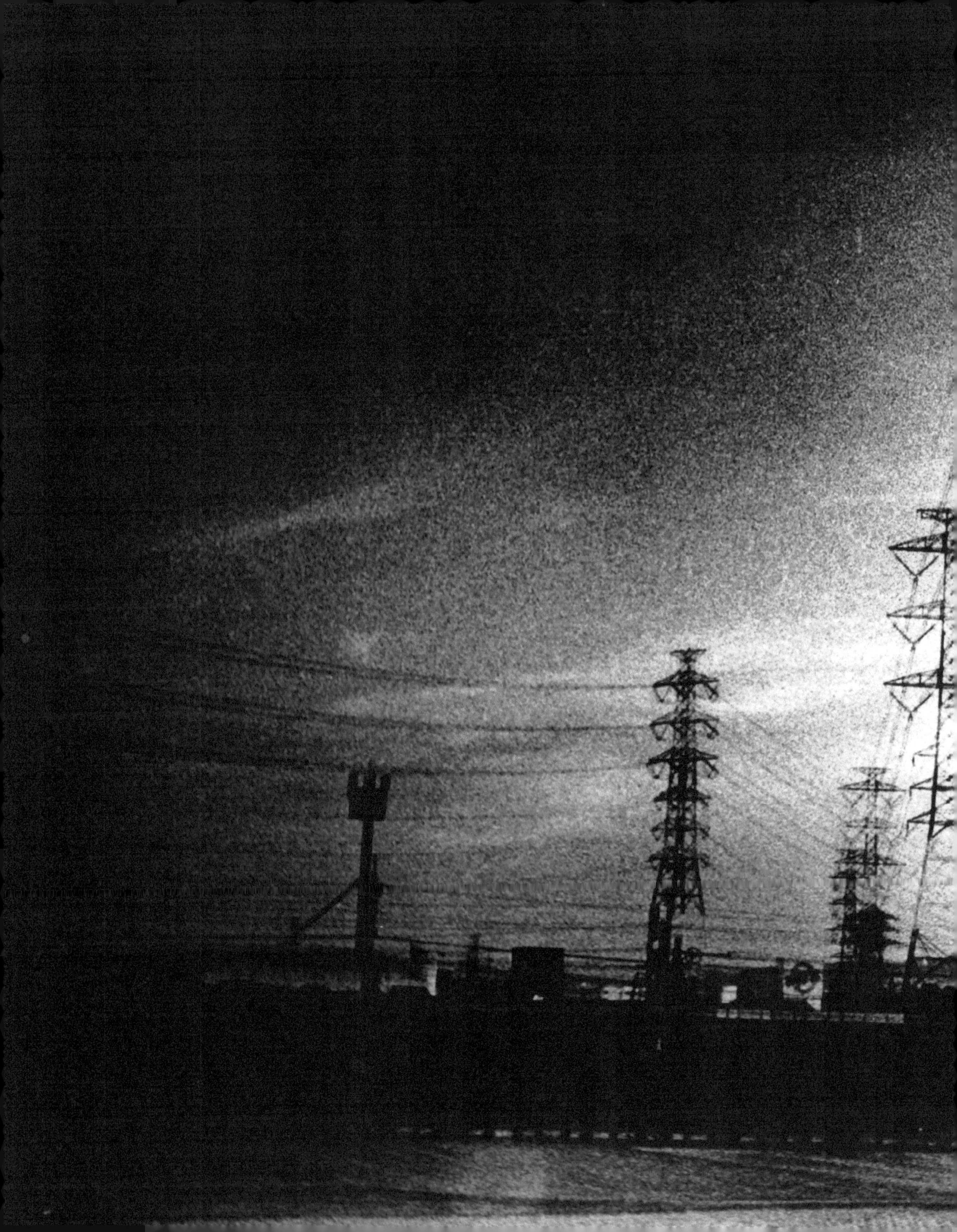

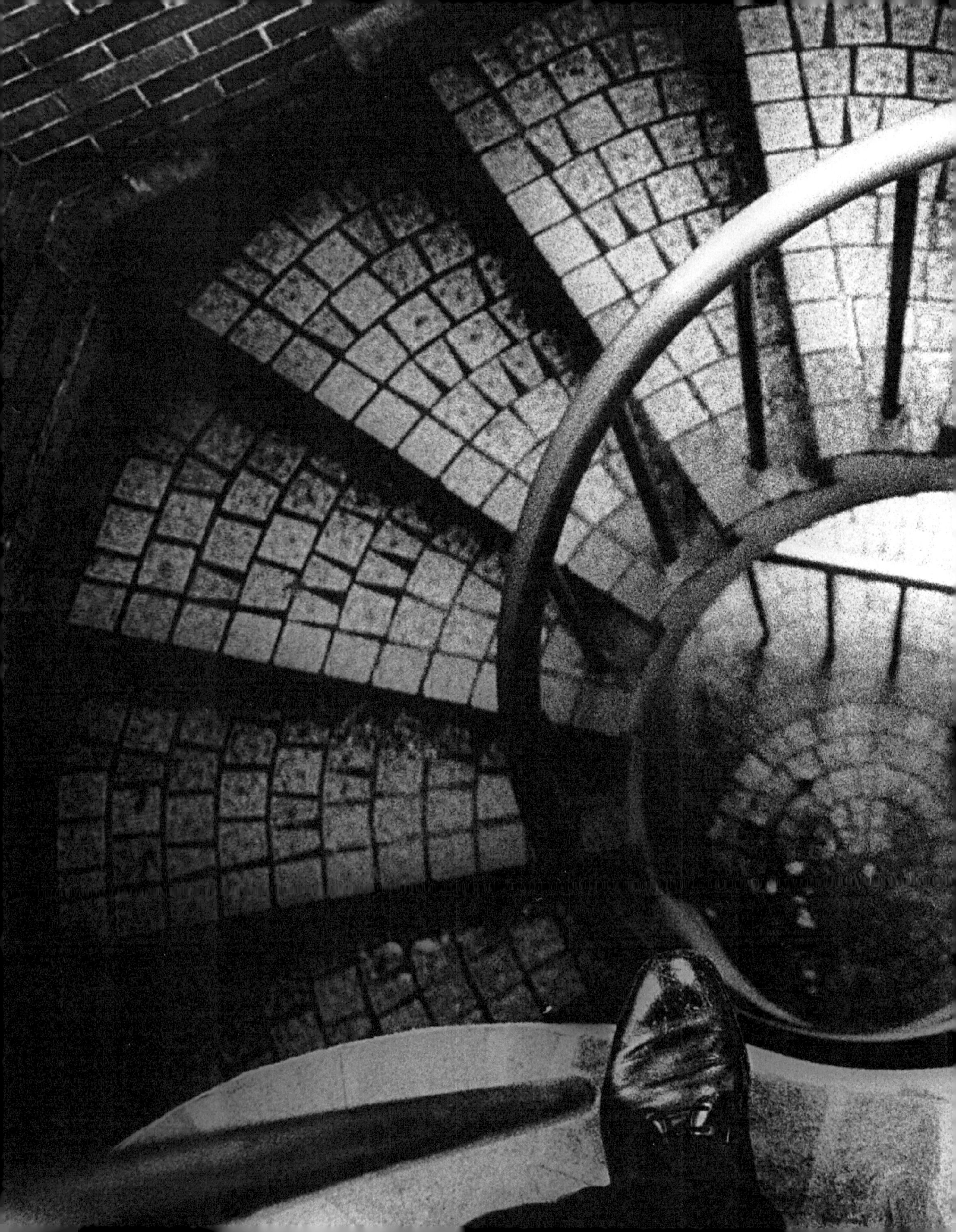

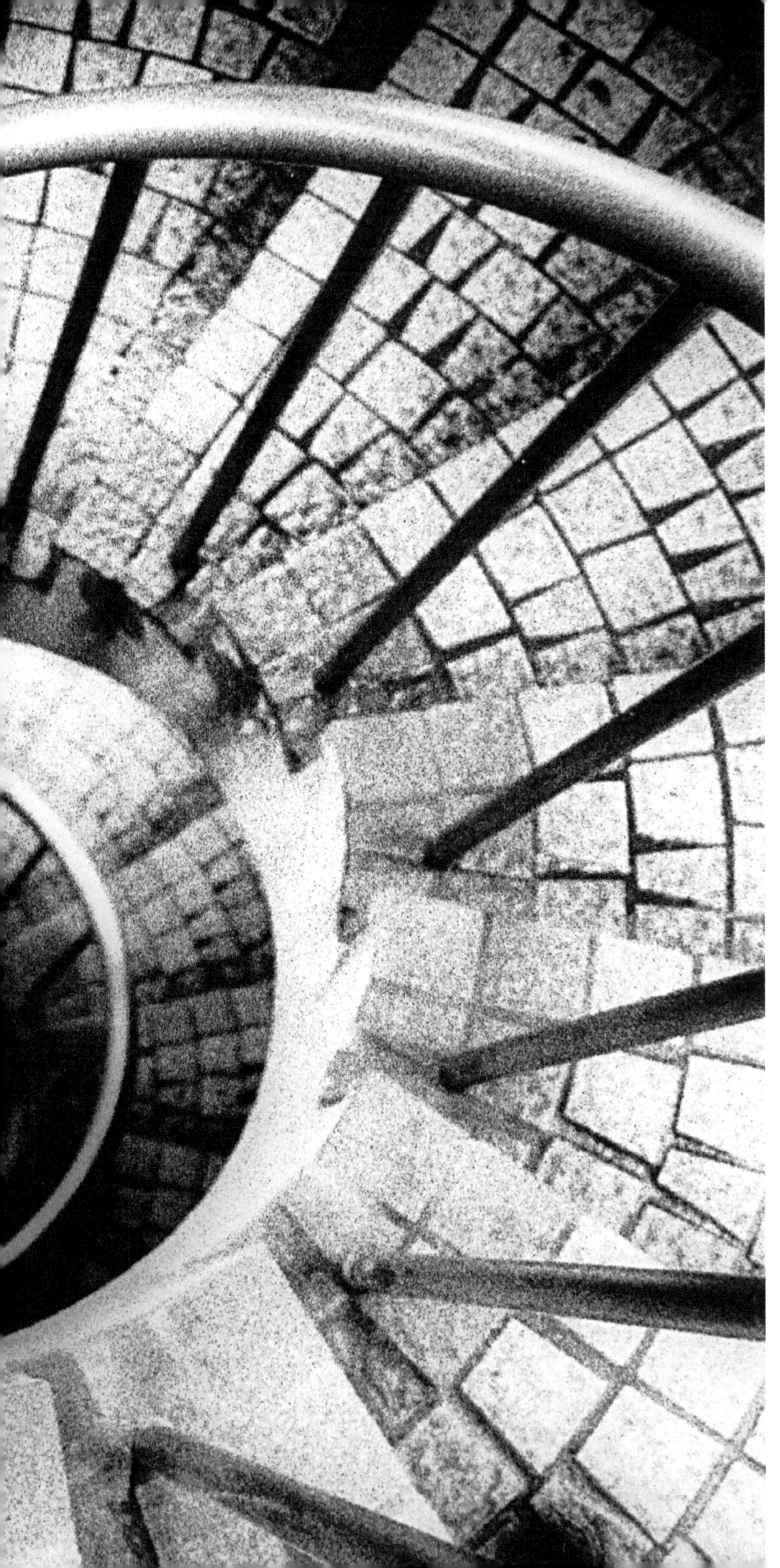

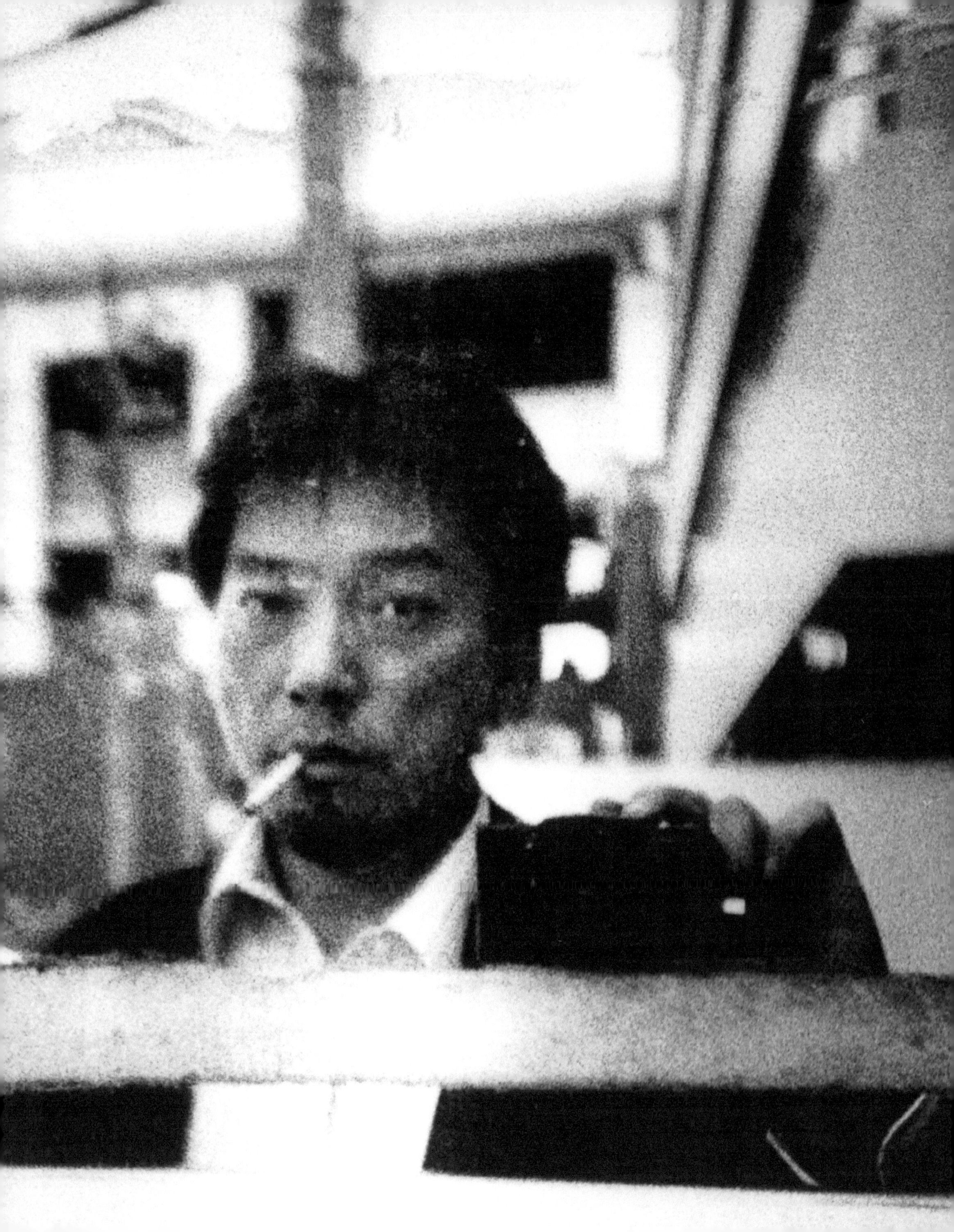

1959年、神戸生まれ
18歳頃から日常にある友人を撮り始める。
ある日、父が私を撮った古いアルバムを見て、自分も家族の写
真を残そうと決意する。
また、WEBで多くの素晴らしい写真に出会ったことを機会に、
私は写真についてもっと真剣に考えようと思い、それを父親に
伝えたところ、彼はアルバムに居た私を撮った古いマニュアル
カメラをくれた。それは2003年の元旦だった。

私はWEBで偶然発見した中平卓馬（PROVOKE雑誌）の写真に
衝撃を受けた。粗粒のモノクロ写真は私の内なる心と一致し
ている。私は試行錯誤を介して自分のドキュメンタリーを残す
ために写真を続けています。

B I O G R A P H Y

I was born in 1959 in Kobe, Japan. When I was 18 years old I started taking pictures of my friends on a daily basis.
One day, much later in my life, I was going through our family album and some of the photographs my father took with his film camera got me thinking about leaving my own photographs in my own family album.
I started looking for good photographs on Internet and thinking about doing photography more seriously.
When I told my father about it, he gave me his old manual film camera; this was the one he was using when he took the photographs for the family album. I remember the date: it was New Year's day, 2003.
Then, by chance, I stumbled upon the work of Takuma Nakahira, one of the "Provoke" photographers, and was deeply affected, almost shocked by their message.
Those grainy black and white photographs matched the state of my mind perfectly.
Since then, I am taking photographs to leave behind the story of my life.